Native Wills from the Colonial Americas

Native Wills

from the

Colonial Americas

Dead Giveaways in a New World

edited by

Mark Christensen and Jonathan Truitt

THE UNIVERSITY OF UTAH PRESS

Salt Lake City

The Defiance House Man colophon is a registered trademark
of the University of Utah Press. It is based on a four-foot-tall
Ancient Puebloan pictograph (late PIII) near Glen Canyon, Utah.

20 19 18 17 16   1 2 3 4 5

LIBRARY OF CONGRESS CATALOGING-IN-PUBLICATION DATA

Native wills from the colonial Americas : dead giveaways in a new
world / edited by Mark Christensen and Jonathan Truitt.
    pages cm
    Includes bibliographical references and index.
    ISBN 978-1-60781-416-0 (cloth : alk. paper) —
ISBN 978-1-60781-417-7 (ebook)
1. Indians of Mexico—History.   2. Indians of Central America—
History.   3. Wills—Mexico   4. Wills—Central America.
5. Mexico—History—Spanish colony, 1540–1810.   6. Central
America—History—To 1821.   I. Christensen, Mark Z., editor,
author.   II. Truitt, Jonathan G., 1977– editor, author.
    F1219.N37 2015
    972'.02—dc23
                                        2015017706

Printed and bound by Sheridan Books, Inc., Ann Arbor, Michigan.

Contents

Illustrations

Abbreviations

AGCA	Archivo General de Centro América (Guatemala City)
AGI	Archivo General de Indias (Seville, Spain)
AGN	Archivo General de la Nación (Mexico City)
AHAY	Archivo Histórico del Arzobispado de Yucatán (Mérida, Mexico)
AHJ	Archivo Histórico Judicial (Oaxaca, Mexico)
AHNE	Archivo Histórico Nacional de España (Madrid, Spain)
AJVA	Archivo Judicial de Villa Alta (Oaxaca, Mexico)
ANEY	Archivo Notorial del Estado de Yucatán (Mérida, Mexico)
ANM	Archivo Histórico de Notarías de la Ciudad de México (Mexico City)
APSM	Archivo Parroquial de San Miguel (Huexotzinco, Mexico)
BNAH	Biblioteca Nacional de Antropología e Historia (Mexico City)
BNP	Biblioteca Nacional de Perú (Paris)
FRAF	Fondo Reservado Archivo Franciscano (Mexico City)
INAH	Instituto Nacional de Antropología e Historia (Mexico City)
LC	Library of Congress (Washington, D.C.)
NL	Newberry Library (Chicago)
TULAL	Tulane University, Latin American Library, Rare Manuscript Collection (New Orleans, Louisiana)
UNAM	Universidad Nacional Autónoma de México (Mexico City)

Acknowledgments

As many know, the process of writing an article or a book is hardly ever a solitary task. In the case of an edited volume that seems an obvious statement, yet for all of the names that appear in the current volume, there are others whose work has proved instrumental in moving this volume forward.

We have benefited from correspondence with Alan Greer, David Chang, Jeani O'Brien, and Noenoe Silva. Additionally, Eric Carlson and Ben Ramirez-shkwegnaabi answered a number of questions regarding British and Anishanabek testaments. The anonymous reviewers who worked with the University of Utah Press provided invaluable feedback that helped to make the final product stronger. We thank them for the time and attention they gave our volume. We have, all of us, benefited from a great number of librarians and archivists across the Americas. We appreciate their dedication to the documents, books, and their craft in general.

The College of Humanities and Social and Behavioral Sciences at Central Michigan University provided a small subvention for the maps that appear in the volume. We thank Dean Pamela Gates for her support of the project.

It is difficult to be a good scholar and a mentor, but both Susan Kellogg and Matthew Restall succeeded. They deserve our gratitude for their inspiring prequel and their encouragement and support of its sequel. Moreover, all of our contributors have been amazing, and we thank all of you for your interest in the project. We also thank our editor at the University of Utah Press, Reba Rauch, who has been supportive and encouraging since the idea was pitched to her in 2008. She has carefully shepherded the project from phase to phase and answered numerous questions (some of them twice).

We wish to thank the late Jim Lockhart for his support of the project. From its inception he supported the idea and spent numerous hours working with many of us to improve our Nahuatl translations. As those who knew him are aware, he was tireless when it came to Nahuatl. Many of the chapters in this volume received his attention, for which we thank him—and his family for sharing him with us. He will be missed.

This project has been a long time in the writing. During this time much has transpired in our families, who surely grew tired of hearing about the fascinating things we continued to discover in testaments of long ago, yet continued to at least feign interest. Feigned interest or real, we thank them for their support and encouragement throughout the project.

Introduction

JONATHAN TRUITT AND MARK CHRISTENSEN

In August of 2006, Jon presented a paper at the Harvard Atlantic World Seminar, two weeks of intense discussion that brought scholars together from across the world. Over the course of the seminar, the usefulness of last wills and testaments became a topic of discussion. Some participants believed that wills were too formulaic, and too controlled by the notaries who wrote them, to be of any significant use for historians. Just starting on his research at that time, and fully enamored with the information that could be gleaned from wills, Jon was surprised that some scholars viewed them as a waste of time.

In 2008, we both presented at the American Society for Ethnohistory in Eugene, Oregon. Following our panel we started discussing our research and documents. We both used testaments, enjoyed *Dead Giveaways* (1998), and wanted to know how scholars were using them today and for which regions. We approached Susan Kellogg and Matthew Restall with the idea of a follow-up volume about the current use of native testaments in the Americas and the new insights they might provide—and they agreed. Like our predecessors, we believe that wills provide "detailed information impossible to find in any other documentary genre" (Restall and Kellogg 1998, 5). This volume joins many other works to further illustrate how employing wills as historical sources is not a waste of time.

The remainder of this introduction has two goals. The first is to provide the reader with a brief and general sense of testament making in the Americas among native peoples. The second is to discuss how native testaments fit into the larger historiography of social history in the Americas, and to further illustrate the important and increasing role testaments have played as historical sources since the first volume of *Dead Giveaways* was published in 1998. Scholarship on native peoples in the colonial Americas has flourished over the past fifteen years, and native wills continue to play a large role in our understanding of the past, often in new and creative ways. Today, research on native testaments includes new regions, new languages, and new actors, revealing regional differences and cultural influences. In short, testaments continue to provide ample fodder for scholars seeking to understand the colonial inhabitants of the Americas. The purpose of this volume is to showcase new information obtained from new testamentary sources interpreted largely through current trends in the historiography. In the process, this volume aspires to illustrate how scholars are using wills to further reveal the diverse ways in which natives responded to colonial life.

The Last Will and Testament
Comes to the Americas

The last will and testament found favor in Europe long before it came to the Americas. Adopting the Roman testamentary tradition, the early Catholic Church employed wills as both secular tools in the legal postmortem settlement of estates, and as spiritual aids that benefited the soul after death. Generally speaking, the Church expected each person to complete a will. In fourteenth-century Spain, this expectation went so far as to deny burial to any who died intestate (Eire 1995, 19–24). However, the tradition of making testaments varied from region to region across Europe. The results are a patchwork of wills that reside in the archives of Europe today.[1] These differences in European testamentary procedures, combined with differences in New World evangelization techniques and efforts to convert native languages into the Roman alphabet, affected the colonial powers' approach to final wills and testaments in the Americas.

For example, Great Britain's evangelization effort in the Americas paled in comparison to that of Spain. Thus, it is no surprise that regions under Spanish rule typically produced more wills than their British counterparts. Moreover, Spanish Catholics generally prepared for death by leaving donations in their wills for masses and rites that would benefit their souls, thus fortifying the document's importance. In contrast, many Protestants of North America approached death through elaborate funerary rituals, thus decreasing the role of a will.[2] Regardless of the general trends, by the early sixteenth century, natives across the Americas were writing wills in a variety of languages (Cline 1998, 14–17).

The successful acceptance of wills among native populations of the Americas was not, however, solely the product of persuasive European ecclesiastics. The cultures included in this volume—from the Andes to New England—had developed oral traditions of chronicles, speeches, and final declarations long before they encountered Europeans. In addition, many of these American cultures practiced some form of precontact historical record keeping, be it, in the words of Elizabeth Hill Boone (2012, 211), "painted, knotted, or threaded." In the end, these established traditions facilitated the acceptance of a written testament in the Roman alphabet (Restall, Sousa, and Terraciano 2005, 12).

Because a great variety exists among the native cultures of the Americas, will making was variously successful. Regions that include what James Lockhart and Stuart Schwartz have called the "imperial sedentary peoples" in Mesoamerica and Peru readily adopted wills, but they are markedly absent among the semisedentary and nonsedentary peoples that inhabited northern New Spain and Florida; if they did exist, they did not survive or have yet to be uncovered (Lockhart and Schwartz 1983, chap. 2). Interestingly, no native wills are known to be extant for the French or Portuguese colonies where semisedentary and nonsedentary peoples abounded. Since wills were clearly a part of both the Catholic Church and Spanish colonial policy in the imperial centers, their absence speaks loudly in regard to the agency of each individual European and indigenous group.

Although the British similarly employed last wills and testaments, they were scarce in British America. In some ways this is surprising, considering both the success of native writing practices in North America (for example, among the Cherokee, Pokanoket, and Dakota) and among the Kanaka Maoli (native Hawaiians). In other ways it is understandable, given the natives' semi- and nonsedentary status, the general lack of British enthusiasm in instructing the natives in testamentary procedures, and the natives' limited access to and involvement with the British legal system in North America. That said, native testaments in North America do exist. For example, the Oklahoma State Historical Society contains testaments in multiple indigenous languages, including Cherokee and Choctaw.[3]

In their simplest form, wills allowed native testators to settle their affairs before God and the local community prior to leaving this world. Although subject to variation, wills composed in Spanish America followed a basic formula. As the testator felt death approaching, he called for the indigenous *cabildo* (town council) to record his testament. How many members appeared other than the town notary varied according to local tradition and situation. Regardless, the notary began the testament with a preamble, generally consisting of an invocation of the Holy Trinity, a supplication, a profession of faith, and an encommendation of the body and soul (Terraciano 1998, 125).[4] Following the preamble, the notary documented bequeathed items and their new owners. The testament concluded with a statement of finality and the signatures of any witnesses. The Pokanoket of colonial New England followed a similar formula, although without the Catholic trappings.

Native Testaments and Social History

The historiography of Latin America, like most historiographies, has followed the path of least resistance. It began with the most accessible sources and then, after exhausting those, moved on to the next easiest or most accessible. This principle—dubbed by Lockhart (1972b, 8) "the law of preservation of energy of historians"—produced a historiography that has evolved from the epic histories of Cortés and Columbus to "ground up" and "subaltern" studies examining native-language texts and testaments.

The first historians to write about colonial Latin America drew upon the most accessible and synthetic sources, most notably the original "histories" of the Spanish conquest, such as the letters Cortés wrote to Charles V, Francisco López de Gómara's history of Cortés and his accomplishments, and the accounts of Bernal Díaz del Castillo. The next wave of historians in the first half of the twentieth century employed the internal records of state institutions. They were followed by scholars employing economic or macrodemographic research in efforts to obtain more direct and systematic information about colonial life. Emigrant registers, ship logs, parish records, tax and tribute rolls, and census records all contributed to a wide variety of macrohistories.

Despite their contributions, however, macrodemographic studies struggle with fitting the local scenario into the larger image. Moreover, historians began to better comprehend the disadvantages in attempting social history from a single source. Thus, the historiography began to employ a variety of sources focused on local settings and actors to produce close studies that nuanced the larger narrative (Lockhart 1968, 1972a; Schwartz 1973). However, because much of the more accessible sources concerned elites or elitist perspectives, scholars into the 1970s commonly portrayed colonized peoples as "little more than a peripheral milch cow from whom a surplus was extracted and sent back to a center or metropolis" (Powers 1995, 4).

As historians continued to expand their sources and focus on local situations within the broader narrative, they produced regional histories that increasingly included the subaltern as actors in their own history.[5] In this vein, scholars would eventually supplement Spanish sources with native-language documents, including testaments. Because central Mexico contained the largest cache of such documents, it was the first region represented in the historiography. Nahuatl testaments became the focus of *The Testaments of Culhuacan* (Cline and León Portilla 1984) and *Documentos nahuas de la ciudad de México del siglo XVI* (García Reyes 1996), and they continually informed many important works on central Mexico (Lockhart 1992; Cline 1986; Kellogg 1995; Haskett 1991; Wood 1991; Offutt 1992; Horn 1997). Moreover, on the eve of the 1998 publication of *Dead Giveaways*, scholars in regions outside central Mexico—particularly Guatemala and the Andes—had already begun employing wills (Hill 1989; Stern 1982; Abercrombie 1998; Powers 1998; Salomon 1988).

Generally speaking, the historiography of social history and its use of testaments in North America followed a similar path as that of Latin America. Using the most available sources, initial scholars told a tale of weak natives being supplanted by superior Europeans in the wake of "civilization." Later, in the 1960s, scholars such as Francis Jennings began writing native-oriented histories from the natives' point of view. The clash and conflict between Europeans and natives eventually gave way to negotiation in works such as Richard White's *The Middle Ground* (1991), which incorporated a wide variety of sources to write a "new Indian history" that placed natives at the center of focus, depicting them as active participants in creating a colonial world. Regarding native testaments, Pokanoket wills appeared in Ives Goddard and Kathleen Bragdon's *Native Writings in Massachusett* (1988). Yet with the notable exception of this work, Native American wills as a genre of research for the colonial period in U.S. and Canadian history are virtually unknown.[6]

As native testaments continued to produce rich studies on specific regions in the Americas, the possibility for comparative studies increased. It was from this vein of thought that *Dead Giveaways* emerged in 1998. Calling attention to a growing corpus of indigenous testamentary documents, the volume employs native wills from Mesoamerica and the Andes to view the intricate negotiations between colonial European and Native American cultures. Unlike previous works, *Dead Giveaways* contained wills from a variety of native cultures to explore the ways in which responses to European culture varied between social and ethnic groups. At its heart, the work exposed how testaments can reveal intersections between Spanish and indigenous cultures, the domestic and the public, the personal and the social, and language and culture. From these meetings emerged the wealth of sociocultural data so desired by scholars interested in the past.

Since the publication of *Dead Giveaways*, historians have continued to expand into new and exciting subfields and subdisciplines of study—and in nearly every one, testaments from natives appear as both minor and major sources. Indeed, the unique details of the various intersections revealed through wills provide scholars with the "thick description" necessary to elucidate intimate regions of study. For example, testaments frequently inform scholars reexamining the roles of native women throughout the Americas (Schroeder, Wood, and Haskett, 1997; Burns 1999; Socolow 2000; Few 2002; Truitt 2010).[7] In addition, wills also appear as documentary sources in studies examining how natives negotiated their identity as intermediaries (Yannakakis 2008), as rulers (Connell 2011), and as participants in colonial religion (Terraciano 1998; Burkhart 2004; Pizzigoni 2007; Osowski 2010; Christensen 2013).

Native wills have also played an important role in a recent historiographic trend that Susan Schroeder has termed "the New Conquest History" (Schroeder 2007),[8] which turns epic histories on their head to illustrate the natives as conquerors (Restall 1998; Wood 2003; Matthew and Oudijk 2007; Matthew 2012). Furthermore, testaments increasingly appear in studies on regions outside central Mexico (Thompson 1999; Terraciano 2001; Abercrombie 1998; Powers 1998; Salomon 1988; Graubart 2007; Ramos 2010; O'Toole 2012; Rappaport and Cummins 2012). Finally, wills increasingly find themselves as the central documentary source and focus of edited volumes and monographs providing new and pathbreaking details on social history (more recently, see Will de Chaparro 2007; Pizzigoni 2007, 2012). In short, since the social history of the colonial Americas evolved to include the wills of everyday individuals, these important sources of history continue to enrich our understanding of those living in the colonial Americas—a point this volume hopes to illustrate further.

Purpose and Structure of the Present Volume

This volume illustrates the continued value of testaments in contributing to contemporary historical inquiry. Most of the contributors do not claim to offer new approaches or theoretical innovation in their use of wills. Rather, the volume presents new information from new sources within current trends in the historiography. To illustrate this in more detail, we have divided the book into three thematic parts. Each section includes a brief introduction outlining its chapters and their contribution to existing trends in the historiography, and further details and insights on both the chapters and their contributions appear in the afterword. Part 1 employs testaments to highlight the "Women of Native America" and how their lives frequently challenged prescribed gender roles and statuses. Part 2 uses testaments to illustrate the "Strategies of the Elite" in both negotiating and maintaining their power in a colonial, Spanish world. Part 3 contributes to our understanding of "The Individual and Collective Nature of Death" by extracting from wills the importance of conversion, kinship, and societal ties in the colonial Americas.

The intent of this volume was to include a broad geographic approach, and at the outset it seemed possible. The first person we approached was Kathleen Bragdon, who had done work with a couple of Massachusett or Natick testaments. Unfortunately, our early success in broadening the geographic scope was short-lived. We approached scholars working on Brazil, French Canada, the Great Lakes region, Costa Rica, and Hawai'i, as well as the Choctaw, Guaraní, and Cherokee, to name a few regions and groups. In some cases we found scholars who were interested in indigenous testaments but had not encountered any in their area. In other places we found indigenous testaments but did not have scholars with the requisite language skills who were interested in working on them. This necessitated a larger focus on Mesoamerica than we had originally intended. That said, the wills do not disappoint. From a possible native Filipino and his *mulata* (of African and Spanish ancestry) wife, to pictorials demarcating property lines, to the Nahuatl testament of a Mixe, such testaments never cease to surprise us with their offered insights—even in a region as well represented as Mesoamerica.

What is new in this volume as compared with its prequel? Although it deals with many of the usual suspects (Nahuas, Mayas, Andeans[9]), it also

TABLE 0.1. Published indigenous-language testaments since *Dead Giveaways* (1998)

Origin Community	Date	Language/Number	Publication
Culhuacan, central Mexico	1577, 1580	Nahuatl/2	Restall, Sousa, and Terraciano 2005[a]
Various, central Mexico		Nahuatl/	Rojas et al. 1999–2004
Toluca, central Mexico	1652–1783	Nahuatl/98	Pizzigoni 2007
Ixil, Yucatan	1766	Yucatec Maya/2	Restall, Sousa, and Terraciano 2005[b]
Ixil, Yucatan	1748	Yucatec Maya/1	Christensen 2013
Ixil, Yucatan	1766	Yucatec, Maya/1	Bricker and Hill 2009[c]
Tekanto, Yucatan	1744	Yucatec Maya/1	Bricker and Hill 2009
Motul, Yucatan	1762	Yucatec Maya/1	Restall, Sousa, and Terraciano 2005[d]
Cobán, Guatemala	1583	Kekchí Maya/1	Restall, Sousa, and Terraciano 2005[e]
Teposcolula, Mixteca Alta	1672, 1691, 1642	Mixtec/3	Terraciano 2001
Teposcolula, Mixteca Alta	1672, 1691, 1633	Mixtec/3	Restall, Sousa, and Terraciano 2005[f]

[a] Both wills are included in Cline and León-Portilla 1984.
[b] Both wills are also included in Restall 1995, 1997.
[c] Will also appears in Restall 1995.
[d] Will also appears in Kellogg and Restall 1998.
[e] Will originally appeared in Dieseldoff 1931.
[f] Two of the three wills appeared in Terraciano 2001.

introduces new actors, such as the Pokanoket of colonial New England, the Mixe of Villa Alta, and a likely Filipino native and his *mulata* wife. As a whole, the volume presents readers with translations and analyses of wills written from the sixteenth to eighteenth centuries in Spanish, Nahuatl, Yucatec Maya, K'iche' Maya, Mixtec, and Wampanoag. As will be seen, these wills offer new insights and details on a wide range of colonial actors from a variety of regions, thus furthering our understanding of indigenous life in the Americas under colonial rule.

Native wills still have much information to reveal, and their value in the historical narrative continues to hold. Yet there are many voices waiting to be discovered. Perhaps in the future we will hear from the Guaraní of Paraguay, the Otomí of central Mexico, the Mapuche of the Araucanía, or the Anishinaabeg of the Great Lakes region. These contributions would further expand our understanding of the similarities and differences between natives' experiences in the colonial Americas. Until then, such valuable details and insights must remain hidden in remote archives—for they are never truly dead giveaways.

Notes

1. For information on early modern British testaments see Carlson 1994 and Marsh 1998. For an excellent study on testamentary procedures in Spain see Eire 1995.
2. For more on the differences between Protestant North America's and Catholic Spanish America's funerary traditions see Will de Chaparro 2007, xv–xxii.
3. Interestingly, the Hawaiian state archives also possess copious wills composed by Kanaka Maoli, many in their native tongue. We thank Noenoe K. Silva for alerting us to this cache of testaments in Hawaii, and David Chang for his assistance. Additionally, we thank Brian Basore of the Oklahoma Historical Society for alerting us to the existence of native-language testaments held in its archival collection.
4. Louise Burkhart (2004, 43–47) does some comparison of encommendation among Nahuatl wills.
5. For a few of many examples, see Gibson 1952, 1964; Taylor 1972, 1979.
6. We thank Kathleen Bragdon and Eric Hinderaker for their insights on the matter.
7. This and the following lists are in no way exhaustive but serve to provide examples.
8. The New Conquest History (Schroeder 2007) is rooted in the reappraisal of conquest wars in sixteenth-century Mesoamerica. At its core is a use of native-language sources to present not just the native side but multiple native perspectives; however, its revisionist spirit reflects the ecumenical direction(s) in which colonial Latin American social history has been going since the 1980s. The history is not just about indigenous viewpoints, but also about African roles and views, as well as Spanish ones. The school seeks to avoid demonizing the Spanish conquistadors and to delve deeper into the archives in order to better understand the multiple perspectives of European protagonists.
9. With all but two of the testaments in the current corpus we are able to identify the ethnic group of the testator in question. In the case of Karen Graubart's Andean testament, it is likely that the testatrix in question was of Cajamarca or Pomamarca descent. The ethnic groups of this region were conquered by the Inca, who also brought other ethnic groups in to help suppress dissent, and thus it is possible from the limited information we have to discern her specific group membership, as would be preferred. For more information see Espinoza Soriano 1976, 135–180. Thank you to Karen Graubart for sharing this source.

References

Abercrombie, Thomas A. 1998. "Tributes to Bad Conscience: Charity, Restitution, and Inheritance in Cacique and Encomendero Testaments of 16th-Century Charcas." In *Dead Giveaways: Indigenous Testaments of Colonial Mesoamerica and the Andes*, edited by Susan Kellogg and Matthew Restall, 249–289. Salt Lake City: University of Utah Press.

Anderson, Arthur J. O., Frances Berdan, and James Lockhart, eds. 1976. *Beyond the Codices: The Nahua View of Colonial Mexico*. UCLA Latin American Studies. Berkeley and Los Angeles: University of California Press.

Boone, Elizabeth Hill. 2012. "Presidential Lecture: Discourse and Authority in Histories Painted, Knotted, and Threaded." *Ethnohistory* 59(2): 211–237.

Borah, Woodrow. 1954. *Early Colonial Trade and Navigation Between Mexico and Peru*. Berkeley: University of California Press.

———. 1963. *The Aboriginal Population of Central Mexico on the Eve of the Spanish Conquest*. Berkeley: University of California Press.

Borah, Woodrow, and Sherburne F. Cook. 1958. *Price Trends of Some Basic Commodities in Central Mexico, 1531–1570*. Berkeley: University of California Press.

Brading, David A. 1971. *Miners and Merchants in Bourbon Mexico, 1763–1810*. Cambridge: Cambridge University Press.

Bricker, Victoria R., and Rebecca E. Hill. 2009. "Climatic Signatures in Yucatecan Wills and Death Records." *Ethnohistory* 56: 227–268

Burkhart, Louise M. 2004. "Death and the Colonial Nahua." In *Nahuatl Theater*, vol. 1, *Death and Life in Colonial Nahua Mexico*, edited by Barry D. Sell and Louise M. Burkhart, 29–53. Norman: University of Oklahoma Press.

Burns, Kathryn. 1999. *Colonial Habits: Convents and the Spiritual Economy of Cuzco, Peru*. Durham, N.C.: Duke University Press.

Carlson, Eric Josef. 1994. "The Historical Value of the Ely Consistory Probate Records." In *Index of the Probate Records of the Consistory Court of Ely, 1449–1858*, Part 1: *A–E*, edited by Elisabeth Leedham-Green and Rosemary Rodd, and Clifford and Dorothea Thurley, compilers. London: British Record Society.

Christensen, Mark Z. 2013. *Nahua and Maya Catholicisms: Texts and Religion in Colonial Central Mexico and Yucatan*. Stanford, Calif.: Stanford University Press.

Cline, Sarah. 1998. "Fray Alonso de Molina's Model Testament and Antecedents to Indigenous Wills in Spanish America." In *Dead Giveaways: Indigenous Testaments of Colonial Mesoamerica and the Andes*, edited by Susan Kellogg and Matthew Restall, 13–33. Salt Lake City: University of Utah Press.

Cline, Sarah L. 1986. *Colonial Culhuacan, 1580–1600: A Social History of an Aztec Town*. Albuquerque: University of New Mexico Press.

Cline, Sarah L., and Miguel León-Portilla. 1984. *The Testaments of Culhuacan*. Los Angeles: UCLA Latin American Center Publications.

Connell, William F. 2011. *After Moctezuma: Indigenous Politics and Self-Government in Mexico City, 1524–1730*. Norman: University of Oklahoma Press.

Dieseldoff, Erwin P. 1931. "A Kekchi Will of 1583." In *The Maya Society Quarterly* 1(1) (December): 65–68.

Dropsie, Moses A., trans. and ed. 1892. *The Roman Law of Testaments, Codicils, and Gifts in the Event of Death*. Philadelphia: T. & J. W. Johnson.

Eire, Carlos M. N. 1995. *From Madrid to Purgatory: The Art and Craft of Dying in Sixteenth-Century Spain*. Cambridge: Cambridge University Press.

Farriss, Nancy M. 1984. *Maya Society Under Colonial Rule: The Collective Enterprise of Survival*. Princeton, N.J.: Princeton University Press, 1984.

Few, Martha. 2002. *Women Who Live Evil Lives: Gender, Religion, and the Politics of Power in Colonial Guatemala*. Austin: University of Texas Press.

García Reyes, Luis. 1996. *Documentos nahuas de la ciudad de México del siglo XVI*. Mexico City: AGN.

Gibson, Charles. 1952. *Tlaxcala in the Sixteenth Century*. Stanford, Calif.: Stanford University Press.

———. 1964. *The Aztecs Under Spanish Rule: A History of the Indians of the Valley of Mexico, 1519–1810*. Stanford, Calif.: Stanford University Press.

Goddard, Ives, and Kathleen Bragdon. 1988. *Native Writings in Massachusett*. Philadelphia: American Philosophical Society.

Graubart, Karen B. 2007. *With Our Labor and Sweat: Indigenous Women and the Formation of Colonial Society in Peru, 1550–1700*. Stanford, Calif.: Stanford University Press.

Haring, Clarence Henry. 1947. *The Spanish Empire in America*. New York: Oxford University Press.

Hill, Robert M. 1989. *The Pirir Papers and Other Colonial Period Cakchiquel-Maya Testamentos*. Nashville, Tenn.: Vanderbilt University.

Horn, Rebecca. 1997. *Postconquest Coyoacan: Nahua-Spanish Relations in Central Mexico, 1519–1650*. Stanford, Calif.: Stanford University Press.

Kellogg, Susan. 1995. *Law and the Transformation of Aztec Culture, 1500–1700*. Norman: University of Oklahoma Press.

Kellogg, Susan, and Matthew Restall, eds. 1998. *Dead Giveaways: Indigenous Testaments of Colonial Mesoamerica and the Andes*. Salt Lake City: University of Utah Press.

Lockhart, James. 1968. *Spanish Peru, 1532–1560: A Colonial Society*. Madison: University of Wisconsin Press.

———. 1972a. *The Men of Cajamarca: A Social and Biographical Study of the First Conquerors of Peru*. Austin: University of Texas Press.

———. 1972b. "The Social History of Colonial Spanish America: Evolution and Potential." *Latin American Research Review* 7(1): 6–45.

———. 1992. *The Nahuas After the Conquest: A Social and Cultural History of the Indians of Central Mexico, Sixteenth Through Eighteenth Centuries*. Stanford, Calif.: Stanford University Press.

Lockhart, James, and Stuart B. Schwartz. 1983. *Early Latin America: A History of Colonial Spanish America and Brazil*. Cambridge: Cambridge University Press.

Marsh, Christopher. 1998. "'Departing Well and Christianly': Will-Making and Popular Religion in Early Modern England." In *Religion and the English People, 1500–1640: New Voices New Perspectives*, edited by Eric Josef Carlson, 201–244. Kirksville, Mo.: Truman State University Press.

Matthew, Laura E. 2012. *Memories of Conquest: Becoming Mexicano in Colonial Guatemala*. Chapel Hill: University of North Carolina Press.

Matthew, Laura E., and Michel R. Oudijk, eds. 2007. *Indian Conquistadors: Indigenous Allies in the Conquest of Mesoamerica*. Norman: University of Oklahoma Press.

Offutt, Leslie S. 1992. "Levels of Acculturation in Northeastern New Spain: San Esteban Testaments of the Seventeenth and Eighteenth Centuries." *Estudios de Cultura Náhuatl* 22: 409–443.

Osowski, Edward W. 2010. *Indigenous Miracles: Nahua Authority in Colonial Mexico*. Tucson: University of Arizona Press.

O'Toole, Rachel Sarah. 2012. *Bound Lives: Africans, Indians, and the Making of Race in Colonial Peru*. Pittsburgh: University of Pittsburgh Press.

Prescott, William H. 1873. *History of the Conquest of Mexico*. Edited by John Foster Kirk. 3 vols. Philadelphia: J. B. Lippincott and Co.

Pizzigoni, Caterina, trans. and ed. 2007. *Testaments of Toluca*. Nahuatl Studies Series No. 8, edited by James Lockhart. Stanford, Calif.: Stanford University Press.

———. 2012. *The Life Within: Local Indigenous Society in Mexico's Toluca Valley, 1650–1800*. Stanford, Calif.: Stanford University Press.

Powers, Karen Vieira. 1995. *Andean Journeys: Migration, Ethnogenesis, and the State in Colonial Quito*. Albuquerque: University of New Mexico Press.

———. 1998. "A Battle of Wills: Inventing Chiefly Legitimacy in the Colonial North Andes." In *Dead Giveaways: Indigenous Testaments of Colonial Mesoamerica and the Andes*, edited by Susan Kellogg and Matthew Restall, 183–214. Salt Lake City: University of Utah Press.

Ramos, Gabriela. 2010. *Death and Conversion in the Andes: Lima and Cuzco, 1532–1670*. Notre Dame, Ind.: University of Notre Dame Press.

Rappaport, Joanne, and Tom Cummins. 2012. *Beyond the Lettered City: Indigenous Literacies in the Andes*. Durham, N.C.: Duke University Press.

Restall, Matthew. 1995. *Life and Death in a Maya Community: The Ixil Testaments of the 1760s*. Lancaster, Calif.: Labyrinthos Press.

———. 1997. *The Maya World: Yucatec Culture and Society, 1550–1850*. Stanford, Calif.: Stanford University Press.

———. 1998. *Maya Conquistador*. Boston: Beacon Press.

Restall, Matthew, and Susan Kellogg. 1998. Introduction to *Dead Giveaways: Indigenous Testaments of Colonial Mesoamerica and the Andes*, edited by Kellogg and Restall, 1–12. Salt Lake City: University of Utah Press.

Restall, Matthew, Lisa Sousa, and Kevin Terraciano, trans. and eds. 2005. *Mesoamerican Voices: Native-Language Writings from Colonial Mexico, Oaxaca, Yucatan, and Guatemala*. Cambridge: Cambridge University Press.

Ricard, Robert. 1966. *The Spiritual Conquest of Mexico: An Essay on the Apostolate and the Evangelizing Methods of the Mendicant Orders in New Spain, 1523–72.* Translated by Lesley Byrd Simpson. Berkeley and Los Angeles: University of California Press.

Rojas Rabiela, Teresa, Elsa Leticia Rea López, Enrique Nieto, Mercedes de los Santos Ortega, and Constantino Medina Lima. 1999–2004. *Vidas y bienes olvidados.* 5 vols. Mexico City: Centro de Investigaciones y Estudios Superiores en Antropología Social, Consejo Nacional de Ciencia y Tecnología.

Salomon, Frank. 1988. "Indian Women of Early Colonial Quito as Seen Through Their Testaments." *The Americas* 44(3): 325–341.

Schroeder, Susan. 2007. "Introduction: The Genre of Conquest Studies." In *Indian Conquistadors: Indigenous Allies in the Conquest of Mesoamerica*, edited by Laura E. Matthew and Michel R. Oudijk, pp. 5–27. Norman: University of Oklahoma Press.

Schroeder, Susan, Stephanie Wood, and Robert Haskett, eds. 1997. *Indian Women of Early Mexico.* Norman: University of Oklahoma Press.

Schwartz, Stuart B. 1973. *Sovereignty and Society in Colonial Brazil: The High Court of Bahia and Its Judges, 1609–1751.* Berkeley: University of California Press.

Silverblatt, Irene. 1987. *Moon, Sun, and Witches: Gender Ideologies and Class in Inca and Colonial Peru.* Princeton, N.J.: Princeton University Press.

Socolow, Susan Migden. 2000. *The Women of Colonial Latin America.* New Approaches to the Americas. Cambridge: Cambridge University Press.

Soriano, Waldemar Espinoza. 1976. "La pachaca de Pariamarca en el reino de Caxamarca, siglos XV–XVII." *Historia y Cultura* 10: 135–180.

Stern, Steve J. 1982. *Peru's Indian Peoples and the Challenge of Spanish Conquest: Huamanga to 1640.* Madison: University of Wisconsin Press.

Taylor, William. 1972. *Landlord and Peasant in Colonial Oaxaca.* Stanford, Calif.: Stanford University Press.

———. 1979. *Drinking, Homicide, and Rebellion in Colonial Mexican Villages.* Stanford, Calif.: Stanford University Press.

Terraciano, Kevin. 1998. "Native Expressions of Piety in Mixtec Testaments." In *Dead Giveaways: Indigenous Testaments of Colonial Mesoamerica and the Andes*, edited by Kellogg and Restall, 115–140. Salt Lake City: University of Utah Press.

———. 2001. *The Mixtecs of Colonial Oaxaca: Ñudzahui History, Sixteenth through Eighteenth Centuries.* Stanford, Calif.: Stanford University Press.

Thompson, Philip C. 1999. *Tekanto, a Maya Town in Colonial Yucatan.* New Orleans: Tulane University Middle American Research Institute.

Truitt, Jonathan. 2012. "Courting Catholicism: Nahua Women and the Catholic Church in Colonial Mexico City." *Ethnohistory* 57(3): 415–444.

White, Richard. 1991. *The Middle Ground: Indians, Empires, and Republics in the Great Lakes Region, 1650–1815.* New York: Cambridge University Press.

Will de Chaparro, Martina. 2007. *Death and Dying in New Mexico.* Albuquerque: University of New Mexico Press.

Wolf, Eric. 1982. *Europe and the People Without a History*. Berkeley: University of California Press.

Wood, Stephanie. 1991. "Adopted Saints: Christian Images in Nahua Testaments of Late Colonial Toluca." *The Americas* 47: 259–293.

———. 2003. *Transcending Conquest: Nahua Views of Spanish Colonial Mexico*. Norman: University of Oklahoma Press.

Yannakakis, Yanna. 2008. *The Art of Being In-Between: Native Intermediaries, Indian Identity, and Local Rule in Colonial Oaxaca*. Durham, N.C.: Duke University Press.

PART 1

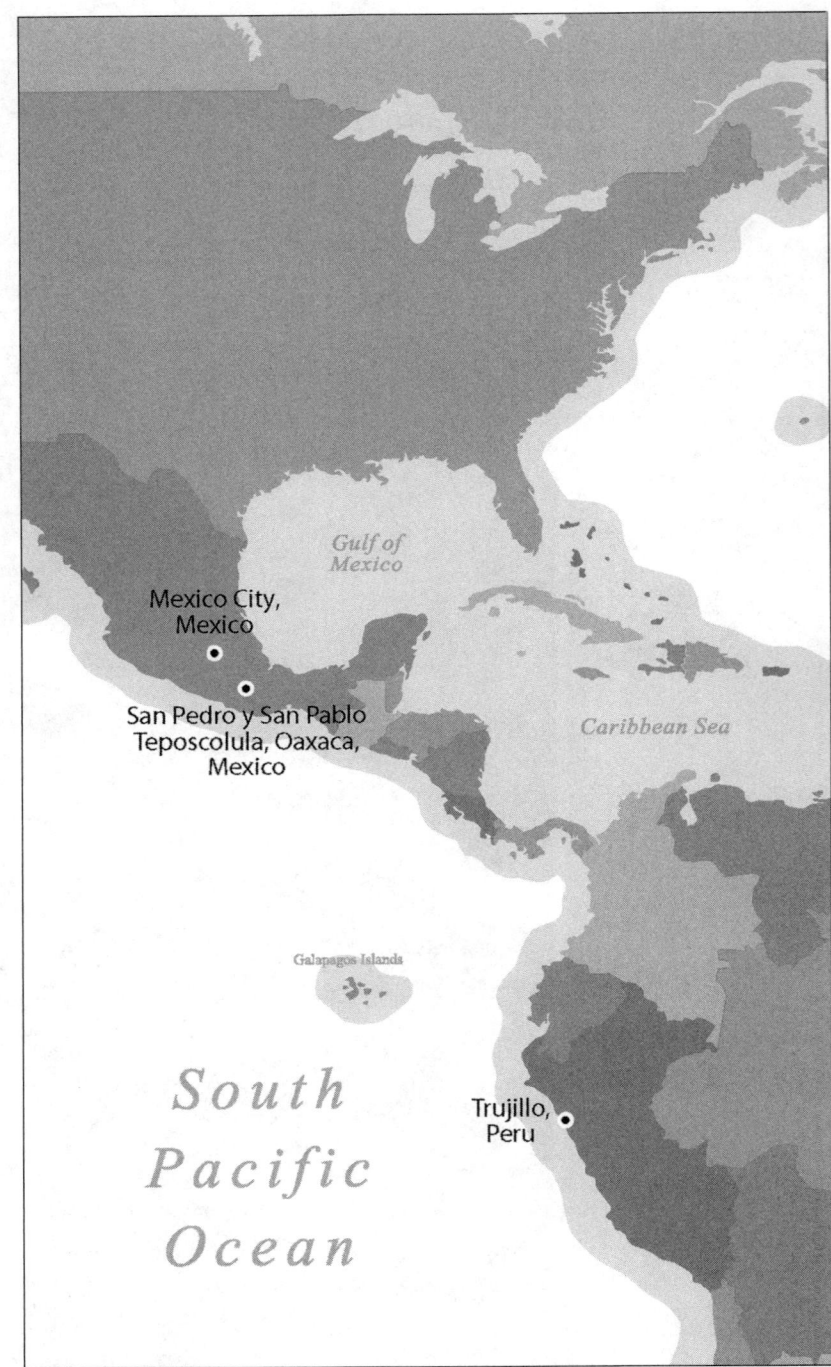

Gulf of
Mexico

Mexico City,
Mexico

San Pedro y San Pablo
Teposcolula, Oaxaca,
Mexico

Caribbean Sea

Galapagos Islands

Trujillo,
Peru

South
Pacific
Ocean

Women of Native America

For years the historiography prescribed a traditional image of colonial life in the Americas sculpted by European, male-driven bureaucracies and institutions. This idea included natives, women, and slaves to be sure, but as passive individuals, not active participants. Then, as scholars explored the subfields of social history, "unexpected" histories emerged, and this image began to crack. Important among many examples is the role of women in colonial society. Works such as *Moon, Sun, and Witches* (Silverblatt 1987), *Sexuality and Marriage in Colonial Latin America* (Lavrin 1992), *Indian Women of Early Mexico* (Schroeder et al. 1997), and *Good Wives, Nasty Wenches, and Anxious Patriarchs* (Brown 1996) all formed part of a new gender history that recognizes the role of women throughout the Americas as contributing historical actors.

The chapters in this section each use wills to uncover aspects of indigenous women's lives in the Americas. Beginning in the Andes, Karen Graubart focuses on the life of Catalina de Agüero. As did many native immigrants, Agüero moved to a city but did not sever ties with her home community. Rather, she found herself in a position between the two. Though she was not of elite status, by the end of her life her social network and estate stood as testament to her success at finding acceptance and prosperity in the Spanish city of Trujillo without abandoning her indigenous roots.

Tatiana Seijas's chapter, "Born Oceans Apart," focuses on a testament from Mexico City, a joint will belonging to a probable Filipino man and a *mulata* woman. As an "indio de las islas filipinas," the testator was eventually considered an indigenous person in legal terms within New Spain. The will uncovers the remarkable and unexpected story of how he started his life in New Spain as a slave, and how his *mulata* wife eventually purchased his freedom. Also employing a will from Mexico City, Jonathan Truitt examines Nicolasa Juana, who belonged to the non-Nahua parish of Mixtecos in Mexico City; it is the only extant document to reveal the Nahua leadership position of the *tenantzin* (people's mother). Closer examination of the will elucidates the ongoing role indigenous women played in the spiritual life of their communities throughout the colonial period.

The focus shifts to southern Mexico with Kevin Terraciano's chapter, "Portrait of a Mixtec Woman Named 6-Crocodile." It starts with a study of the contents of the will, both the items listed and the specific language used, to pinpoint 6-Crocodile's economic and social position in Mixtec society. Terraciano finds that she, as well as other women mentioned in her testament, held an economic position between that of commoner and hereditary elite. Following his examination of the will, he provides an important background on Mixtec as an alphabetic language. Terraciano then applies the information to the testament, demonstrating how colonial notaries and modern scholars use/d the language.

None of the women studied in this section held the noble title of *doña*, but three of them—Catalina de Agüero, Lucía Hernández Ñuquihui (6-Crocodile), and María de la Concepción—were financially secure. Despite not having similar wealth, Nicolasa Juana occupied a position of social importance nonetheless. Although women—and women of subaltern status, in particular—have all too often been written out of the historical record in patriarchal societies, it by no means indicates a complacency on their parts for the assumed status quo. Rather, as demonstrated by María de la Concepción's purchase of Miguel's freedom, women were quite capable of taking action on behalf of the men in their lives. As scholars look closer at the mundane documents of life, they find that women worked within the prescribed strictures of the imposed colonial societies to find a way to secure stability for themselves, their families, and their communities.

References

Brown, Kathleen M. 1996. *Good Wives, Nasty Wenches, and Anxious Patriarchs: Gender, Race, and Power in Colonial Virginia.* Chapel Hill: University of North Carolina Press.

Lavrin, Asuncion. 1992. *Sexuality and Marriage in Colonial Latin America.* Lincoln: University of Nebraska Press.

Schroeder, Susan, Stephanie Wood, and Robert Haskett, eds. 1997. *Indian Women of Early Mexico.* Norman: University of Oklahoma Press.

Silverblatt, Irene. 1987. *Moon, Sun and Witches: Gender Ideologies and Class in Inca and Colonial Peru.* Princeton, N.J.: Princeton University Press.

CHAPTER 1

Catalina de Agüero

A Mediating Life

KAREN B. GRAUBART

The city of Trujillo, Peru, on the Pacific coast some 500 miles north of the Spanish viceregal capital of Lima, was the site of seismic social changes in the sixteenth century. The colonial city was founded in 1534 in a sparsely settled region of the Moche Valley, a desert valley irrigated by rivers that descend from the Andean peaks. The Spanish conquistadors who two years earlier had accompanied Francisco Pizarro to the momentous meeting with Atahualpa at Cajamarca emerged wealthy from Inca gold and silver, and twenty-nine of them settled in Trujillo as *encomenderos*, awarded the right to demand tribute from indigenous communities on the coast and in the nearby highlands. These soldiers-turned-founding citizens were joined by merchants, bureaucrats, priests, treasure seekers, and artisans eager to make their careers in what rapidly became an important secondary port city, part of an Atlantic network linked to Lima and Panama by ocean, and to highland cities such as Cajamarca, Chachapoyas, Quito, and Loja by mule train.

Because of its key position on the coast en route to Lima-Callao, Trujillo became home to Spanish-owned cattle ranches, sugar estates, and wheat farms, labored on by indigenous *mita* (forced labor rotation) and wage workers, and, increasingly, African slaves. Indigenous communities, hard hit by epidemics and forced migration, produced the crops and products required by the *encomenderos* (particularly wheat, poultry, corn, cloth, and silver) as well as for their own needs. Over the next few decades (and despite periodic environmental disasters stemming from El Niño events) Trujillo became a vibrant participant in the growing Atlantic economy, feeding the Panamanian isthmus and Peru, and purchasing European clothing, wine, and luxury goods, along with enslaved Africans.[1]

While Spaniards formally founded the city, most of the city's immigrants were not Europeans. In 1604, one of the earliest dates for which we have a reasonable population estimate, the city's 3,188 inhabitants were nearly equally divided (according to the categories of the census taker) among "Spaniards and mestizos" (1,021), "blacks and *mulatos*" (1,073), and "Indians" (1,094).[2] The number of Afro-Peruvians is worth remarking, as many enslaved men and women were manumitted and formed a free black community alongside the many enslaved laborers, artisans, and domestic servants.[3] The indigenous residents of Trujillo were almost entirely immigrants too: while there were likely some displaced communities in the area "founded" by Spaniards, they were too few or too disempowered to show up in the legal record.[4] On the other hand, the city and its employment opportunities exercised an inexorable pull on many indigenous residents of the region's small towns. At times this pull was coerced, and many Andean men and women left natal communities because their labor was claimed by Spaniards with power over them. But many immigrated voluntarily, hoping for relief from increasing tribute rates and decreasing tributaries, or attracted by the novelty of the city. These indigenous immigrants (like the Spaniards and Afro-Peruvians) came to reimagine their ethnicities through their collective actions, but also through their interactions across racial and ethnic boundaries in the Atlantic world.[5]

Urban life was not particularly easy for indigenous immigrants. Regular work was scarce; if not employed in elite households, women and men sought patchy incomes selling commodities in the markets or apprenticed to learn the skills necessary to hold a trade such as tailoring or shoemaking. A great many became the marginal poor who lived on the outskirts of the *traza* (center of the city). A smaller number found economic stability or prosperity, and some even purchased the desirable *solares* (urban plots) in the *traza* where Trujillo's wealthiest housed themselves.[6] But the city also had a significant group of indigenous residents who, while by no means wealthy, found ways to make do, sometimes by plying a variety of trades that connected them to both rural communities and the new Atlantic economy.

Excavating these early urban lives through wills demonstrates some important truths about colonial interdependence. First, it was not inevitable that indigenous immigrants lost ties with their rural kin, nor did they fall readily into simple categories of "acculturated" or not. Many successful immigrants appear to have embraced the diversity of their present, mediating easily between what might be falsely set off as a prehispanic past and an Atlantic future. We cannot know whether these individuals saw themselves as embracing novelty or simply as making do with the options open to them, but their wills illustrate the variety of terms through which urban residents presented themselves.

In February of 1570, an indigenous woman named Catalina de Agüero came before the Spanish notary Juan de Mata in Trujillo to record what she believed to be her last wishes.[7] She was suffering from a serious illness and hoped to establish the inheritances of her children and also to place her soul "on the road to salvation." She had been born shortly after the conquest of Peru in a small town in the highlands of Cajamarca, a few days' journey west of coastal Trujillo. Agüero does not seem to have been a member of the native elite: she was not called *doña* in her will, as indigenous women of even remotely noble lineage commonly were (Charney, this volume). Yet she ended her life the owner of multiple properties in Trujillo and the mother of two mestizo children, with a modest estate and a social network that included powerful elite Spanish men.

Taken in the context of other archival documents, Agüero's will describes a life lived at a profound moment of transformation, from the chaotic world of Inca civil war and the eventual Spanish conquest into a colonial society linked to Europe and Africa, and she lived as an intermediary between those worlds. It also provides a glimpse of how an indigenous woman who appears at first glance to have lacked options in a world that marginalized both Indians and women was able to build a life that filled her needs in a way that might have been unrecognizable to her predecessors and taken for granted by her descendants.

Routes to the City

Catalina de Agüero was born in Pomamarca, one of the seven *guarangas* of Cajamarca.[8] This moderate-sized community was, after the Spanish conquest, assigned in *encomienda* by Francisco Pizarro in 1535 to the *comendador* Melchor Verdugo, famed not only for his military prowess alongside Pizarro, but also his many abuses of power.[9] Pomamarca itself was the subject of a famous litigation between Verdugo (and, after his death, his widow, doña Jordana Mejía) and a series of recipients of pieces of the *encomienda*, which was subdivided by the viceroy in 1542 for being too large for a single income (Del Busto Duthurburu 1981, 76). Catalina de Agüero presumably was at some point a tributary of Verdugo's and likely had an even closer relationship than that, given the description in her will of a personal bequest from him of certain "Castilian sheep."[10]

Agüero's will does not mention how she arrived in Trujillo, but it speaks of her "service" to Diego de Olivares and his daughter, Ana, from whom she requested her salary. We may surmise, then, that Agüero, like many indigenous women, arrived in the city as a domestic servant to a Spanish family (Glave 1989; Graubart 2007).[11] Agüero likely worked in the household of Olivares, who was then a prominent citizen of Trujillo (where he had been *alcalde*, or magistrate) and of Chachapoyas (where he had been *alguacil mayor*, or chief constable). Olivares also had a close friendship with Melchor Verdugo and Jordana Mejía, and the three were regular business partners in the collection of Cajamarca's tribute and the sale of indigenous textiles and African slaves, among other things (Zevallos Quiñones 1996, 1:199, 2:255).

Agüero might have come to the Olivares family from service in Melchor Verdugo's household. She spoke, as noted, of a "legacy" of some sheep. During his last illness, in 1566, Verdugo had a crisis of conscience over his mistreatment of the indigenous communities of Cajamarca. In particular, he repented of his abuse of "personal service," obliging the Indians of his encomienda to work in his and his friends' houses and haciendas, and in the region's mines—all without pay. In his will Verdugo left a portion of his fortune for these workers' salaries, as well as to endow a hospital and other charitable works. In one clause he left 100 sheep and 10 rams to Catalina de Agüero "for the good services which she has done me and for the long time she has served me" (Zevallos Quiñones 1996, 2:244).

Agüero's service to Verdugo probably began while she was a small child, removed from her natal community and placed in a Spanish household. Her will lacks even the most basic information about her family: neither mother, nor father, nor spouse is named in the first lines, where such a statement was expected. The declaration of the testator's parents had paramount importance since when there were no surviving children, the parents were the *herederos forzosos*, or compulsory heirs of the estate. Catalina de Agüero's will omits most of this information, only indicating her birth in Pomamarca and her legal/cultural status as *yndia ladina* (Spanish-speaking Indian). We see the same omission in the wills of other women who worked as domestic servants from a young age, including Catalina Chumbi, who drafted a will in 1574 and noted explicitly that "she did not know her parents."[12]

But this silence goes deeper into the will. Although Agüero maintained her herd in Cajamarca, they were "in the power of don Pablo Malcadan, nobleman of Cajamarca." Malcadan was a *guaranga* in Cajamarca, and Agüero was certainly referring to its *kuraka*, whom she might have known through Verdugo and his circle (Ramírez 2002, 31–32; Rostworowski and Remy 1992, 1:108). Beyond don Pablo, the will names only two other indigenous members of the Cajamarca community, her niece and her niece's husband. Everyone who currently played an important role in her life—her executor, the guardian she named for her children, the man with whom she left some pesos for "investment"—were *vecinos* of the city of Trujillo, and Spanish men. In his study of domestic servants in the eighteenth-century Andes, Miguel Glave discovered that "many…[indigenous domestic workers] were lacking in ties to family networks in rural towns and *ayllus*" (Glave 1989, 337). While Glave characterized this as a "cultural uprooting," there is no reason to see the adoption of a new community as necessarily culturally unhealthy.

Finally, we might consider her surname: de Agüero. By the last decades of the sixteenth century, indigenous men and women were required to baptize their children, giving them a Spanish first name such as "Catalina." Surnames in local rural areas were almost always derived from indigenous languages: an administrative inspection carried out in rural Cajamarca in the 1570s registered most residents with a Christian baptismal name and a Quechua or Mochic surname (e.g., "Juan Colquemoro," "Andres Chal"). Pomamarca's registers do not include a single Agüero nor any Spanish surname whatsoever (Rostworowski and Remy 1992, 1:189–207). In contrast, many of Trujillo's indigenous residents carried the same surnames as Spaniards, and these commonly indicated a form of intimacy: godparentage, unacknowledged parentage, or simply being raised in the household of a family with that name (as was also the case for slaves). Although wills rarely clarify this issue, many indigenous women with Spanish surnames used their wills to collect salaries and other debts from Spanish men with the same last name (Graubart 2007, 108–109). These rather oblique cases suggest that either parentage or employment preceded the shared surname.

We know little of Agüero's later career. She cared for the sick, as in the case of the daughter of her master, Olivares; healing was a common occupation among indigenous women in colonial cities, and many had a multiethnic clientele, drawing upon the reputation of Indians as "witches" or curers (Osorio 1999). Within an elite household, a servant had access to a variety of people, from enslaved Africans to the elite of Trujillano society, who might need her services during an illness or when seeking remedies for lost love or bad luck. A servant might also draw upon a reputation as a healer when trying to widen her social network and create a base for other businesses.

Lacking additional sources, we cannot guess how Agüero earned her keep, but it is clear that she had more resources than a servant's salary, which in this period was generally between ten and fifteen pesos a year plus some clothing, a bed, and meals (Graubart 2007, chap. 2). Nor did she receive significant income from her herd of sheep; apparently she obeyed Verdugo's final instructions not to sell them, and the small herd had nearly doubled by 1570. In any case, at the time of her death she had far more property than most servants.

In the first place, Agüero owned various pieces of real estate. Her will speaks of three *solares* in the center of the city, previously reserved for prominent Spanish citizens but, as the economy boomed and busted, an increasingly multiethnic location (Noack 2005). She had purchased two of these from Antonio Martín, "for a hundred pesos," and the third from "Falcon, schoolmaster." While buying real estate on credit was common, Agüero indicated clearly that she bought hers with cash, and, in contrast with many colonial wills (including several described in this volume), hers did not speak of loans or debts beyond the pesos Olivares owed her in salary.

These property purchases were intended to serve as her daughter's dowry, "for which purpose I bought them for her." Moreover, she had placed 100 pesos in silver in the hands of Diego García Trujillo, a business associate of Diego de Olivares, to invest, also to assure her daughter's future.[13]

It was a long journey from her beginnings in Pomamarca to Catalina de Agüero's status as a woman of some property and investments in the city of Trujillo, which had barely existed at the time of her birth. We are not speaking solely of economic stability, but also of a process of transculturation, or the adaptation of the symbols and techniques of colonial society as an integral part of her adult existence: a new name, the ability to speak Spanish, and a social network that replaced her kin networks in the *sierra*. Her will allows us to understand how she forged this new ethnic identity in a key moment of urban colonial history.

The Formation of a Social Network

However she arrived there, Catalina de Agüero seems to have found her way in Trujillo. Not only did she purchase properties and amass funds, but she also lived the part of a woman of status: she worshipped prominently in a Catholic Church and dressed in a colonial fashion, mixing styles and fabrics that were imported as well as local and regional. She also formed part of a network that transcended economic class and ethnicity.

In her hour of need she called upon a notary to prepare her will and adeptly followed standard legal and religious practices rather than ones that marked her as belonging elsewhere (see Hosselkus, this volume, for a comparative case). She knowledgeably detailed her burial (dressed in a Franciscan habit), her final resting place, and the full complement of masses and offerings. She was assisted in this matter by two Franciscan friars and, having no compulsory heirs—legitimate children or living parents—she chose her own soul as heir, indicating that once her debts and bequests were paid, the remainder of her estate would be spent on masses to assure the quick passage of her soul from purgatory: "I name and leave as my universal heir in all of it my soul, so that everything be turned over to…my executor, and that he sell it all and distribute its value in doing good for my soul, as he sees fit, by saying masses for my soul and the discharge of my conscience."

The process of evangelization in the sixteenth century was quite slow in most highland communities, where indigenous elites were required to perform acts identifying themselves as Christians, such as giving family members burial in a church, in order to hold their offices, but most did little other than receive baptism.[14] In the cities, however, Christianity offered opportunities for indigenous immigrants, particularly through membership in a confraternity, a religious society generally open to people of all classes and ethnicities. Confraternities offered material benefits as well as spiritual ones, including loans and charitable assistance, and the presence of large numbers of mourners at one's funeral.[15] Many indigenous men and women joined confraternities, and even more left small bequests to the church for masses and pious works, suggesting that urban residents constructed meaningful communities through these means.

Although she chose her soul as her final heir, Agüero had two children for whom she left careful bequests. They were "natural" children, signifying that neither their mother nor father was married at the time of birth—not to each other or anyone else. Legally, she was not required to recognize them in her will, but she did, in the paragraphs directly following her spiritual desires, underlining their importance in her life and plans. In contrast with some other mothers of illegitimate children, she did not use her will to identify a powerful or wealthy father who might take on responsibility for their care; she simply referred to "a Spaniard now deceased" and "Juan Herrera, mestizo." Herrera did not figure in any other part of her will, and it appears that he had no ongoing relationship with either mother or son.

Berta Ares Queija (1997) and Elizabeth Kuznesof (1995) have argued that a great part of the first generation of "Spaniards" born in the New World were, biologically, mestizos because of the relative absence of Spanish women in the colonies and the obvious discrepancies between the large numbers of births registered as "Spaniards" and the small number as "mestizos." They find that the children of Spanish conquistadors and indigenous women (to whom they were rarely married) were categorized as Spaniards if they lived with their father, and thus were able to inherit their father's estate. Mestizos, on the other hand, were thought of as persons without material wealth, status, or legitimate parentage. But Ares and Kuznesof both posit just two outcomes for these ethnically mixed children: those recognized by their fathers and considered Spaniards, and those not recognized by their Spanish fathers and raised by their mothers as Indians in indigenous communities. In the case of Catalina de Agüero a third possibility arises: those raised with their mother in an urban setting, with a more complicated ethnicity—that of an urban mestizo.

Urban mestizos lacking legal recognition or material support from their fathers shared characteristics with another new group, *indios criollos*: indigenous men and women born in cities, away from rural kin networks.[16] Although colonial bureaucrats often preferred to place subjects into crude categories such as "Indians" and "Spaniards," urban inhabitants in the sixteenth century had their own associations and also might migrate from one category to another, or even avoid colonial categories entirely depending upon their social status, profession, or other qualification (Cahill 1994; Cope 1994). Trujillo's archives demonstrate this through wills left by men of African parentage who were called *vecinos* (citizens) rather than *mulatos*, and through evidence of indigenous women losing the marker *yndia* as they gained wealth and came to be addressed as *doña* (Graubart 2007). What is common among these cases is that they all found social and economic mobility, creating their own cultural place in a multiethnic urban center. Contextualized studies of these transitional characters are few, but Catalina de Agüero's instructions for her illegitimate children offer some clues as to how status could be created and passed intergenerationally.[17]

Agüero distributed her estate between her children quite explicitly. Francisco would receive two mattresses and the proceeds from the sale of most of her sheep in Cajamarca. Her daughter, Juana, received 100 pesos in silver, two *solares* (worth another 100 pesos), a bedspread, and two mattresses. Juana's bequest was intended for her dowry, an indication that a bit of capital might erase some of the social "stains" that accompanied illegitimacy and *mestizaje*. In 1570, neither bequest was a fortune—Diego de Olivares provided dowries of 3,000 pesos to each of his four illegitimate daughters that same year—but a few hundred pesos in cash could make the difference between a marginal existence and one with promise.[18]

In her study of illegitimacy in colonial Latin America, Ann Twinam (1999, 159) suggests that this "condition" generated a series of problems for children as well as adults: an insecure childhood, poverty, even the inability to contract a favorable marriage or acquire a public office. Evidently, this kind of future preoccupied Catalina de Agüero, and she dedicated herself not only to providing financial resources for her children but also a supporting social network. Choosing Hernando Estebes, a Spanish *vecino*, as guardian for her children (as well as her executor) indicated her intent to construct a secure environment for them, even beyond the cash bequests. With this social connection they could expect to be marriageable, to have access to financial capital for their businesses, and to have a support system based in the most important institutions of the colonial city: the *cabildo*, the church, and the elite. Thus the two children would have a beginning very different from that of their mother: rather than "Indians" leaving their rural community for the life of a domestic servant in a new home, they would be residents of a city where they could count upon at least the limited protection of powerful friends and patrons. Their mother's achievements should not simply be evaluated by the property and luxury goods she amassed during her lifetime, but also by the social network she constructed for the maintenance of her family in the city.

Conclusions: Dressing for Difference

Finally, we can comment upon material life and *mentalité* through an examination of the most common objects in indigenous wills: clothing. Agüero's estate included a collection of clothing Andean in style, but many items were made from imported European and Asian textiles. She had, for example, indigenous-style *anacos* (wrap dresses) and *lliquillas* (large shawls), but rather than being woven with local cotton or wool, these were made of Rouen cloth (a French cotton) and *olanda* (fine linen). Although not the most expensive textiles in American markets, Rouen cloth and *olanda* represented luxury goods, and by using them, Agüero presented herself as socially ascendant. She also wore clothing made of *cumbi*, a textile whose use had once been restricted to the Inca nobility as a potent social symbol but which was now available for anyone able to purchase it, indigenous or Spanish (Murra 1962; Niles 1992). While not as wealthy or elite as don García Pilco Guaman, the *curaca* of the nearby Jequetepeque Valley, who had dual wardrobes that allowed him to demonstrate his elite status either as a high-ranking Andean lord or a wealthy European, Agüero rethought her Andean clothes through a European textile vernacular that was becoming available to her through the Atlantic economy.[19]

Nearly a century later, Francisca Ramírez, another indigenous resident in Trujillo, would move away from indigenous-style *lliquillas* and *anacos*, even in imported materials, toward a fully Hispanicized wardrobe as she grew wealthier and more purposefully disconnected from her rural roots. She began as a *chicha* vendor, dressed in the style of an Andean peasant, but ended calling herself *doña*, dressing in fully European garments, and operating a store whose clientele were all Spaniards. Agüero, formulating an urban ethnicity as Trujillo's economy was just beginning to open itself to Atlantic wares and status symbols, presented herself as a member of a changing society; by Ramírez's time, a woman could make herself less distinctive from Spaniards while calling herself (likely spuriously) a member of the indigenous elite.[20]

Indigenous immigrants to Trujillo in the sixteenth century exhibited a strong self-consciousness of their social position as "Indians" who had left their communities and were now residents of a city. They did not have a substantial middling group, as in Lima, which became nearly indistinguishable from plebeian Spaniards, dressing in an Atlantic vernacular and accustomed to buying and owning African slaves. They modified their garments less rapidly, wearing a wardrobe that gestured to both Andean and European fashion, differentiating themselves more clearly from the city's blacks, mestizos, and Spaniards. Like Agüero they purchased clothing and real estate, and participated in institutions that spoke to their new status, but without entirely changing their physical appearance. The children of these immigrants, however, might have seen themselves as part of a new urban culture, without ties to rural communities or the economic status of tributaries. In her will Agüero requested that all of her clothing be auctioned off to pay for masses; she did not leave her daughter the *lliquilla*, *topo*, or *mamachumbe*, which had signaled the status of tributary. She left Juana only property, cash, and European bedclothes—resources that she could use in the life Agüero imagined for her.

Thus Catalina de Agüero physically presented herself as an urban, transculturated indigenous woman, dressed in a wardrobe that spoke of her birth community and her ancestors—the colonial indigenous uniform of *anaco* and *lliquilla*—but also indicated the changes to her status, her occupation, and her residence in the city. She could purchase expensive textiles like Andean *cumbi*, but also imported European linens. In this sense, Agüero was a mediator between these now-linked cultures. We cannot guess how she experienced this mediation. Did she see herself taking sides in a cultural collision, or was this all perfectly normalized for her? But certainly she recognized the duality of her situation, and she understood that her children would not experience the colonial world in the same way.

Catalina de Agüero is representative of processes that took place in Atlanticizing cities such as Trujillo during the final decades of the sixteenth century. Born an indigenous tributary, she was removed from her rural community at a young age, raised with emotional and material ties to elite Spaniards, and spent the rest of her life as yet another urban immigrant. As such, she acquired the accoutrements of urban colonial life: a close relationship with the Catholic Church, clothing appropriated from various cultural traditions, and professional and sexual relationships with Spanish

and mestizo men. Her will demonstrates that this process of transculturation can be seen not as a cultural loss, but as a creative reinvention of
community that took place parallel with the preservation of certain rural
ties, however weak.

On the other hand, Agüero's children were creole residents of the city,
with only distant ties to an indigenous community. They likely spoke only
Spanish, dressed like plebeian Spaniards, and, with luck, married into "de-
cent" families. Because of the struggles and strategies of their immigrant
mother, they would not have doubted their own social position.

Testament of Catalina de Agüero

Transcription
*(Archivo Regional de La Libertad,
Protocolos Notariales, leg. 11, fol. 42r [25.2.1570])*
En el nombre de dios nro nño sr e de la sienpre virgin ma su bendita
madre y señora nña sepan quantos esta carta vieren como yo Cata de
Aguero yndia ladina en la lengua española natural q̃ soy de las probincias
de caxamalca de la guaranga de pomamarca otorgo e conosco por esta
presente carta que hago e ordeno este my testamento y prostimera
boluntad a onrra y gloria de dios nño sor e de su bendita madre en quyen
creo y adoro firmemente que la santa madre ygleçia de roma lo tiene e
cree en la forma e manera siguyente.

Yten mando que si dios nño sor fuere serbido de me llebar desta
presente enfermedad que my cuerpo sea enterrado en la ygleçia del sor
San Franco desta çibdad arriba de la pila del agua bendita en la parte
q̃ a mis albaçeas paresciere y que acompañan my cuerpo la cruz alta y
los curas de la ygleçia mayor desta çibdad y q̃ por todo ello se pague la
limosna acostumbrada.

Yten mando que el dia de mi entierro si fuere ora y si no otro dia
siguyente me digan en la dha ygleçia del sor Franco una misa de requyen
cantada ofrendada al paresçer de mys albaçeas y otro dia siguyente me
digan otra mysa de requyen cantada en la dha ygleçia y monesterio por
la mysma orden que la de cuerpo presente y por todo ello se pague la
limosna acostumbrada.

Yten mando que me entierren con el abito del sor san franco y que se
pague la limosna acostumbrada.

Yten mando que en la dha ygleçia del s^{or} san fran^{co} desta cibdad me
digan quatro misas resadas por [mi] anyma.

Yten declaro que tengo por mis hijos naturales a juana nyña mestiza
hija de un español ques muerto.

Yten declaro que tengo por mi hijo natural a fran^{co} mestizo my hijo y
hijo de juan herrera mestizo.

Yten declaro que tengo en poder de diego garcia de trug^o çien pos
en plata que le di p^a que sean y case con ellos los quales le di e tengo
señalados pa la dha Juana my hija p^a su casamiento mando q se le den con
todo lo que con ellos se obiere granjeado.

Y ansimismo mando a la dha juana my hija dos solares que tengo en la
traza de esta cibdad i compre de antonio mỹn en cien pos los quales dhos
solares mando a la dha my hija pa su casamiento por quanto los compre
pa ella e siempre los e tenido e tengo señalados p^a la susodha p^a el dho
efeto mando q̃ se le den e que sean sus bienes propios e con mas los cien
p^{os} questan en poder del dho diego garcia de trug^o e proçedido dellos.

Yten declaro que tengo en las probinçias de caxamalca çiertas obejas
de castilla q̃ seran como dozientas las quales proceden de una manda q̃
me mando el comendador M^{or} Verdugo las quales estan en poder de don
pablo malcaden prençipal de caxamalca mando q̃ della se den treynta
obejas a andres yndio q me sirbio y esta casado con una sobrina mya y las
demas se bendan y se de el proçedido dellas al dho fran^{co} my hijo.

Yten declaro que tengo por mis bienes un solar q̃ compre en p^{os} de
falcon maestro de muchachos mando que se benda con los dhos mis
bienes pa hazer della bien my anyma como de yuso va declarado.

Yten declaro q̃ tengo en my cama quatro colchones y una frezada
mando que los colchones se den a la dha juana mi hija con mas la frasada
y los otros dos colchones se den al dho fran^{co} my hijo.

Yten mando a las mandas forsosas lo acostumbrado doze a cada una
dellas.

Yten declaro q̃ tengo mas por mis bienes los siguientes
quatro piezas de ropa de lana cumbi
una liquilla de algodon de colores
dos liquillas de tafetan la una colorada y la otra amarilla
seis tiras de red
un paño de manos de olanda labrada de seda carmesi
otro paño de manos labrado de seda verde y colorado

dos almohadas labradas grana no tienen mas de un hazerico
dos tiras de almohadas labradas de grana
una tabla de manteles de castilla
niebe pañezuelos de mesa de castilla y de algodon
dos mamachumbes de lana
una delantera de cama de red
dos cortinas de algodon
una cestilla con çiertos adereços cortados y otros cosillas de ruan
una almohada bieja labrada de negro
un anaco y una lliquiyda de olanda traydo
otro anaco de ruan
dos topos de plata dorados
otros tres topos de plata dorados mas chicos
un dedal de oro y unos pedacillos de oro
dos cucharas de plata
un poco de franja de algodon
treze obillos de hilo de algodon chicos y grandes
una tira de red de almohada
una [ilegible] labrada de azul
tres collares de ruan con sus polaynas pa camisas bastas
una ymagen de nra sa de bidrio sin guarneçer
un lienço de colchon de algodon traydo
tres madejas de seda una colorada y otra blanca y otra amarilla
una sabana de algodon trayda
una caxa con su llabe
dos mantas de lonas y costales
sesenta pos que me deben los bienes de dio de olibares los veynte q̄
mando su hija ana de olivares porque la cure y serbi y los quarenta que me
mando el dho de serbiçio en su enfermedad

Yten dexo y nonbro por tutores curador de las personas e bienes de
los dhos juana y franco mys hijos a herdo estebes vecº desta cibdad el qual
quyero e mdo sea tutor e curados de sus personas e bienes.

Yten pa cumplir e pagar este my testamto y las mandas y legatos y
obras pias y demas cabsas en el contenydos dexo y nombro por my
albaçea y testamentario a herdo esteves vecº desta cibdad questa presente
al qual doy poder cumplido tal qual de dr̄o en tal caso se requiere pa q̄
entre todos mys bienes e los benda y remate en puca almoneda y fuera

della y de su balor cumpla y pague este my testam^to y las mandas y legatos
en el contenidos aunque sea pagado el año de albaçeasgo.

Y en el remanyente que quedare e fincare de todos mys bienes d^ros y
acciones dexo y nombro por my unibersal heredero en todos ellos a mi
anyma p^a que todos ellos esten en poder del dho her^do estebes my albaçea
e los benda e su balor distribuya en hazer bien por my anima a su pareçer
e boluntad asi q̄ dezir mysas por my anima y descargo de my conçiençia
porquesta es mi ultima e postrimera boluntad.

Y por este mi testam^to y prostimera boluntad reboco e anulo e doy
por ningunos todos e qualesquier testamentos codicilios clausulas
mandas que hasta el dia de oy aya fho e otorgado por escrito o por palabra
que auyero que no balgan ny fagan fee en juizio ny fuera del salbo este
my testam^to y prostimera boluntad del qual quiero que balga por my
testam^to e codiçilio o por escritura pu^ca a como mejor de dr̄o aya lugar
en testimonyo de lo qual otorgue esta carta segun dho es ante el escri^o
publico e testigos de yuso escritos ques fha e otorgado en esta çibdad de
trug^o del piru en beynte y çinco dias del mes de heb^o de mill e quy^os e
setenta a^s t^os que fueron presentes a lo q̄ dho es luys rrodriguez e luis de
montalbo e luys mȳn e fray xpobal lopez y fray ju^o de la conseçion de la
orden del s^or Sn Fran^co y en dho otorgante a la qual yo el escrivano doy
fee conosco no firmo porque no supo firmaron por ella dos t^os en este
registro.

Soy t^o Luis Rrodriguez [rúbrica] por t^o luys de montalvo [rúbrica]
fho ante my Ju^o de Mata
esc^o pu^co

Translation

In the name of God our lord and of the always virginal María his blessed
mother and our lady, let all who see this letter know that I, Catalina de
Agüero, a Spanish-speaking Indian woman, native that I am of the provinces of Cajamarca, of the *guaranga* of Pomamarca, execute and recognize
by this letter that I make and put in order this my last will and testament,
to the honor and glory of God our lord and of his blessed mother in whom
I believe, and I firmly worship whatever the holy mother church of Rome
holds and believes, in the following form and manner.

Item, I order that if God our lord were pleased to take me from this
present illness, that my body be buried in the church of San Francisco in

this city, above the holy water font, in the place chosen by my executors; and that the high cross and the priests of the Cathedral church of this city accompany my body; and that the customary offering be paid for this.

Item, I order that on the day of my funeral, if there is time, and if not on a following day, a requiem mass be sung in the church of San Francisco, as my executors see fit, and another subsequent day they sing another requiem mass in the said church and monastery, in the same manner as that with the body present, and for all of this the customary offering be paid.

Item, I order that they bury me in the habit of San Francisco, and that the customary offering be paid.

Item, I order that they say four low masses for my soul in the church of San Francisco in this city.

Item, I declare that I have for my illegitimate children [sic] Juana, a young girl, a mestiza, daughter of a Spaniard who is dead.

Item, I declare that I have for my illegitimate son, Francisco, mestizo, my son and the son of Juan Herrera mestizo.

Item, I declare that I have one hundred pesos in silver, being held by Diego García of Trujillo, which I gave to him to invest for me; I have designated them for the said Juana, my daughter, for her marriage; I order that she be given these plus all the accumulated profits.

And likewise I leave for the said Juana my daughter two solares, which I have in the traza of this city; and I bought them from Antonio Martin for one hundred pesos; the said solares I bequeath to my said daughter for her marriage because I bought them for her and I have always designated them for this purpose, that they be given to her, and that they be her property, in addition to the one hundred pesos that the said Diego García of Trujillo is holding, and the proceeds from those.

Item, I declare that I have, in the provinces of Cajamarca, certain Castilian sheep, which should be some two hundred, which proceed from a bequest left to me by the comendador Melchor Verdugo; these are in the hands of don Pablo Malcaden, nobleman of Cajamarca; I order that of these, thirty sheep should be given to the Indian Andrés, who served me and is married to my niece, and the rest be sold and the proceeds given to the said Francisco my son.

Item, I declare that I have as my property a solar which I purchased from Falcon, the schoolmaster; I order that it be sold with my property in order to do good for my soul, as will be declared below.

Item, I declare that I have in my bed four mattresses and a bedspread; I order that two mattresses be given to my daughter Juana along with the bedspread, and the other two mattresses to my son Francisco.

Item, I leave for the mandatory charitable gifts the customary amount, twelve [*sic*] to each.

Item, I declare that I have as my property the following:

Four pieces of clothing made of woolen cumbi cloth

A *lliquilla* [shawl] of colored cotton

Two *lliquillas* of taffeta, one red and the other yellow

Six pieces of net

A hand cloth made of fine linen embroidered with red silk

Two scarlet-embroidered cushions, very small ones.

Two strips of scarlet-embroidered cushion.

A tablecloth from Castile

Nine small tablecloths, some Castilian, some cotton.

Two woolen *mamachumbes* [large woven belts]

A net bed spread

Two cotton curtains

A small basket with bits of cloth and ornament

An old cushion, embroidered in black

An *anaco* and *lliquilla* of fine linen, worn out.

Another *anaco* made of *ruán* [cotton cloth manufactured in Rouen]

Two silver *topos* [pins], gold plated

Three more silver *topos*, gold plated

A gold thimble and some little bits of gold

Two silver spoons

A bit of cotton fringe

Thirteen skeins of cotton thread, large and small

A strip of a net cushion

Three basted *ruán* collars with matching cuffs for shirts

An undecorated glass image of Our Lady

A cotton mattress, worn out

Three skeins of silk thread, one red, another white, and the other yellow.

A worn-out cotton sheet

A wooden chest with its key

Two canvas blankets and bags

Sixty pesos owed to me by the estate of Diego de Olivares; the twenty that his daughter Ana de Olivares left me because I healed her, and the forty that Diego de Olivares left me for my service during his illness.

Item, I leave, and name as tutor and guardian of the persons and estates of the said Juana and Francisco, my children, Hernando Esteves, citizen of this city, whom I wish and order that he be their tutor and guardian of their property

Item, in order to complete and pay for this my will and the bequests and legacies and charitable acts and other things contained within it, I leave and name as my executor and testamentarian Hernando Esteves, citizen of this city who is now present, to whom I give full power of attorney, as necessary by law, so that he may take possession of my property and sell and liquidate them in public auction or elsewhere, and with the proceeds carry out and pay for this my will, and the bequests and legacies contained within, as long as these are paid within the year allowed by law.

And, for whatever is left over from my estate and lawsuits, I name and leave as my universal heir in all of it my soul, so that everything be turned over to the power of Hernando Esteves, my executor, and that he sell it all and distribute its value in doing good for my soul, as he sees fit, by saying masses for my soul and the discharge of my conscience, because this is my final will.

And by this last will and testament I revoke and annul all other testaments, codicils, clauses, bequests, which made before today, executed in writing or orally, have no value in court or out of court, except this my last will and testament, which I desire to be valid as my will and codicil, by public statement as law sees fit, in testimony of which I execute this letter before the public notary and witnesses written below, which is written and executed in this city of Trujillo of Peru, on the twenty-fifth day of the month of February of the year one thousand, five hundred and seventy, before the witnesses who were present who are Luys Rodriguez and Luis de Montalbo and Luys Martin and fray Cristobal Lopez and fray Juan de la Concepcion of the Franciscan Order, and the said deponent, whom I the notary swear I know, did not sign because she did not know how, and two witnesses signed the document on her behalf.

In witness: Luis Rodríguez [signature] As witness: Luys de Montalvo [signature]

Before me, Juan de Mata, notary public

Notes

1. On Trujillo's early economy, see Ramírez 1986, chaps. 2–3; and the introduction in O'Toole 2012.
2. Romero 1925, 91–93. The manuscript cites a census carried out by the *corregidor* don Felipe de Lazcano in 1604 and includes the inhabitants of local haciendas as well as those resident within the city walls.
3. On Africans in colonial cities see O'Toole 2012; Bowser 1974; Cope 1994; and Seijas, this volume.
4. In contrast with Lima, which had a significant displaced population (whose leaders later sued Spanish authorities) as well as good-sized regional communities. See Charney, this volume; and Graubart 2007, 13–16.
5. On ethnicity in the Atlantic world, see Graubart 2013.
6. While Indians were legally excluded from owning *solares*, *cabildo* records show that some, including plebeians, were indeed granted these properties. See, for example, Concejo Provincial de Trujillo 1969, 109, 150.
7. Testamento de Catalina de Agüero, Archivo Regional de la Libertad (ARRL), Protocolos Notariales (PN), leg. 11, fol. 42r (25.2.1570).
8. *Guaranga* is a Quechua term meaning "1,000," used to indicate a sociopolitical unit composed of *pachacas* (units of 100). The two terms were commonly used in the Cajamarca region to denote a community, as opposed to *ayllu*, which was used by the Incas and reintroduced into Cajamarca by Spaniards after the conquest. See Rostworowski and Remy 1992, 1:73.
9. Verdugo was present at the second (and definitive) founding of the city, in March 1535, when he was presented with "yndios de repartimiento" by Pizarro. See Consejo Provincial de Trujillo, 1:391–392.
10. As differentiated from *carneros de la tierra* (llamas and alpacas).
11. Nearly half of the 1,094 indigenous residents in the 1604 Trujillo census were living as servants in Spanish households (Romero 1925, 93).
12. Testamento de Catalina Chumbi, ARLL, PN, 32, reg. 7, fol. 355v (1574).
13. Olivares's businesses with García are laid out in his will: Testamento de Diego de Olivares, Archivo General de la Nación (Lima) (AGN), Real Audiencia (RA), Procedimientos Civiles, leg. 21, cuad. 105, fols. 60–92v (1583).
14. See, for example, Guillermo Cock's (1986) analysis of the 1580 will of don García Pilco Guaman, *curaca* of the nearby Jequetepeque Valley.
15. On confraternities in Peru, see Lowry 1989 and Charney 1998.
16. On *indios criollos*, see Graubart 2009.
17. Still the best study of the complex relations between race and class in this period is Cope 1994. On the case of Afro-Peruvian women and intergenerational wealth, see Graubart 2013.
18. He provided 2,000 pesos each to his illegitimate sons, having "not given them more than ordinary sustenance." Testamento de Diego de Olivares, AGN, RA, Procedimientos Civiles, leg. 21, cuad. 105 (1583).
19. Cock 1986, 176.
20. On Francisca Ramírez and her five extant wills, see Graubart 2007, 1–3, 73–74).

References

Ares Queija, Berta. 1997. "El papel de mediadores y la construcción de un discurso sobre la identidad de los mestizos peruanos (siglo XVI)." In *Entre dos mundos: Fronteras culturales y agentes mediadores*, edited by Berta Ares Queija and Serge Gruzinski, 37–60. Seville: Escuela de Estudios Hispano-Americanos.

Bowser, Frederick P. 1974. *The African Slave in Colonial Peru, 1524–1650*. Stanford: Stanford University Press.

Cahill, David. 1994. "Colour by Numbers: Racial and Ethnic Categories in the Viceroyalty of Peru, 1532–1824." *Journal of Latin American Studies* 26: 325–346.

Charney, Paul. 1998. "A Sense of Belonging: Colonial Indian *Cofradías* and Ethnicity in the Valley of Lima, Peru." *The Americas* 54(3): 379–407.

Concejo Provincial de Trujillo. 1969. *Actas del Cabildo de Trujillo*, vol. 1, 1549–1560 (Lima).

Cock, Guillermo, 1986. "Power and Wealth in the Jequetepeque Valley During the Sixteenth Century." In *The Pacatnamu Papers*, edited by Christopher Donnan, 171–180. Los Angeles: UCLA/Museum of Cultural History.

Cope, R. Douglas. 1994. *The Limits of Racial Domination*. Madison: University of Wisconsin Press.

Del Busto Duthurburu, José Antonio. 1981. "El infante: Melchor Verdugo." In *La hueste perulera*. Lima: Pontificia Universidad Católica del Perú.

Glave, Luis Miguel. 1989. *Trajinantes: Caminos indígenas en la sociedad colonial, siglos XVI/XVII*. Lima: Instituto de Apoyo Agrario.

Graubart, Karen B. 2007. *"With Our Labor and Sweat": Indigenous Women and the Formation of Colonial Society in Peru, 1550–1700*. Stanford, Calif.: Stanford University Press.

———. 2009. "The Creolization of the New World: Local Forms of Identity in Urban Colonial Peru, 1560–1640." *Hispanic American Historical Review* 89(3): 471–499.

———. 2013. "Los lazos que unen: Dueñas negras de esclavos negros en Lima, ss. XVI–XVII." *Revista Nueva Corónica* [Lima] 2.

———. 2014. "Ethnicity." In *The Princeton Companion to Atlantic History*, edited by Joseph C. Miller, 192–196. Princeton, N.J.: Princeton University Press.

Kuznesof, Elizabeth. 1995. "Ethnic and Gender Influences on 'Spanish' Creole Society in Colonial Spanish America." *Colonial Latin American Review* 4(1): 153–176.

Lowry, Lyn. 1989. "Religiosidad y control social en la colonia: El caso de los indios urbanos de Lima." *Allpanchis* 20(32): 11–42.

Murra, John. 1962. "Cloth and Its Functions in the Inca State." *American Anthropologist* 4: 710–728.

Niles, Susan. 1992. "Artist and Empire in Inca and Colonial Textiles." In *To Weave For the Sun: Ancient Andean Textiles*, edited by Rebecca Stone-Miller, 50–66. Boston: Museum of Fine Arts.

Noack, Karoline. 2005. "Catalina Rodríguez, 'hechicera y alcahueta' de Trujillo: La cultural popular urbana del siglo XVI." In *Represión, transgresión y sentimientos en la historia cultural andina,* edited by H. Tomoeda and L. Millones, 43–69. Lima: Congreso de la República.

Osorio, Alejandra B. 1999. "*El callejón de la soledad*: Vectors of Cultural Hybridity in Seventeenth-century Lima." In *Spiritual Encounters: Interactions between Christianity and Native Religions in Colonial America,* edited by Nicholas Griffiths and Fernando Cervantes. Lincoln: University of Nebraska Press.

O'Toole, Rachel Sarah. 2012. *Bound Lives: Africans, Indians, and the Making of Race in Colonial Peru.* Pittsburgh: University of Pittsburgh Press.

Ramírez, Susan E. 1986. *Provincial Patriarchs: Land Tenure and the Economics of Power in Colonial Peru.* Albuquerque: University of New Mexico Press.

———. 2002. "Don Melchior Caruarayco: A Kuraka of Cajamarca in Sixteenth-Century Peru." In *The Human Tradition in Colonial Latin America,* edited by Kenneth Andrien. Wilmington, Del.: Scholarly Resources.

Romero, Carlos A. 1925. "Fragmento de una historia de Trujillo." *Revista Histórica* 7(1–2): 86–118.

Rostworowski, María, and Pilar Remy. 1992. *Las visitas a Cajamarca, 1571–1572/ 1578.* Lima: IEP.

Twinam, Ann. 1999. *Public Lives, Private Secrets: Gender, Honor, Sexuality and Illegitimacy in Colonial Spanish America.* Stanford, Calif.: Stanford University Press.

Zevallos Quiñones, Jorge. 1996. *Los fundadores y primeros pobladores de Trujillo del Perú.* Trujillo: Fundación Pinillos Goicochea.

CHAPTER 2

Born Oceans Apart

The Joint Testament of
a *Chino* Slave and His *Mulata* Wife

T A T I A N A   S E I J A S

The joint testament of Miguel de Silva and María de la Concepción testifies to the reach of the slave trade to Spanish America and demonstrates how slavery shaped interracial relations in seventeenth-century Mexico.[1] María, a free *mulata* (of mixed Spanish and African descent), looked beyond outward markers of difference and embraced Miguel, a *chino* slave, whom she married and freed with her own inheritance. They made a life together and achieved considerable social mobility and economic success. Their story tells us that legal and racial categories were ambiguous and malleable at the individual level. That said, Miguel and María still lived in a society with a wide social rift that divided Spaniards from everybody else.

Prior to their marriage, Miguel and María led completely different lives. He was the slave of his namesake, Miguel de Silva, who was an affluent spice trader and master of various other slaves (ANM, Fernando Veedor, 4601, fol. 221 [1657]). María, on the other hand, was the wife of a rich man named Alonso Hernández.[2] When he died, María inherited a small fortune (more than 5,000 pesos), which gave her economic security and financial independence. At this point, María could have made a desirable marriage and further increased her social standing. Instead, she followed her heart and married Miguel, a penniless slave, using part of her inheritance to purchase his freedom.[3] The relationship was helped in this by Mexico's relatively open slave system, which allowed and even encouraged manumission (Proctor 2006). Miguel was manumitted in 1661, more than a decade prior to the abolition of *chino* slavery by the Spanish crown in 1672.[4] Their union, therefore, allowed Miguel to live in liberty many more years than he would have otherwise.

A global trading system supplied slaves from both Asia and Africa to the Spanish colonies. Miguel was brought to Mexico on the Manila Galleon as part of the transpacific slave trade, which operated from the late sixteenth century through the end of the seventeenth.[5] Despite their many linguistic, religious, and other differences, these slaves were divided on arrival into just two categories: *negros* (blacks) or *chinos* (in vague reference to China, which represented Asia in the popular imaginary).[6] We do not know where Miguel was actually born, but it is possible that he came from the Spanish Philippines. If so, he would have been one of many native Filipinos who were enslaved and sent to Mexico despite the royal prohibitions on indigenous slavery.[7] Alternatively, Miguel may have been the descendant of slaves brought by Portuguese traders to the Philippines from elsewhere in Asia (Seijas 2008). Regardless of his precise origins, once in Mexico, Miguel was considered a *chino* slave—chattel like all the others.

Given that most Africans brought to Mexico during this period came through the Middle Passage, we can say with some certainty that one or more of María's ancestors were slaves from Africa, even though she herself was free.[8] María was described as a *parda* (dark brown) and categorized as a *mulata*, denoting mixed African and European parentage. Despite their different backgrounds, colonial society would have viewed both Miguel and María as carrying the stain of slavery, meaning they would have had a common experience with racial prejudice.[9] They had to make great efforts to advance in a society that categorized them according to assumed physical differences.

Miguel and María's economic success speaks to the vibrancy of the colonial economy. By the time they set down their testament in 1672, eleven years into their marriage, they were on sound financial footing and each other's sole heirs. They owned significant property, had no personal debts, and planned to leave substantial sums of money as gifts, providing handsomely for their adopted children. They had a daughter, Francisca de la Concepción (described as *española* [Spanish]) and a son, Miguel, who was not categorized in the documentation. According to the testament, Francisca was to be given 600 pesos when she either joined a convent or married, and Miguel was to receive 300 pesos when he came of age. Notably, the couple decided not to set aside money for masses for their souls, as was commonly done.[10] Their one significant donation to a religious institution was for the Confraternity of the Holy Sacrament and Charity, which was founded to aid orphan girls of Spanish parentage (Cuebas, Guerrero, and Pan 1946). Perhaps they made this bequest to support the organization that had helped their own adopted daughter.

Miguel and María started their marriage with her inheritance but grew wealthier from Miguel's "trading and contracting." Miguel first followed in the footsteps of his previous master, who sold spices in the city's main market in the *plaza mayor* (main plaza).[11] In the seventeenth century, the market was said to be one of the largest and most abundant in the Americas, selling everything from locally made crafts and goods to Asian silks and spices. Miguel probably learned about the business as his master's assistant, which was common among *chino* servants. Once free, he likely used part of María's dowry as capital to set up his own *tendejón* (stall) in the market, allowing him to trade at the epicenter of Mexico's economy. He started with spices but then moved on to other commodities and investment opportunities.

In evident recognition of slavery's economic importance, Miguel also invested in human chattel. Mexico City had the largest slave market in the viceroyalty; it supplied slaves for urban industries and domestic service as well as faraway mines and haciendas. In 1664, for example, the diarist Gregorio Martín de Guijo (1953) reported the arrival of 600 *piezas de negros* (black pieces). These men and women would have been sold at a public auction under the portals of the main plaza, "where slaves walked in circles while buyers made their bids" (AGI, Escribanía 291B [1636]; quoted in Vila Vilar 1977, 225). Miguel, who had likely been sold in this very same place decades earlier, came back as a free man to make his own sales and purchases. He was a slave owner just a few months after manumission, selling a black woman named Lucia in 1661 (ANM, Diego de los Rios 3847, fol. 111 [1661]). Miguel was a talented trader and acute businessman, and at this time slaves were a sound investment.

The testament did not itemize all of their assets, but their real estate suggests that they were quite wealthy. The most valuable properties were two new buildings, which had liens amounting to 3,000 pesos. These liens (or mortgages) would have been part of a credit arrangement called a *censo*, an agreement to pay the noted lenders—in this case, a convent and a private investor—a certain amount each month in lieu of interest. The couple may have taken out these loans to construct the said buildings or to undertake additional projects. Their real estate investments and access to credit show that Miguel and María had strong social networks and a sound financial reputation, which made social and economic mobility possible.

In 1677, Miguel and María filed a codicil to their testament claiming to have experienced some financial setbacks. Their declaration of "poverty," however, was likely exaggerated and somewhat disingenuous, since the value of their property had not changed since the original will. The codicil's sole aim was to revoke the gift to their adopted daughter, Francisca, who had married Juan Antonio de Tobar in the intervening years. They did not explain the disinheritance, but the codicil does imply that Miguel and María were disappointed with Francisca's spouse and that they resented the couple's presence in their home.

At the time of Francisca's marriage, Miguel and María had given Juan Antonio a very significant dowry of almost 1,300 pesos (significantly more than the 600 pesos designated for Francisca in their will). Given the large dowry, the couple was likely pleased, at first, to marry their daughter off to this individual, but he apparently fell out of their favor. Miguel and María likely felt that Juan Antonio and Francisca were taking advantage of their generosity. They could not allow them to draw on their finances indefinitely. Their only recourse was to exclude Juan Antonio and Francisca from their will and force their independence.

The family conflict may have been related to their son-in-law's status. The codicil did not record Juan Antonio's racial category, but he was most likely Spanish. He was a goldsmith, and the goldsmith guild in Mexico City prohibited slaves and free *castas* (people of mixed descent) from working in this craft (Barrio Lorenzot 1920, 139). Spanish artisans organized guilds to promote their particular crafts, foster corporate solidarity, and regulate production. From their perspective, these objectives required exclusivity, so they explicitly forbade non-Spaniards from their ranks, especially slaves, whether "black or other color" (Barrio Lorenzot 1920, 46, 124, 229). Slaves were particularly threatening because their association with a craft diminished the status of all its practitioners. Juan belonged to an organization that disdained slaves and their labor, and he probably shared this attitude. If so, Juan likely treated his parents-in-law with certain condescension, coloring their relationship. Miguel and María may have disinherited the

young couple out of personal insult and a generalized resentment for the
social and economic privileges enjoyed by Spaniards in colonial society.

Miguel and María likely wanted to leave their fortune in the hands
of more deserving heirs—people like themselves who had struggled for
their position. They shared a common experience at the bottom of society
that brought them together. As was the case among other plebeians, class
trumped race (Cope 1994). The racialized caste system did not separate
them because Miguel and María had other struggles and a mutual drive
for social and economic advancement. Nonetheless, race was all-important
at the highest level of colonial society. Regardless of the solidarity among
different peoples in the lower strata, it was nearly unimaginable for someone with the taint of slavery to be considered the equal of a Spaniard. Their
adopted daughter and her husband likely made this all too clear.

Archivo Histórico de Notarías de la Ciudad de México

Transcription

Nicolas Bernal 457, exp. 61, fols. 82r–85r

En el nombre de dios nuestro padre todo poderosso y de la sacratissima
virgen María nuestra señora concevida sin pecado original su bendita
madre amen = Sepan quantos esta carta vieren como nos Miguel de Silva,
chino libre, veçino de esta ciudad de Mexico y natural de la de Manila =
y Maria de la Consepcion de color pardo libre de cautiverio su lixitima
muger veçina y natural de esta ciudad hija legitima de Alonsso Hernandez
difunto, ambos marido y muger juntos de mano comun estando como
estamos a onrra y gloria de dios nuestro señor buenos y sanos de nuestra
boluntad y con entera salud y creiendo como bien y berdaderamente
creemos en el misterio gloriossissimo de la santissima trinidad padre
hijo y espiritu santo tres personas distintas y un solo dios berdadero y
en todo lo demas que tiene cre y confiessa nuestra santta madre yglessia
catolica romana devajo de cuia fee y creencia emos bivido y protestamos
vivir y morir como catolicos xptianos ymbocando como imbocamos
por nuestra intersessora y abogada a la santissima reyna de los angeles la
virgen maria nuestra señora para que intersede con su pressiossissimo
hijo nuestro señor Jessu christo por nossotros y le pida perdon de
nuestras culpas y pecados y nos lleve a su ssanta gloria dessimos que
por quanto no tenemos seguridad en la vida humana ni ora cierta para

morir previniendo los futuros contingentes que pueden suseder y
deseando poner nuestras almas en carrera de salvacion tenemos tratado
y consertado haser y otorgar nuestro testamento ultima y prostimera
boluntad en la forma y manera siguiente.

~Lo primero encomendamos a dios nuestro señor nuestras animas
que las crio y redincio con su pressiosa sangre passion y muerte y el
cuerpo a la tierra de que fueron formados y quando su divina boluntad
fuere servico de llevarnnos y a qualquiera de nos de esta pressente vida
queremos que nuestros cuerpos sean sepultados en la Yglesia parte y
lugar que paresiere al que de nos quedare bivo y a disposicion de nuestros
alvaseas y no mandamos desir ningunas missas por no tener de que

~ytten mandamos de limosna en fallesiendo cualquiera de nossotros
un peso a los lugares santos de Jerusalem y a la cofradia del santissimo
sacramento y caridad fundada en la santa yglesia catedral otro pesso = y a
la hermita de nuestra señora de guadalupe otro pesso = y a nuestra señora
de los remedios otro pesso

~ytten mandamos a las mandas forssosas y acostumbradas quatro
reales dos por cada uno de nosotros con que las escluimos de nossotros

~ytten declaramos que al pressente no devemos nada a ninguna
persona por escriptura ni de palabra para el descargo de nuestras
conciencias

~ytten declaro yo el dicho Miguel de Silva que diferentes personas me
deven diferentes cantidades de pessos por escripturas cedulas y quentas
de libro que las que son constara por ellas a que me rremito mando se
cobren

~ytten declaro yo la dicha Maria de la Consepcion que antes que
contraiesse matrimonio con el dicho Miguel de Silva fui cassada segun
orden de nuestra madre yglecia con Alonsso Hernandes difunto y
durante el dicho matrimonio no tubimos ningunos hijos ni a mi noticia a
benido que el dicho Alonsso Hernandes los hubiesse tenido naturales y
haviendo fallecido me dejo por su heredera lixitima

~ytten declaramos que somos cassados y belados segun orden de
nuestra santa madre yglecia y al tiempo yevando contraimos dicho
matrimonio lleve yo la dicha Maria de la Consepcion por dote y caudal
conosido a poder del dicho Miguel de Silva mi marido cinco mill y beinte
y seis pessos de oro comun y me mando en arras mill pessos como consta
de la escriptura de dotte que esta en nuestro poder su fecha en onse

de agosto del año pasado de sessenta y uno ante Bentura de Cardenas
escrivano real y entonses yo el dicho Miguel de Silva no tenia ningun
caudal porque era esclavo y con el caudal de dicho dotte me liberte y e
tratado y contratado con el asta oi durante y el dicho matrimonio no
emos tenido hijos ni hijas ningunos declaramos assi para descargo de
nuestras consiensias

~ytten declaramos por nuestros vienes unas cassas altas nuevas de
piedra que son en esta ciudad en la calle de la asequia real frontero del
colegio de nuestra señora de todos santos las quales tienen ympuestos y
cargados a sesso redimible tres mill pessos de oro comun, los dos mils y
trescientos de ellos en favor del convento de religiosas de santa theressa
de esta ciudad y los settecientos de ellos cumplimiento a dicha cantidad
en favor de doña Maria donsella veçina de esta ciudad y los reditos estan
pagados asta el dia de oi y no tienen otro senso ypoteca no otra ajenacion

~ytten mandamos que se le den a Juan Galvan nuestro compadre
cientto y cinquenta pessos de oro comun en reales de lo mexor y mas
cien parado de nuestros bienes para que haga de ellos lo que le tenemos
comunicado para el descargo de nuestras conssiensias y esto se entiende
fallesiendo cualquiera de nossotros sin que por ningun pretesto caussa
ni rrason se le pida quenta de su distrivuicion porque asi es nuestra
boluntad

~y para cumplir y pagar nuestro testamento mandos y legado en el
conttenido nos dejamos el uno al otro y el otro al otro por alvaseas del
que primero muriere el cual aya de ser tenedor de vienes y assi mismo
nombramos por nuestro alvasea al dicho Juan Galvan nuestro compadre
veçino de esta ciudad para que en compañia del que quedare bivo de
nossotros dos entre nuestros bienes y ambos qualquiera ynsolidun los
benda y remate en almoneda o fuera de ello como les pareciere y de su
prosedido cumplan este testamento que siendo nessesario nos damos
poder el uno al otro y por falta de ambos sea tenedor de los dichos
nuestros bienes el dicho Juan Galvan nuestro compadre con la mesma
facultad del que quedare bivo

~ytten declaramos que tenemos en nuestra compañia una niña
española nombrada Francisca de la Consepcion que emos criado en
nuestra cassa que sera de edad de dose años poco mas o menos y por
la mucha boluntad y amor que le tenemos le mandamos se le den
seisscientos pesos los trecienttos de ellos en reales y los trescientos en
bienes muebles para el estado que dios nuestro señor fuere servido de

darle de religiosa o cassada, y si la ssusodicha fallesiere antes de tenerle buelban al tronco de nuestros bienes sin obligacion de darle reditos de ellos por ninguno de nosotros

~ytten declaramos que emos criado a Miguel de Silva niño huerfano que sera de edad de ocho años poco mas o menos y por el amor y boluntad que le tenemos le mandamos se le den trescientos pessos de oro comun para el estado que dios nuestro señor fuere servido de darle y si el sussodicho muriere en la edad pupilar buelban los dichos trescientos para el tronco de nuestros bienes sin obligacion de darle ningunos

~Y cumplido y pagado este nuestro testamento mandas y legados en el contenidos en el remaniente que quedare de nuestros bienes derechos y acciones que nos pertenescan y puedan perteneser en cualquier manera nos constituimos y nombramos el uno al otro y el otro al otro nos marido y muger por eredores legitimos para que el que de los dos quedare bivo los gosse aia y herede y disponga dellos a su boluntad en la forma que le pareciere con la bendision de dios en atencion a no tener como no tenemos herederos forsosos asendientes ni desendienttes

~y por el pressente revocamos y anulamos y damos por ninguno y de ningun balor ni efecto otros qualesquier testamentos cobdicilios poderes para testar y otros qualesquier manera para que no balgan ni aganse judicial ni extrajudicialmente el qual otorgamos por nuestra ultima y postrimena voluntad y para que ella bia y forma que mexor aya lugar en derecho que es fecho en la ciudad de Mexico a veinte y dos dias del mes de mayo de mill y seisscientos y settentta y dos años y los otorganttes a quien yo el escrivano doi fee que conosco los quales a lo que nottoriamente paresse estaren su acuerdo y cumplida memoria y assi lo otorgamos y no firmaron porque dijeron no saver a ssu rruego lo firmaron los testigos que supieron siendolo Juan de Cevericha Anttonio de la Avva Bernardo de Solis y Domingo Flores y Rafael de la Auua vexinos de Mexico. Ante mi Nicolas de Bernal escrivano de su magestad

Nicolas Bernal 460, exp. 61, fols. 75v–76r
Cobdicilio. En la ciudad de Mexico a treinta dias del mes de Agosto de mill seiscientos y setenta y siete años ante mi el escrivano y testigos Miguel de Silva chino libre tratante en cajon de espeseria en la plaza mayor della, y Maria de la Consepcion mulata su legitima muger asi mismo libre veçinos desta ciudad a quienes doy fee que conosco estando en salud sin achaque que les obligue aser cama y estando en su entero

juicio y cumplida memoria y de un acuerdo y conformidad dixeron
que por quanto hisieron y otorgaron su testamento ante el presente
scrivano su fecha en esta ciudad en veinte y dos de mayo del año pasado
de mill seiscientos y setenta y dos en el qual dejan nombrado alvaseas
y herederos y por una clausula del declaran que tienen en su compañia
una niña nombrada Francisca de la Consepcion española que criaron en
su casa y por la mucha voluntad y amor que le tenian le mandaron se le
diesen seiscientos pesos, lo trescientos dellos en reales y los trescientos
restantes en vienes muebles para el estado que dios fuese servido darle de
religiosa o casada y si antes de tenerle fallesiese volviesen al tronco de sus
vienes sin obligacion de darles reditos por ningunos de los susodichos,
y porque mediante la voluntad de dios nuestro señor que fue servido
de que la dicha Fransisca de la Consepcion contrajese matrimonio con
Juan Antonio de Tobar tirador de oro y veçino desta ciudad que los an
tenido y tienen en su casa y compañia y al tiempo y quando se efectuo
dicho matrimonio le dieron en dote y casamiento estos otorgantes un
mill doscientos y ochenta y dos pesos y quatro reales los trescientos
dello en reales y lo demas en vienes muebles y otras cosas como consta
de la escriptura de dote que paso ante el presente escrivano en sinco de
octubre del año pasado de seiscientos y setenta y tres y por aver benido
a pobresa y averle entregado la dicha cantidad por bia de cobdicilio y
por el presente revocan la dicha clausula del dicho testamento en que
le mandaron a la dicha Fransisca de la Consepcion dichos seiscientos
pesos para que no tenga por si ni por el dicho su marido accion a ellos
por ningun pretexto causa ni rason y en quanto a lo demas expresado y
declarado en dicho testamento de suso citado quieren y es su voluntad
se guarde cumpla y execute en lo que no fuere contrario lo uno a lo otro
y asi lo otorgaron y no firmaron por no saver escrivir firmolo a su ruego
un testigo siendolo Andres Enriques de Rivera escrivano de su magestad
Juan Cortes y Fransisco de la Cueba veçinos de Mexico

Translation
Testament
In the name of God our Lord all powerful and of the most sacred Virgin
Mary our Lady conceived without original sin his blessed mother amen.
   Know whoever sees this letter that we, Miguel de Silva, a free *chino*,
resident of this city of Mexico and native of Manila, and María de la Con-

cepción, color brown, free from captivity, his legitimate wife, also resident and native of this city, legitimate daughter of Alonso Hernandez, deceased, both husband and wife joined in common hand, in honor and glory of God our Lord, good and well, and of our own free will and in full health, and in true belief of the glorious mystery of the Holy Trinity, Father, Son, and Holy Spirit, three distinct persons and one true God, and of everything else professed and confessed by our Holy Mother Roman Catholic Church, under whose faith and belief we have lived and propose to die as Catholic Christians, invoke as our intercessor and advocate the holy queen of the angels, the Virgin Mary our Lady, so that she may intercede for us with her precious son our Lord Jesus Christ, and ask him to pardon our faults and sins, and take us to his glory.

We say that as we have no security in human life, nor certainty of the hour of death, and in order to forestall the future contingencies that may arise, and desirous to place our souls on the road to salvation, we have concerted to make our last testament and do so in the following manner.

First, we commend our souls to God our Lord who created and redeemed them with his precious blood, passion, and death in body on earth from which it was formed. When it favors his divine will to take either one of us from this present life, we desire to be buried in a church, the place and location to be chosen by the one of us who remains alive and in accord with our executors. We do not have the means to order any masses.

Item, we order at the departure of either one of us the payment of one *peso* in alms to the sacred places of Jerusalem, another peso to the confraternity of the Holy Sacrament and Charity, founded at the Holy Cathedral, another peso to the hermitage Church of our Lady of Guadalupe, and another peso to our Lady of Remedies.

Item, we order the payment of four reales for the forced and customary demands, two for each of us, with which we exempt ourselves.

Item, we declare, on our consciences, that at present we have no common debts to anyone in writing or word.

Item, I Miguel de Silva declare that various people owe me different amounts of pesos, which is certified by obligations of payment and in account books. I order that the remaining debts be collected.

Item, I María de la Concepción declare that prior to contracting marriage with the said Miguel de Silva, I was married by order of our Holy Mother Church to Alonso Hernandez, deceased, and that during the said marriage we had no children, nor has it come to my attention that the said Alonso Hernandez had children out of wedlock. He left me as his sole heir at the time of his death.

Item, we declare that we were married and veiled by order of our Holy Mother Church. At the time, I María de la Concepción brought to the marriage as dowry and common property the amount of 5,026 pesos, now in the power of the said Miguel de Silva, who granted 1,000 pesos for my sake, as noted in the dowry contract in our possession, dated August 11, 1661, before Bentura de Cardenas, royal notary. Then, I Miguel de Silva, who did not have any property because I was a slave, used part of the dowry to purchase my freedom. I have since used the rest to engage in trade. We further declare on our consciences that we have not sired sons or daughters during the said marriage.

Item, we declare as our property a number of tall brick houses, newly built in this city on the street of the royal irrigation channel, in front of the College of Our Lady of All Saints, which carry mortgages totaling 3,000 pesos in common gold, 2,300 in favor of the convent of the nuns of Saint Teresa of this city, and 700 in favor of doña María Doncella resident of this city. All payments are up to date. The houses have no other liens or financing.

Item, we order a payment in cash in the amount of 150 pesos in common gold to our friend Juan Galvan, in addition to 100 pesos more from the sale of our property, so that he may do what we have already agreed upon to discharge our consciences. This will be done at the time of either one of our deaths, without any pretext, and under no reason will he be asked to give account of his disbursement. That is our will.

Item, we name each other as executors and whoever survives the other as sole heir. In order to complete our testament, we also name as executor the said Juan Galvan resident of this city, so that he may assist the surviving spouse in the sale and distribution of our property, as the two of them see fit. And if both of us were to die, we name the said Juan Galvan sole executor.

Item, we declare that we have in our company a Spanish girl named Francisca de la Concepción, whom we have raised in our home, who is now approximately twelve years old. For the goodwill and love that we have for her, we order that she be given 600 pesos, 300 in cash and 300 in movable assets, to support her in whatever life our Lord gives her, be it as a religious or in marriage. If she were to die prior to committing to either life, the amount would return to our common property without further obligation.

Item, we declare that we have also raised an orphan boy named Miguel de Silva, who is now approximately eight years old. For the goodwill and love that we have for him, we order that he be given 300 pesos in common gold to support him in whatever life our Lord gives him. If he were to die prior to legal age, the amount would return to our common property without further obligation.

Once this our testament has been completed and the orders paid, we declare that the remainder of our property is the inheritance to the surviving spouse, whom we each declare to be our sole legitimate heir. Whoever remains alive will be able to enjoy, inherit, and dispose of this inheritance according to his or her own free will with the blessing of God. We do this in attention of not having any compulsory heirs or descendants.

For the present, we revoke, annul, and discount any previous testaments, codicils, or powers, of any judicial form, and grant this testament as our last will and testament, made in the best legal form in the city of Mexico, dated May 22, 1672.

I, the notary, give faith that I know the said grantors, and that they are in complete accord and with full mental powers. The grantors did not sign because they said they did not know how to do so, and requested the signatures of their witnesses Juan de Cevericha, Antonio de la Ava, Bernardo de Solis, Domingo Flores, and Rafael de la Ava, residents of Mexico. Before me Nicolas de Bernal, his majesty's notary.

Codicil

In the city of Mexico, on August 30, 1677, before me the notary and witnesses, appeared Miguel de Silva, a free *chino*, who owns a spice stall at the Plaza Mayor, and María de la Concepción, a *mulata*, his legitimate wife, also free, residents of this city, whom I certifiably know, both in good health and without any ailment that would confine them to bed. With full discretion and complete memory, they said in accord and agreement that they had made their testament before the present notary in this city on May 22, 1672, with noted executors and heirs. In a clause of that testament, they declared that they had in their company a girl named Francisca de la Concepción, a Spaniard, whom they reared in their household. For the goodwill and love that they had for her, they had then ordered that she be given 600 pesos, 300 in cash and 300 in movable assets, to support her in whatever state God gave her, as a nun or married woman, and that if she died the amount was to return to their common property without further obligation. Since then, it has been the will of God our Lord that the said Francisca contracted marriage with Juan Antonio de Tobar, a goldsmith, resident of this city, both of whom now live in their house and company. At the time of the marriage, the said grantors gave her as dowry 1,282 pesos and 4 reales, 300 in cash and the rest in movable assets, as certified in the dowry contract drawn up by the present notary on October 5, 1673. Having now succumbed to poverty, and having given her the said amount, they now revoke with this said codicil the clause in that testament, in which they had ordered payment of 600 pesos to the said Francisca de la Concepción. They do this to prevent her or her husband from taking legal action against them, for whatever pretext. In regard to whatever else is expressed and declared in their testament, it is their will that it be completed and executed as written. And this is what they declared and did not sign because they do not know how to write. At their request, signed one witness Andres Enriquez de Rivera, royal notary, Juan Cortéz, and Francisco de la Cueva, residents of Mexico.

Notes

1. The following reconstruction is based on four documents from the ANM: a testament, a codicil, and two slave titles.
2. The name "Alonso Hernández" appears in the documents as María's deceased husband as well as her father; both men may have had the same name, or the confusion may be due to scribal error.
3. The manumission likely cost approximately 350 pesos, the typical purchase price for a slave at the time (Seijas 2014).
4. The decree was part of the Crown's ongoing efforts to abolish indigenous slavery on the northern frontier; the prohibition grouped *chinos* with Indians, partly in acknowledgment that some *chinos* were, in fact, from the Spanish Philippines and therefore legally *indios* who should have been protected from enslavement. AGN, Reales Cédulas Duplicadas 30, 45, fol. 78r (1672); AGI, Indiferente 537, leg. 7, fol. 43v (1672). Part of the documentation is transcribed in González Claverán 1989.
5. For an analysis of the slave trade and the experience of *chino* slaves in Mexico, see Seijas, 2014; and Oropeza Keresey 2011. The classic study on the Pacific trade is Schurz 1959.
6. The slaves were originally from East Africa, Portuguese India, the Muslim

sultanates of Southeast Asia, and the Spanish Philippines. African slaves were also called *cafres* (a derogatory term meaning "pagans").

7. All natives of Spanish colonies were considered *indios* (Indians) after the New Laws and thus protected from slavery as vassals of the Crown. The Spanish king prohibited the enslavement of Indians as early as 1526, but exceptions were regularly made, such as for native men captured in "just wars" or *moros* (Muslims) from Mindanao. The laws were summarized in the Laws of the Indies under the section "On the Liberty of the Indians"; see *Recopilación* (1943) and Hidalgo Nuchera 1994.

8. Estimates of the volume of the transatlantic slave trade to Mexico need scholarly revision, but one of the more widely cited figures is that 50,525 Africans reached New Spain between 1595 and 1622 alone (Palmer 1976, 16).

9. For a discussion of the Spanish preoccupation with purity of blood, see Martínez 2008.

10. They left the bare minimum—4 *reales*—to pay the "forced and customary demands," which were a kind of additional mortuary taxation imposed by the Church.

11. Miguel's namesake master (Miguel de Silva) had a "cajón de especies." ANM, Fernando Veedor 4601, fol. 221 (1657). The stalls of the *plaza mayor* were generally reserved for Spanish traders, but several free *chinos* successfully petitioned for special licenses to sell varied goods there. See, for example, AGN, General de Parte 7, exp. 221, fol. 147r (1632); and AGN, Indios 13, exp. 126, fol. 111v (1641).

References

Barrio Lorenzot, Juan Francisco del. 1920. *El trabajo en México durante la época colonial: Ordenanzas de gremios de la Nueva España*. Mexico City: Secretaría de Gobernación.

Cope, R. Douglas. 1994. *The Limits of Racial Domination: Plebeian Society in Colonial Mexico City, 1660–1720*. Madison: University of Wisconsin Press.

Cuebas, Juan de, Juan Guerrero, and Pedro de Pan. 1946. "La Cofradía del Santísimo Sacramento y Caridad." *The Americas* 2(3): 369–376.

González Claverán, Virginia. 1989. "Un documento colonial sobre esclavos asiáticos." *Historia Mexicana* 38(3): 523–532.

Hidalgo Nuchera, Patricio. 1994. "¿Esclavitud o liberación? El fracaso de las actitudes esclavistas de los conquistadores de Filipinas." *Revista Complutense de Historia de América* 20: 61–74.

Martín de Guijo, Gregorio. 1953. *Diario, 1648–1664*. Vol. 2. Mexico City: Editorial Porrúa.

Martínez, María Elena. 2008. *Genealogical Fictions: Limpieza de Sangre, Religion, and Gender in Colonial Mexico*. Stanford, Calif.: Stanford University Press.

Oropeza Keresey, Déborah. 2011. "La esclavitud asiática en el Virreinato de la Nueva España, 1565–1673." *Historia Mexicana* 61(1): 5–57.

Palmer, Colin. 1976. *Slaves of the White God: Blacks in Mexico, 1570–1650*. Cambridge, Mass.: Harvard University Press.

Proctor, Frank T., III. 2006. "Gender and the Manumission of Slaves in New Spain." *Hispanic American Historical Review* 86(2): 309–336.

Recopilación de leyes de los reinos de las Indias, mandadas imprimir y publicar por la Majestad Católica del Rey Don Carlos II. Vol. 2. 1791. Madrid: Consejo de la Hispanidad, 1943.

Schurz, William Lytle. 1959 (1939). *The Manila Galleon*. New York: E. P. Dutton.

Seijas, Tatiana. 2008. "The Portuguese Slave Trade to Spanish Manila: 1580–1640." *Itinerario* 32(1): 19–38.

———— 2014. *Asian Slaves in Colonial Mexico*. New York: Cambridge University Press.

Vila Vilar, Enriqueta. 1977. *Hispanoamérica y el comercio de esclavos: Los asientos portugueses*. Sevilla: Escuela de Estudios Hispano-Americanos.

CHAPTER 3

Revelations on Mexico Tenochtitlan

The 1648 Testament of Nicolasa Juana

JONATHAN TRUITT

The layout and organization of colonial Mexico Tenochtitlan was one fraught with political infighting between different indigenous families and groups, mendicant and secular priests, and Spanish politicians. Under its initial consideration the *altepetl* (ethnic-state) of Mexico Tenochtitlan was established as the *doctrina* (a parish specifically for people new to the faith) of San Josef de los Naturales. By design this placed the souls of its indigenous population under the purview of the Franciscan order. The 1550s witnessed an attempted shift to reorganize the *doctrina* of San Josef into secular-controlled parishes. The plans of then-archbishop Montúfar did not come to full fruition, but with the help of the Spanish government and political maneuvering within the indigenous community, he was able to split the *doctrina* into four sections based on prehispanic *altepetl* organization. However, the control of the four newly established parishes remained in the hands of the mendicant orders. Over the course of the next sixty years, two additional parishes were established, those of Santa Cruz and Mixtecos.[1] Though both were established later, it is Mixtecos, the only formally non-Nahua indigenous parish in Mexico Tenochtitlan, that is the focus of this chapter.[2]

In 1610 the Dominican order argued for the establishment of the parish of Mixtecos for Mixtec migrants from southern New Spain (Javier Pescador 1992, 28).[3] Their argument was based on the fact that the native language of the Mixtecs was not Nahuatl. Since the Dominican order (as the principal order in southern New Spain) had friars who spoke Mixtec, they believed they should establish an indigenous parish at their friary in the chapel of Nuestra Señora del Rosario for these migrants. In 1639 the Dominicans were on the defensive in regard to their parish. Mixtecos had no geographical boundaries within the city, and as such, their parishioners lived within the jurisdictions of other parishes. The other religious orders argued that the Dominicans' indigenous parishioners should be attending the chapels within the parish boundaries where they lived, especially since many of them spoke Nahuatl. Ultimately, the Dominicans were allowed to maintain their parish (AGN, Indios, vol. 11, e. 122, fols. 98v–101v).

Nine years later Nicolasa Juana, a Dominican indigenous parishioner, died. Her death in and of itself was not remarkable, but of approximately ninety known wills from Mexico Tenochtitlan, hers is the only extant testament from Mixtecos.[4] Intriguingly, though the will was written nine years after the Dominicans reasserted the need for the parish, it was not written in Mixtec, Nahuatl, or any other indigenous language, but in Spanish, and the only loanword to occur in the document is Nahuatl. A closer examination of her will provides a window into aspects of indigenous politics and religion in colonial Mexico Tenochtitlan. By looking very closely, it is even possible to catch a glimpse of the unwritten role of female leadership within the community.

Generally, in order to be a member of a particular parish in Mexico Tenochtitlan, a parishioner needed to be born within its geographical jurisdiction. If the parishioner later moved to another part of the city, he or she would still be associated with their original parish and could be buried there, as was the case with Francisco Juárez in 1644 (UNAM, FRAF, caja 96, e. 1413). In the case of Mixtecos a person was supposed to be of Mixtec descent, though over time it included other migrant natives, including Zapotecs and Filipinos (O'Hara 2010, 40).[5] Nicolasa Juana's tie to the parish of Mixtecos is established in her desire to be buried at the chapel of Santa María del Rosario and the notary's confirmation of the validity of the council and *cabildo* of the said chapel within the body of the testament. The geographical diversity of the parish is supported by Nicolasa Juana's tie to the barrio of San Pablo (in the southeastern portion of the *altepetl*), whereas the chapel of Santa María del Rosario was located in Santa María la Redonda (in the northwestern portion).

With her connection to the parish established, the question becomes why was she a member of this parish instead of the parish of San Pablo, within whose jurisdiction she lived, or San Josef, from which her husband originated? It is possible to gather some of the pertinent information from her testament, yet it still remains perplexing. According to the establishment guidelines of the parish of Mixtecos, members were to be non-Nahua natives (AGN, Indios, vol. 11, e. 122). In the case of Nicolasa Juana this is difficult to prove. Her parents predeceased her, and both she and her husband were born in Mexico Tenochtitlan, so if she was of a different native background, it had to be her parents or an earlier ancestor who migrated to the capital city. Another place to look would be the language used to write the document—in this case, Spanish. In some instances where an indigenous woman's testament was written in Spanish rather than her native language, it was indicated in the document that the testatrix in question was a *ladina* (a woman fluent in Spanish) (AGN, Bienes Nacionales, vol. 387, e. 1). Nicolasa Juana's will makes no mention of such fluency, but neither does the document have any note stating that it was translated by the notary or that there was a need to speak to Nicolasa in a language other than Spanish, as other wills occasionally indicate. For example, Clara López was identified in her will as an "india ladina," and no translator was provided. In contrast, Nicolasa de los Angeles was identified as "ladina mediante" (partially fluent), and an interpreter was provided for her when they wrote her will. Other wills include a note stating when the document was translated (AGN, Bienes Nacionales, leg. 1096, e. 8; leg. 293, e. 1, fols. 242–243). Unfortunately, since the will fails to mention any sort of language translation skills on the part of Nicolasa Juana or an appointed translator, whose Spanish was near perfect, it is impossible to verify the accuracy of the Dominicans' language-need claims in relation to Nicolasa Juana or her family.

An examination of the general material goods found in Nicolasa Juana's will indicates that she was neither particularly wealthy nor destitute at the time of her death. When her parents died, they left her a house that, based on the amount Nicolasa expected to receive for it, would appear not to have been overly fancy. In fact, in exchange for her house she asked that she receive a very modest burial at the chapel of Nuestra Señora del Rosario and that some of the money from the sale go toward masses for her soul. She states that she had no other assets. If there was any money left after that point, it was to go for four high masses for her parents' souls and two low masses for the souls of her godparents. Should her spouse/executor have any money still left from the sale of the house, he was directed to spend it on additional masses for her soul. This is telling, because other than a couple of religious images, she did not leave anything to her spouse: all of the money went to the Catholic Church in the form of masses, and all of those went to people on her side of the family.

In the area of religious items there is nothing remarkable about her collection of saints' images, yet her distribution and disposal of them are intriguing. At her death she possessed one of Nuestra Señora de la Candelaria, two of San Nicolás, and another Nuestra Señora (probably de la Candelaria as well), all sculptures in the round. One San Nicolás and the unnamed Nuestra Señora went to her husband, Juan Antonio, and the other San Nicolás went to her aunt Ana María. However, the Nuestra Señora de la Candelaria went to her *comadre* Francisca specifically for use in the benediction. The location of the benediction was not mentioned; however, the use of personally owned saints' images in religious ceremonies was established by the early seventeenth century (Grijalva 1985, 162). But men, not women, tended to hold positions of prominence when it came to officially sanctioned church responsibilities during the colonial period, the notable exception being the *cihuatepixque* (see below). Yet here we have a woman in control of an image used in a benediction ceremony passing it along to another woman for use in future ceremonies. Though reading more into this is tempting, it would be naught but speculation at this time.

Nicolasa Juana's collection of images also included another small, unknown quantity that she did not entrust to anyone. This again is unique: of the extant wills from Mexico Tenochtitlan to mention effigies, only three of them discussed images that were not left to the care of another person. In the case of the other two wills, the unbequeathed images were either under construction at the time of the testator's death or being refinished. But Nicolasa Juana took a different route. The images she bequeathed were made in the round, so they were statues constructed of some type of durable material, probably wood. Her other effigies, however, were old woodcuts, engravings, and painted panels, and the saints' likenesses had probably faded over time, as she states that they "were no good anymore." Moreover, she did not, as others had, have them refinished; instead she burned them.

Her act of burning the images is a bit surprising at first because one gets a sense from reading other sources that the natives of central Mexico believed the saints were actually present in their images—a sort of window onto the world of humanity. If this were the case, burning the images may have been the equivalent of destroying an avenue of access to one's intercessors. Yet the images were faded. Nicolasa Juana's burning of them then suggests that she at least, if not other Mesoamericans, believed that the saints had left those images, so burning them may have been a way of disposing of the holy vessels. Whether or not she believed these things, it is probable that her disposal of the images was appropriate; after all, she acted as the caretaker of an image tied to the benediction in one of the local chapels.

Nicolasa Juana's mention of the material her saints were created from is also informative. Scholars know that images have been made out of many different materials, but for Mexico Tenochtitlan this is one of the only references to a market of cheap consumable images, likely directed at both the general popularity of the cult of the saints as well as poorer ranks of society. And her disposal of the images may be tied to the ease with which others of this type could be obtained. By 1648 the woodcuts and engravings were being created locally in Mexico City as well as imported from Europe and were generally 4 inches by 2.5 inches. Some were given away at shrines, while others were sold at a profit. It is difficult to know the exact material they were made from because the Spanish terms used to reference them in wills varied. The painted tablets were even more common by this point and a bit larger: 10 inches by 5 inches (give or take). They were especially popular in rural areas as they traveled better than statues or canvases (Kelly Donahue-Wallace, pers. comm.). Despite the potential durability of some of these images, those belonging to Nicolasa Juana had apparently faded to the point that they were not nice enough to pass on to any of her friends or relatives. Perhaps it is due to the cheapness of the effigies that Nicolasa Juana figured no one would want them. Images of these types had been available in Mexico City since the 1560s, and hers is the only indigenous will to mention them by name and to physically dispose of a collection of images (Truitt 2009, chap. 1). They may have been available even earlier than this, as Hernán Cortés is known to have left woodcuts of the Virgin Mary in indigenous temples on his march toward Tenochtitlan. Additionally, fray Pedro de Gante appears to have favored woodcuts and engravings as pedagogical tools for both direct evangelization and training in a European art style (Donahue-Wallace 2007, 328–329). Until more indigenous testaments are uncovered with similar references to effigies, it will be difficult to understand why she burned these particular images.

Perhaps the most intriguing element of Nicolasa Juana's testament is the Nahuatl word it employs, *tenantzin* (people's beloved mother). The word is found on folio 18 and is used in regard to the title of the person holding the wills of her parents: "I declare that the testament that my parents made is in the custody of a woman called Ana who raised me, who lives in the barrio of San Pablo, and she is the *tenantzin* of the people of Teocaltitlan." The reference is fascinating in that it is the only reference to such a position of which I am aware. The closest similar position for women was likely the *cihuatepixqui* (woman in charge of people), but the latest reference to *cihuatepixqui* for Mexico City comes from 1581 in Tlatelolco (Truitt 2010, 435). This testament then, alongside other documents, provides support for the argument that a recognized, if informal, leadership position continued to exist for indigenous women in Mexico Tenochtitlan until at least the middle of the seventeenth century. Additionally, the reference to the position occurred at a time when indigenous women were appearing less regularly in colonial-era legal documents as witnesses and were starting to disappear from the historical record in general. This reference thus suggests that though male notaries did not regularly record women's actions in the written record, women were still active participants within their communities. Moreover, by stating that Ana was the "*tenantzin* of the people of Teocaltitlan," the will suggests the existence of women of similar title and status. Teocaltitlan was one of a multitude of small neighborhood units known as *tlaxilacalli*. The fact that Ana was tied specifically to Teocaltitlan hints at the possibility of other women in similar roles in other *tlaxilacalli* across the *altepetl*.

So what exactly did a *tenantzin* do? In this area there is very little information, but what is suggested by her will is promising. *Tenantzin* Ana cared for other people's documents, and it appears, at least in the case of Nicolasa's testament, that she raised orphans, though this may have been an isolated case. Even though Nicolasa was married by the time of her death, it appears that Ana continued to play some role in her life as she still possessed the wills of Nicolasa's parents and some of her moveable goods, such as four metates (grinding stones). Beyond the obvious role that Ana played in Nicolasa's life, she does not appear to have played a very major role in her death, as Nicolasa requests that her parents' wills and other paperwork be retrieved and that goods in Ana's care be sold for masses. While it is possible that Ana may have had the responsibility of purchasing some of the masses, this is not indicated by the testament. Unfortunately, additional information is not available from this will or the surrounding documentation.

Buried within the general mix of folders and disorder that make up the Bienes Nacionales *ramo* (or subset) of documents in the Archivo General de la Nación in Mexico City, Nicolasa Juana's testament is easily missed, especially since many of the documents that precede it in its folder are written in Nahuatl. The hand of the notary who wrote the testament is unremarkable, and it is easy to see why the will has not received any special attention. Indeed, I barely gave it a second look initially, and it was only on a closer reading of the Nahuatl documents that I was encouraged to spend more time with Bienes Nacionales 1766 in its entirety. Based on the only extant information we have on Nicolasa Juana, she led a life similar to other average indigenous people in Mexico Tenochtitlan, yet her will provides a more vibrant picture of life at that time than other, similar testaments available in Nahuatl or Spanish. Perhaps similar documents related to topics found in this testament, such as Mixtecos or the *tenantzin*, will eventually be found.

Testament of Nicolasa Juana

Transcription

[fol. 17]

En el nonbre de dios todopoderoso Sepan cuantos esta carta vieren como
Yo . nicolasa Juana natural de mexico al Bario de san pablo huerfana
de padre y madre Casada que soy de leJitima matrimonio con Juan
antonio segun horden de la Santa madre yglesia y natural desta ciudad
de mexico al barrio xihuitongo digo que estando enferma en la cama de
una enfermedad de la cual segun su asidente me apresura la muerte y asi
estando en mi entero Juicio sano el entendimiento y libre la voluntad .
otorgo y ago mi testamento por mi ultima voluntad creyendo como creo
firmemente en dios padre y dios yJo y dios espiritu Santo tres personas
distintas y un solo dios - verdadero y creo en todo lo que cree y enseña

la santa madre yglesia catolica rromana y nonbro por mi abogada a la
Santisima virgen maria nr̄a señora y al santo āJel de mi gª.- y asi ago mi
testamento en la forma y manera que se sigue_____

    Primeramente encomiendo a dios mi alma que la crio y rredimio con
su presiosa sangre y el cuerpo a la tierra de que fue formado

    Yten declaro que mi cuerpo se entierre en la yglesia y capilla de nr̄a
señora del rrosario que tienen los naturales en santo domingo desta
ciudad de mxº con muy moderada ponpa

    Yten declaro que tengo unas Casas las cuales me las dexaron mis
padres porque no tubieron mas yJos que yo y estas casas quiero y es mi
boluntad de que se bendan y de todo lo que por las dichas casas dieren
sera para que se rreparta en lo primero para mi entierro porque no tengo
otras bienes sino es de todo segundo quiero y es mi bolunta de lo que
que[fol. 17v]dare se me digan algunas misas por mi alma segun lo que le
paresiere a mi albasea y marido Juan antonio –

    mas declaro que de lo rremaniente de todo lo que quedare demas de
las dichas casas quiero y es mi boluntad de que se digan cuatro misas
cantadas por mis padres y dos misas rresadas por mis padrinos –

    y esta es mi ultima boluntad.

    Yten declaro que si sobrare alguna cosa desta casa que cunplido
todas mis mandas se lo dejo a mi marido Juan antonio para que me digan
algunas misas por mi alma conforme a su pareser y en todo se lo dexo a su
boluntad.

    tanbien declaro que tengo una ymajen de nr̄a sra. de la candelaria
de bulto y que quiero y es mi boluntad de que se quede en poder de mi
comadre frca. por la bendicio y que nadie se la pida que es mi ultima
boluntad

    tanbien digo y declaro que tengo otro san nicolas que la tiene mi tia
ana maria y es de bulto y es mi boluntad de que se quede en su poder y
que nadie se la pida porque es mi ultima boluntad.

    V̲ mas tengo que es mio otro san nicolas pequeño y otra hechura de
nr̄a sra. de bulto ambas piesas es mi boluntad que se que de an poder de
mi marido Juan antonio y todas las demas estanpas de papel y de tablas
viejas los queme me[sic] porque no estaban ya buenas y asi nadie tiene
que pedirle a mi marido

    V̲ yten declaro que que[sic] me dexo aguardar una madrina mia
que se fue fuera de mexico cuatro metates sin manos y una caja y una

mesa si bineeren por ello se lo den y todo esta en poder de Juan martin sonbrerero que yo se lo dexe tanbien aguardar [fol. 18]

Yten declaro que el testamento que mis padres ySieron esta en poder de una muger que me crio que bibe en el barrio de san pablo llama ana y que es tenantsin de los de teocaltitlan mando y quiero que se cobren los dichos testamentos con otros papeles que estan con ellos.

yten de declaro que tengo cuatro metates en poder de la dicha ana y es mi boluntad que se cobre mas tengo dos huipiles ya traidos y uno colorado tanbien ya traido mas dos fresadas biejas y una cubija de rruan y una caxa para q̃ se me diga algunas misas por mi alma _____

y para que se cumpla y se guarde este mi testamento nonbro por mi albasea a Juan antonio mi marido y por amor de dios lue [sic] rruego asete el nonbramiento por estarme bien que asi es mi boluntad.

y rreboco y anulo otros cuales quier testamento legados codisilios que antes desta ubiere hecho y es mi boluntad que esta valga y aga entera y en testimonio de verdad yo pedro rrodrigues escribano nonbrado –

por el cabildo y rreximiento que los naturales tienen en la capilla de nr̃a sra del rrosario desta ciudad de mexico Cuyo nonbramiento doy fe esta en los archibos y papeles de dicha cofradia y rreximiento y a la dicha otorgante a quien doy fe que conosco otorgo ante mi este testamiento y no firmo por que no supo firmar siendo testigos lucas de herrera y Juan miguel naturales y vesinos desta ciudad de mexico ante mi

+

Pedro Rodriguez

Escribano nonbrado

Translation

[fol. 17]

In the name of God omnipotent, know all who see this letter that I, Nicolasa Juana, native of Mexico City in the barrio of San Pablo, orphaned by mother and father, legitimately married as I am to Juan Antonio according to the orders of the Holy Mother Church, and he is a native of Mexico City in the barrio of Xihuitongo, say that being sick in bed of sudden illness which is hastening my death, and being entirely in my senses, sound of mind and free of will, I decree and make my last will and testament, believing firmly as I do in God the Father, God the Son, and God the Holy Spirit, three distinct persons but only one true God. And I believe all that the

Holy Mother Roman Catholic Church deems true and teaches, and I name as my advocate our lady the most holy Virgin Mary and my holy guardian angel. Thus I make my testament in the form and manner that follows.

First, I commend my soul to God who created it and redeemed it with his precious blood, and the body to the earth from which it was formed.

Item, I declare that my body is to be buried in the church and chapel of Nuestra Señora del Rosario that the natives have in [the friary] of Santo Domingo here in Mexico City with very modest pomp.

Item, I declare that I have a house which my parents left to me, because they had no other children than I. I desire and it is my will that these houses be sold and that all that is received for the said house is to be distributed first for my burial, because I have no other assets, for that is all, and second I desire and it is my will that from what is left [fol. 17v] some masses be said for my soul as my executor and husband Juan Antonio should think best.

Additionally, I declare that from the remainder of all that is left over from the said house, I want and it is my will that four high masses be said for my parents and two low masses for my godparents, and this is my final will.

Item, I declare that if there is something left over from this house after all my commands are fulfilled, I leave it to my husband Juan Antonio so that they will say some masses for my soul as he thinks best; I leave it all up to his will.

Also I declare that I have an image of Nuestra Señora de la Candelaria in the round and that I desire and it is my will that it remain in the custody of my *comadre* Francisca for the benediction,[6] and that no one is to demand it from her; it is my final will.

Also I say and declare that I have another [image, a] San Nicolás,[7] that my aunt Ana María has, it is in the round and it is my will that it stay in her custody. No one is to demand it from her, because it is my will.

V Additionally, I have another small San Nicolás and another figure of Nuestra Señora in the round. It is my will that both pieces stay in the custody of my husband Juan Antonio. I burnt all the others, the engravings[8] and the old ones on boards, because they were no good any more. So no one is to demand them from my husband.

V Item I declare that when a godmother of mine left Mexico City she left four metates[9] without pestles, a chest, and a table in my care. If they should come for it then give it [to them;] it is all in the power of the hat maker Juan Martín, to whom I in turn left it to take care of. [fol. 18]

Item, I declare that the testament that my parents made is in the custody of a woman called Ana who raised me, who lives in the barrio of San Pablo, and she is the *tenantzin*[10] of the people of Teocaltitlan. I order and want that the said testaments be retrieved along with the other documents that are with them.

Item, I declare that I have four metates in the custody of the said Ana and it is my will that they be collected. Additionally, I have two worn *huipiles*,[11] a red one, also worn, two old rough blankets, a cover of Rouen cloth; and a chest so that some masses can be said for my soul.

And to carry out and take care of my testament I name my husband Juan Antonio as my executor. For the love of God I ask him to accept appointment as a favor to me, for thus is my will.

I revoke and annul whatever other testaments, bequests, or codicils I should have made before this one. It is my will that this one should be valid and be entirely [credited] and in testimony of its truth I Pedro Rodríguez, appointed notary— [place here my signature]

For the cabildo and council that the natives have in the chapel of Nuestra Señora del Rosario here in Mexico City, the appointment of which I attest is in the archives and papers of the said confraternity[12] and council, and as for the testator, I attest that I know the person who issued this testament before me. She did not sign because she does not know how to.

The witnesses were Lucas de Herrera and Juan Miguel, natives and citizens of Mexico City here. Before me

+

Pedro Rodríguez,
appointed notary.

Notes

I am very appreciative of the invaluable help I received from the late James Lockhart with the translation and transcription of the will. Tatiana Seijas, Ken Ward, and Mark Christensen provided help at key points as well. I would also like to thank Stafford Poole for his continual insight into some of the lesser-known aspects of the Catholic faith. As always, all mistakes are my own.

1. The parish of Santa Cruz was another Nahua parish and seems to have been created through the political machinations of ambitious Nahuas within its boundaries. For more information on this parish as well as the *doctrina* of San Josef and 1550s change to parish status, see Truitt 2009, chap. 1.

2. A mixed confraternity of Filipinos and Nahuas in the parish of San Sebastián suggests that at least one other parish started including migrant natives by the end of the seventeenth century (Truitt 2009, chap. 4).

3. Special thanks to Tatiana Seijas for directing me to this source.

4. AGN, Bienes Nacionales, vol. 1766, e. 7, fols. 17–18.

5. While the church eventually included Filipinos, it is unknown whether Miguel de Silva, from Tatiana Seijas's chapter, was buried here as a specific burial location was not named in his will.

6. This was potentially an evening service organized by a confraternity during which they sang canticles in front of a statue of the Virgin Mary—in this case, Nuestra Señora de la Candelaria. For more information see *Catholic Encyclopedia*, http://www.newadvent.org/cathen/02465b.htm.

7. This is likely an image of San Nicolás de Tolentino, who, by the date of this document, had become the patron saint of Mexico City after being credited by Nahuas and Spaniards for saving the lives of both a Spanish and Native woman (as well as some children) during an earthquake. See Chimalpahin Quauhtlehuanitzin 2006, 191–193.

8. Woodcuts and engravings are listed regularly in inventories as *estampas de papel* (Kelly Donahue-Wallace, pers. comm.).

9. Metates are flat stones used for grinding corn.

10. Literally, "people's mother."

11. Traditional indigenous female upper garment.

12. A confraternity is not specifically named in the document, but it probably went by the same name as the chapel, Nuestra Señora del Rosario.

References

Boone, Elizabeth Hill. 2000. *Stories in Red and Black: Pictorial Histories of the Aztecs and Mixtecs*. Austin: University of Texas Press.

Chimalpahin Quauhtlehuanitzin, Domingo de San Antón Muñón. 2006. *Annals of His Time*. Edited and translated by James Lockhart, Susan Schroeder, and Doris Namala. Stanford, Calif.: Stanford University Press.

Donahue-Wallace, Kelly. 2007. "Picturing Prints in Early Modern New Spain." *The Americas* 64(3): 325–349.

———. 2011. Email correspondence. February 24.

Grijalva, Juan de. 1985. *Crónica de la orden de N.P.S. Agustín en las provincias de la Nueva España: En cuatro edades desde el año de 1533 hasta el de 1592*. Mexico City: Editorial Porrúa.

Javier Pescador, Juan. 1992. *De bautizados a fieles difuntos: Familia y mentalidades en una parroquia urbana Santa Catarina de México, 1568–1820*. Mexico City: El Colegio de México.

Lockhart, James. 1992. *The Nahuas After the Conquest: A Social and Cultural History of the Indians of Central Mexico, Sixteenth through Eighteenth Centuries*. Stanford, Calif.: Stanford University Press.

O'Hara, Matthew D. 2010. *A Flock Divided: Race Religion, and Politics in Mexico, 1749–1857*. Durham, N.C.: Duke University Press.

Osowski, Edward W. 2006. "Carriers of Saints: Traveling Alms Collectors and Nahua Gender Roles." In *Local Religion in Colonial Mexico*, edited by Martin Austin Nesvig, 155–186. Albuquerque: University of New Mexico Press.

Sedano, Francisco. 1974. *Noticias de México: Crónicas de los siglos XVI al XVII*. 3 vols. Mexico City: Colección Metropolitana.

Truitt, Jonathan. 2009. "Nahuas and Catholicism in Mexico Tenochtitlan: Religious Faith and Practice and La Capilla de San Josef de los Naturales, 1523–1700." Ph.D. dissertation, Tulane University.

———. 2010. "Courting Catholicism: Nahua Women and the Catholic Church in Colonial Mexico City." *Ethnohistory* 57(3): 415–444.

CHAPTER 4

Portrait of a Mixtec Woman
Named 6-Crocodile

KEVIN TERRACIANO

The will of a Mixtec woman named 6-Crocodile is a rich source for expos-
ing the paradoxes that abounded within colonial society. From her reten-
tion of an indigenous name based on the ancient Mesoamerican calendar
to her evident success as a local businesswoman involved in the cloth trade,
the will and inventory of Lucía Hernández Ñuquihui (ñu = 6; *quihui* =
crocodile) provide a portrait of a seventeenth-century woman that joins
those presented by Graubart and Truitt, and others before them, to challenge traditional assumptions about indigenous women as powerless in a
patriarchal colonial society. This chapter not only reveals this "unexpected"
side of a woman, but also illustrates the many insights to be gained from
language analysis. Understanding wills requires more than a translation of
the source. Indeed, a philological examination of the Mixtec in Hernández
Ñuquihui's will provides valuable information about the author's training
and writing conventions, his engagement with a Spanish colonial system,
and the regional traditions of which Hernández Ñuquihui was a part.

The *escribano* Andrés de Jeréz wrote the Mixtec-language last will
and testament of Lucía Hernández Ñuquihui in the Mixteca Alta region
of Oaxaca, Mexico, in May of 1633 (AHJ, Teposcolula, Civil 3, 287 [older
numeration]: fols. 24-26v).[1] Hernández Ñuquihui identified herself as a
member of a *ñuu siqui* called Dzumañuu (tail of the pueblo) within the
yuhuitayu of Yucundaa. This one sentence reveals three levels of sociopolitical organization: *siqui* was one of two terms used in the Mixteca Alta
to refer to a constituent unit of a ñuu. Spaniards referred to the *siqui* as a

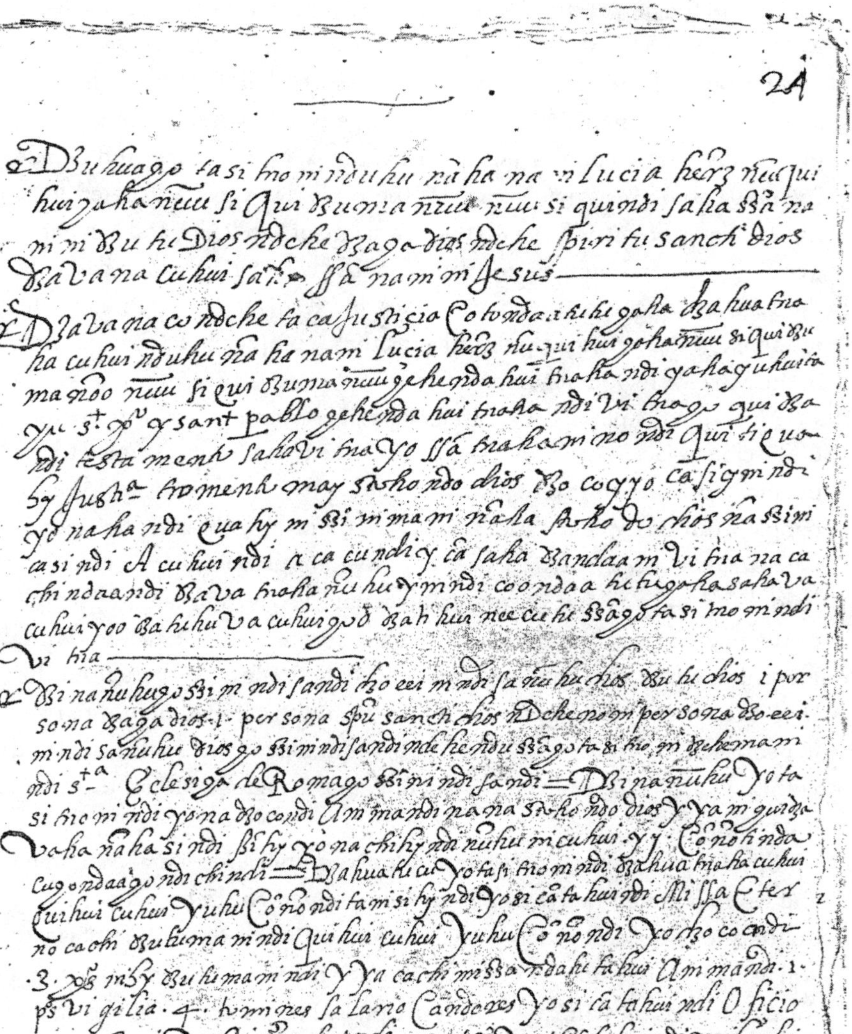

FIGURE 4.1. Testament of Lucía Hernández Ñuquihui. (Archivo General del Poder Ejecutivo del Estado de Oaxaca, AHJ Teposcolula, Civil 3, 287, older numeration: fols. 24–26v.)

barrio, and the ñuu as a *pueblo*; the *siqui* and ñuu might also be considered Mixtec equivalents of the Nahua *calpolli* (or *tlaxilacalli*) and *altepetl*, respectively.[2] The term *yuhuitayu* (reed mat seat) denoted a ñuu that was allied with other ñuu through the marriage of its dynastic rulers. In the preconquest-style codices and other paintings, pairs of male and female rulers seated on reed mats represent the *yuhuitayu*. Spaniards referred to the *yuhuitayu* of Yucundaa with the new name of San Pedro and San Pablo Teposcolula, combining patron saints' names with a place-name based on the Nahuatl language. The many names and terms in the opening of the testament reflect the sociopolitical and ethnic complexity of communities in the Mixteca region of Mesoamerica.

Mixteca is the plural form of the Nahuatl *mixtecatl*, referring to "people of the cloud place," a term that Nahuas from central Mexico assigned to the people of this northwestern part of the modern state of Oaxaca. However, people from the Mixteca Alta referred to themselves in their writings as *tay ñudzahui* or *tay ñudzavi*, "people of the rain place" (*tay* = "person" or "people"; *ñu* = "place"; *dzavi* = "rain"); it could also be translated as "people of the place of Dzahui." Dzavi or Dzahui (pronounced "dawi") was the Ñudzahui equivalent of the Nahua rain deity, Tlaloc.[3] Writers used this term in both the earliest and latest texts from the colonial period to refer to people, their language, the region, communities, and artifacts associated with the local culture area. Many people in the region still use the name today to refer to themselves.

Speaking of names, Lucía Hernández Ñuquihui and several other men and women mentioned in her testament retained Ñudzahui names based on the ancient 260-day sacred calendar, indicating that many people were still using it by this time in 1633, even though it was forbidden by the friars for its association with preconquest rituals. Names based on the calendar persisted until the eighteenth century in many parts of the Mixteca. Hernández Ñuquihui had both Spanish and Mixtec surnames. If indigenous elites were the first and commoners were the last to adopt Spanish surnames in the colonial period, then Hernández Ñuquihui's possession of two last names in 1633 (one Spanish, the other indigenous) reflects her "middling" status, as does the common but not plebeian Spanish surname ending in "-ez," "Hernández."

In her testament Hernández Ñuquihui made careful plans for her body and soul, setting aside money for multiple masses, saints, and the singers who would attend her funeral. She requested burial in the church, next to the altar of Santa Inés, and refers to a confraternity dedicated to a black image of the Holy Mary. She then divided her property among her children and grandchildren. She left her oldest child, Pascual Sánchez, and his son eighty pesos, thirty magueys, and several fields, including properties that she had purchased separately from two men and a woman. Pascual was to use the money to pay the royal tribute and to say masses on behalf of Hernández Ñuquihui's soul during saints' feast days. Magueys were a valued possession in Oaxaca; many men and women referred to owning them and bequeathed them to relatives in their testaments. Hernández Ñuquihui left another child, Petronilla, sixty pesos, four fields, and a house. It is important to note that Hernández Ñuquihui gave land to a daughter, indicating that women possessed landholdings even though the division of labor in this society did not associate women with agriculture. She left a third child named Clemente and his daughter, Juana, five houses, a sweatbath, magueys, the patrimonial land on which the houses stood, and four other fields associated with named places, which were to contribute to masses for her soul. She instructed Clemente not to sell any of the land and chose not to give him any money because he had already spent eighty pesos (in compensation) for wounding a man with a knife.

Hernández Ñuquihui's testament is accompanied by an inventory made in June 1633 (after her death) of cloth and money that she owned or was owed. The inventory includes 10 pounds of white cotton yarn and cloth, and 7.5 pounds of blue and black wool yarn. She also possessed the goods of Andrea Camaa, her son's mother-in-law, which included 6 pounds of cotton yarn, 4.5 pounds of blue and black wool yarn, 4 pounds of woolen cloth, at least 1 pound of cotton cloth, maguey cloth, cloaks, shirts, trousers, skirts, *huipiles* (shifts worn by women that extended from neck to ankle), collars, doublets, and more than forty *cascabeles* (small ornamental bells). The inventory features a mixture of indigenous and European-style fabrics, including cotton, wool, sayal wool, taffeta, maguey, and possibly silk. The meaning of "fine cloth" in one entry is unclear, as is a reference to a "skirt made from cloth here." The inventory concludes with a list of monies amounting to 446 pesos. Three women are mentioned here: Isabel Delgado, who presented 100 pesos; the deceased Andrea Camañe, who left 118 pesos to Hernández Ñuquihui; and a María from the town of Tilantongo, who had 25 pesos. It is interesting to observe how several women in

Hernández Ñuquihui's social circle possessed appreciable amounts of money. The inventory suggests that the sum of 446 pesos represents additional funds rather than an approximate value of the listed goods.

I have found no other mention of Lucía Hernández Ñuquihui in the historical record. As is true for most indigenous people from this period, we catch only a glimpse of Hernández Ñuquihui in the archival record and know little more about her life. We do know something about her social type, however. Hernández Ñuquihui was a *toho*, an esteemed member of her community, a *principal* whose social rank was somewhere between the *ñandahi* commoners and the *yya toniñe* hereditary elites. Most notably, Hernández Ñuquihui was involved in the production and sale of cloth for silver. Since Mixtec women owned property separately from their husbands, Hernández Ñuquihui possessed a considerable amount of wealth for an indigenous person. Most Mixtec men and women had little cash; many indigenous testators bequeathed their few pesos or *tomines* (coins valued at one-eighth of a peso) to the church for masses and saints. Hernández Ñuquihui, however, was able to leave 140 pesos to her children, and as many as six people, including three women and three men, owed her money, ranging from 2 to 22 pesos. The total of 446 pesos listed at the end of the inventory appears to be related to her cloth business. Again, it is a respectable sum, especially considering that money and credit were scarce in New Spain between the 1620s and 1650s, when Hernández Ñuquihui's testament was written.

The sale of cloth was one of the few ways that Mixtec men and women could earn pesos in this period. Many records show that the cloth goods brought by Mixtec long-distance merchants to Guatemala and Mexico City were produced or managed by women like Hernández Ñuquihui. Often, married couples collaborated, one producing and the other transporting and selling. The fact that Hernández Ñuquihui's husband owned mules suggests that he used them to transport goods. Many of these traders were *toho* who had familiar surnames such as Hernández and López. In the sixteenth century, many amassed small fortunes of hundreds and even thousands of pesos. The cloth trade was a preconquest tradition that was adapted to include the exchange of new materials (wool), new forms of transport (mules), and new markets (Puebla, for example) in a new money economy that required learning a new numbering system (Arabic).[4] If at first some indigenous traders prospered from selling cloth in local and distant markets, Spaniards eventually took over this trade by the latter part of the seventeenth century, as they did with every other profitable sector of the economy, limiting Mixtec producers and traders—women and men— to local markets.[5]

Notes on Mixtecan Languages

Because the study of Mixtec-language texts written in the Roman alphabet is still so nascent in comparison to scholarship on Nahuatl, it is appropriate if not necessary to make some general remarks about the language of the documents with which I am working, focusing on the testament examined in this chapter. Lucía Hernández Ñuquihui's testament was written in the heart of the Mixteca Alta region of Oaxaca, where Mixtec-language writing originated in the second half of the sixteenth century and flourished for a period of more than 200 years. In my collection of some 400 Mixtec-language texts from this period, nearly half are last wills and testaments. Wills are the earliest and latest surviving writings (1571 and 1807) other than church-sponsored books and manuscripts.

What is meant by the "Mixtec" language? Today, Mixtecan is one of eight branches of the Otomanguean family of languages, which accounts for about a third of all indigenous language speakers in Mexico. Mixtecan and Zapotecan are two of the largest and most internally diversified branches of this family; together they are used in most of the modern state of Oaxaca. At the time of the Spanish conquest, the Mixtec language group was one of the largest in Mesoamerica, with well over a million speakers. Today Mixtecan languages are spoken by about a quarter of a million people in the states of Oaxaca, Guerrero, and Puebla. Thousands more Mixtecan speakers have migrated to the north, to places such as Mexico City, the borderlands, and California.

In the sixteenth century, friars recognized various distinct versions of the *lengua mixteca* and significant phonetic variation throughout the four areas of the Mixteca region: Alta, Baja, Costa, and Valle. Fray Antonio de los Reyes compiled the first published grammar of Mixtec (1593) in the community of San Pedro y San Pablo Teposcolula, where Hernández Ñuquihui's testament was written forty years later. Reyes observed that the language often differed in nuance not only from one community to the next, but within the same pueblo, and even from one barrio to another. Despite these qualifications, he concluded that all of the variations constituted "one single Mixtec language" covering a large area. The fact that native writers in the Mixteca Alta made frequent references in the colonial period to a *dzaha ñudzahui* (Mixtec language) or *dudzu ñudzahui* (Mixtec speech) seems to confirm the idea of a common Ñudzahui language, at least in the Mixteca Alta.[6]

In the preamble to his work, Reyes addressed orthography and pronunciation, or "the ways of speaking and writing the language." He delineated the various geographical and "dialectal" areas of the Mixteca, summarized the phonetic differences of various regions, and noted the ways different variants were written. Reyes was able to describe how the language was both spoken and written because his work was not printed until at least three decades after native-language alphabetic writing had begun in the area. As early as 1571, fray Antonio appeared as a witness to a last will and testament written in the Ñudzahui language. Doña María López, the *cacica* of Tlazultepec, requested him to say masses on her behalf (AGN, Tierras 59, 2). Because he had worked in various areas of the Mixteca, Reyes was very attentive to recording regional and local differences. He considered the Teposcolula area dialect to be most perfect in that "one could write more fully with all the letters" (Reyes 1593, v, viii). The fact that he lived in Teposcolula for many years may have influenced his assessment.

A fellow Dominican, fray Francisco de Alvarado, published a *vocabulario* (Spanish-to-Mixtec vocabulary) in the same year, also working in Teposcolula. Like Reyes, Alvarado used the notes and manuscripts of his predecessors to compile more than 10,000 entries packed into 204 folios. Reyes oversaw Alvarado's work and checked the final product with several Mixtec aides and other friars before recommending it for publication. In the prologue, Alvarado affirmed that although the principal debt for the conception and compilation of the publication was owed to the friars, much of the work was actually done by unnamed "Indians, who are the best teachers and thus were the authors" (Alvarado 1593). The compilations of Reyes and Alvarado, printed in 1593, were the only instructional language texts for Mixtec published in the colonial period. San Pedro y San Pablo Teposcolula was a Dominican center for the study of Mixtec in this period.

Mundane archival records written by native speakers confirm the existence of multiple variants or languages. The extant documentation reveals at least five areas in which orthographic variation, corresponding to phonetic and morphological distinctions, was consistent and somewhat predictable: (1) the Baja area around Huajuapan; (2) the Valley of Oaxaca around Cuilapan; (3) the Alta around the Valley of Nochixtlan, including Yanhuitlan and Coixtlahuaca; (4) the Alta around the Valley of Tamasulapa, including Teposcolula; (5) and the Alta around the Valleys of Tlaxiaco, Achiutla, and Chalcatongo. These five areas correspond roughly with Reyes's observations in the late sixteenth century and are confirmed by modern data. Today most linguists agree that there are multiple, mutually unintelligible Mixtecan languages, some with their own variants or dialects.

The differentiation of variants and languages in the colonial period, and today, is intensified by the existence of contrasting local and regional tonal systems. This extreme variation has evolved over the course of at least two millennia and has accelerated since the Spanish conquest. As groups and native speech communities were reduced in size and became increasingly isolated by the growth of Spanish-speaking centers throughout the colonial and postcolonial periods, many divergent variants evolved into distinct languages.

Let us consider some general characteristics of Mixtecan languages. Word roots (or stems) are characteristically bisyllabic, and stress invariably falls on the first of these two syllables. The bisyllabic root is a nucleus to which other syllables can be added, without disturbing stress placement, and is the basis for all word and phonological phrase constructions (Josserand 1983, 180–181). Mixtecan languages have multiple tones, glottal stops, and both oral and nasalized vowels. Tone is a feature of all vowels. Tone was not represented in colonial transcriptions using the Roman alphabet, nor were devices established to mark tone consistently with diacritics.[7] The inability of the friars to mark tone is understandable; even today different analysts interpret and transcribe tone differently. Tonal variation among Mixtecan languages or dialects is so great that it is often the first feature distinguishing the speech of one community from that of others (Josserand 1983, 158).

Aside from relying on the usual phonetic meaning assigned to Roman alphabetical characters, the friars adapted some standard conventions to represent sounds. Alvarado usually marked the glottal stop with the letter *h*, especially between identical vowels, to indicate a re-enunciation of the second vowel rather than a simple lengthening (e.g., *ñuhu* as opposed to *ñuu*). This convention, also used in Nahuatl, was not always used for other occurrences of the glottal stop, between unlike vowels or preceding consonants, and was used rather inconsistently (as it was in Nahuatl).

Those who studied the language in the sixteenth century noted that Mixtec had no equivalent sounds corresponding to the following Castilian letters: *b, f, g, l* or *ll, p, r* or *rr, v*.[8] They also acknowledged that Mixtec possessed sounds that were unknown to Spaniards. Drawing on the work of their predecessors, Reyes and Alvarado used some digraphs or syllable sequences that combined conventional consonants to represent sounds not found in Castilian, such as *dz* and *nd*. Of *dz* he wrote "in the pronunciation of the dz we strike softly on the d and more strongly on the z" (Reyes 1593, 2). In the Teposcolula area, this *dz* seems to represent [d], a voiced interdental fricative or a voiced counterpart of theta (eth). This convention appears in the first word of the testament of Lucía Hernández Ñuquihui, *dzuhua* (thus), and throughout the text. To indicate a prenasalized stop, Reyes used *nd*, as in *ndehe*; for [t] followed by a nasal vowel, he used *tn* (plus the vowel), as in *tnaha*. Actually, this was simply [t] followed by a nasal vowel, but it is such a common syllable-initial occurrence that it seems as if it were an invented digraph. Hernández Ñuquihui's testament illustrates these conventions: in the first line, she refers to herself with the pronoun *nduhu* (I) and employs a common verb throughout the will, *yotasitnonindi* (I declare).

Reyes described the pronunciation of *vu* as "striking both the letters *vu* so that only one is heard clearly and distinctly." This sound approximates [w]. According to this scheme, *vu* plus a vowel was distinguished from *hu* plus a vowel in that the latter marked a medial glottal before [w]. However, more often than not, the distinction between *hu* and *vu* made by Reyes and Alvarado was either unknown or ignored by native writers and by some friars, including fray Benito Hernández in the first edition of his *Doctrina en lengua misteca*, published in 1567 and again in 1568. The words *dzavui* (rain) and *yuvui* (mat or *petate*), for example, were often written as *yuhui* and *dzahui*. Likewise, for the syllable-initial glide [w], *huitna* (today) was often written as *vuitna*. In Hernández Ñuquihui's testament, for example, the convention proposed by Reyes is often ignored: *yuvui* (mat) is written as *yuhui*; *dzavua* (also) is *dzahua* (and is written once as *dzava*); and *quivui* (crocodile) appears as *quihui* in Lucía's calendrical name (*ñuquihui*).[9] Likewise, *huitna* appears as *vitna* and *huahi* (house) as *vahy*.

The *escribano* of Hernández Ñuquihui's testament from Teposcolula, Andrés de Jeréz, followed many of the conventions described above and also borrowed from Spanish to describe introduced, colonial concepts. Loanwords appear for Christian concepts such as souls (writing "anima" for *animas*), purgatory (*purgatorio*), and anguish (writing "tromentu" for *tormento*). He especially uses loan vocabulary to refer to introduced cloth and related items, including trousers ("calçone" for *calzones*); a shirt ("camissa" for *camisa*); pieces of taffeta ("pedaço tapita" for *pedasos de tafetán*); a doublet ("jompon" for *jubón*); small round bells ("cascabela" for *cascabeles*); collars ("cuilo" for *cuellos*); a large collar ("balona" for *valón*); a course woolen cloth ("seal" for *sayal*); and woolen cloth in general ("paño"). The *escribano* also employed another word for woolen cloth that is not based on the Spanish loanword but is derived from Mixtec: *yuhua ticachi* (sheep cloth). Like the Nahuas, Mixtecs identified the introduced sheep with cotton (*cachi*) and referred to them as *ticachi* (literally "cotton animal," applying the *ti-* animal prefix to a common noun).

Finally, Andrés de Jeréz referred to the weight of goods in pounds (*libras*) and also occasionally noted ounces in the margin. He employed Arabic numerals as well as Mixtec numbers, writing *hoho dzico* (five twenty) for the number 100 (i.e., 5×20) and *usi dzico* (ten twenty) for 200, based on the Mesoamerican vigesimal counting system. He referred to the worth of goods in terms of *pesos* and *tomines*, the introduced currency based on silver.

In the end, Lucía Hernández Ñuquihui's will provides a variety of insights into life in seventeenth-century Oaxaca. Paradoxically, she was a middling native woman with an indigenous name and substantial wealth derived from a successful business. She not only owned much of her wealth separately from her husband, but bequeathed it in ways contrary to traditional divisions of labor. Her success included a role as a creditor. Linguistically, the document also contributes important details about a particular language variant within the Mixteca and how this variant was written. The orthography, vocabulary, and loanwords Jeréz employed provide a fleeting yet intimate view of the fluid and selective negotiations between Mixtec and Spanish societies—both of which Hernández Ñuquihui negotiated in her own lifetime.

Transcription of the Last Will and Testament of Lucía Hernández Ñuquihui, Written in 1633[10]

Transcription

[beginning on fol. 24 of original archival document]

1 v Dzuhua yotasitnoni nduhu ñaha nani lucia he$\overline{rz}$ ñuquihui yaha ñuu siqui dzumañuu ñuu siquindi saha ssaº nanini dzutu Dios ndehe dzaya dios ndehe spiritu sancti dios dzava nacuhui saha ssaº nanini Jesus –

2 v Dzava nacondehe taca Justiçia Cotondaa tutu yaha dzahua tnaha cuhui nduhu ñaha nani luçia he$\overline{rz}$ ñuquihui yaha ñuu siqui dzumañoo ñuu siqui dzumañuu yehe ndahuitnahandi yahayuhuita yu s.^{t} p^u y sant pablo yehe ndahuitnahandi vitna yoquidzandi testamentu saha vitna yossātnahaninondi quiti quahi Justi^a tromentu may stohondo dios dzoco yyocasiynindi yonahandi quahy nissinimaniñaha stohodo dios ñassini casindi Acuhuindi acacundi ycā saha dzandaani vitna nacachindaandi dzava tnaha ñuhuynindi coondaa tutu yaha saha vacuhui yoodzatuhu vacuhui yoodzatihui neecutu ssā yotasitnonindi vitna –

3 v dzina ñuhu yossinindisandi dzo eei ni ndisa ñuhu dios dzutu dios i persona dzaya dios i persona spū sancti dios nDehe noni persona dzo eei ni ndisa ñuhu dios yossinindisandi ndehe ndussa yotasitnoni dzehe mani ndi s^{ta} Eclesiya de Roma yossinindisandi = Dzina ñuhu yotasitnonindi yonadzocondi animandi nana stohondo dios yya niquidza vahañahasindi ssihy yonachihyndi ñuhu nicuhui .yy. coñotindacu yondaa yondichindi = Dzahua tucu yotasitnonindi dzahua tnaha cuhui quihui cuhui yuhu Coñondi tanisihyndi yosicatahuindi Missa Eterno cachi dzutumanindi quihui cuhui yuhu Coñondi yodzocondi 3. pºs nihy dzutumanindi yya cachi missa ndatutahui animandi .1. pºs vigilia .4. tumines salario Candores yosicatahuindi Oficio yaa qhmi yotniñoyahuindi .12. to^s yosicatahuindi yni huahy ñuhu ssā yodzica s^{to} sacramentu altar saa yodzica s^{ta} ynes condusicoñondi yotniñoyahuindi .4. pºs yosicatahuindi Cruz maga dziñuhu quaa 4 tomines yotniñoyahuiñadzaña .4. to^s yotniñoyahuiñadzaña saha canda caa ssihy yosicatahuindi dzuchi yti sta Cruz dzuchi yti s^{ta} maria tnoo quihui Cuhui yuhu Coñondi = dzahua tucu yotasitnonitucundi quihui qh tnaha .9. nicuhui yuhu coñondi yosicatahuindi .1. [fol. 24v] Missa candada cachi dzutumanindi ssihy yonaCahatucundi .1. ca missa yosicatahuindi nana s.^{t} Miguel yodzocondi .1. pºs. yotniñoyahuindi

4 v̲ Dzahua tucu yotasitnonitucundi dzahua tnaha cuhui quihui qh
tnaha misaa .29. Cuiti niquinisihyndi [c]uiyeni qhnay tumines vahy ñuhu
cachi dzutumanindi yosicatahuindi Missa E terno yodzocondi .3. pᵒs .1.
pᵘs vigilia .4. tumines yahui candores meo yodzocondi nana s̲t̲a̲ maria
meᵒ nana sᵗ pᵒ meᵒ nana .Sᵗ· npablo. meᵒ nana sᵗ·ctiego meo yodzocondi
saha anima yyo purgatorio ndehe dzahua yaha yotasitnonindi saha tniño
saha animandi –

5 v̲ Dzahua tucu yotasitnonindi ssā conay dzayayehuandi ñaha
nani pasqual sanchez 80 pᵒs ssā yonayhuahandi saha nidzico .3. molla
taañanda quihui nitnahaninondi quahy nissiniñuhu dzahua tomines dza
oco psᵘ yaha nindoo yona nihymayña yonacuhuandiña ytu nidzico ñu
Ana grᵃ ndoho conayña ndehe dzahua yaha missa yotasitnonindi Conay
dzayayehuandi pasqual sanchez = ssihy mayña conducu ndaha stohondo
Rey ssihy yotasitnonitucundi saha mayña coca Missa saha animandita
quihui sᵗᵒ ñanaca vico sᵗᵒ cocācā tauiña missa saha Animandi

6 v̲ Ytu dzini saha yosahandi dzayandi pasqual sanchez ssihy ytu
yuhuyahy conay dzayandi pasqual ssi dzayandi pᵒ tanda dzava conayña

7 v̲ Dzahua tucu yotasitnonitucundi sā conay dzayañanindi dzaya
Dzayandi pasqual sanchez .pᵒ· sanches .60. ssihy cotnaha .30. yahui nihy
si saha cuhui yahui Cuita ssā candisi si ssihy ytu tadzahua ytu nidzico ñu
domingo sisa ssihy ytu yodzohuaya ytu nidzico franco garçia quaha .10. pus

8 v̲ dzahua tucu yotasitnonitucundi ssā nihy dzayandi ñaha nani
pᵒnilla sanches .60. pᵘs nihyña ssihy ytu yuhundiye ytu yodzoyuhusichi
ssi hi ytu nidzico Juo bautista quaha .5. pus ssihy ytu nidzico diego cama
nihy tucu ña .1. huahy cadzo nino nihyña

9 v̲ Dzahua tucu yotasitnonitucundi sᵃ nihy dzaya cuhui vhuindi tay
nani Clemente Ramirez dzayamayta ssa dzuchi nani Juᵃ. Ramires ho ho
vahy ñehe Cotnaha chiyo sata vahy ndayahui ñoho cañandi tacuhui yahui
caa quihy tnaha qhni ñuhu cuhui missa saha animandi ytu saha yucundaa
nihy si ssihy ytu CahuaCundi ssihy ytu nduhua

[fol. 25] Ychi ndehe dzahuayaha ssa nihy dzayandi nani Juᵃ vacuhui
cuhui yahui dzahua dzayandi Clemente Ramirez ssa yonahamay 80 pᵒs
ña .psᵒ qhmi dzico nidzandehendi ssihy ña quivi nisiyoña vahy quihui ni
tuhuiyuchiña Juᵒ ñuhundihui Cahy ca quachi ninducuña ssihy ñatuhui ca
ssā dzico ña neecutu ssā yosahandi dzayandi vacuhui dzacaninoña dzava
ni yo ssa ndehe neecutu ssa simayndi…

10 <u>v</u> dzahua tucu yaha yondaa Memoria dzahua tnaha ñaha yonayyeca tomines mayndi maria lopez yonay .22. pᵒs = loreço de chavez .14. pᵒs = Juᵒ gomez .3. pᵒs = franca cōchi yonay .2. pᵒs mᵃ nacusi .6. pᵒs — sebastian qhnoo tay st Juᵒ yonay .2. pᵒs ndehe dzava yaha ssā simayndi ndaca alguaçia cuhui Missa saha animandi –

11 <u>v</u> dzahua tucu saha Cuhui quiye tniño tniño yondaa tutu yaha yocootasindi yosahañahandi poder .si. pᵒ· mariscal Dionisio delcado ndehe nduhui toho ya ha dzanomi tniño saha animandi hoho yaha qhnay toˢ huahy ñu[hu] cachi dzutu missa ssihy maytu quaytnoni neecutu ssā nihy dzayandi [t]a ñaha ca ssā ña ninacāhandi ycasaha maytu ndehe nduhui taCuhui alguaçiandi maytu naquaytnoni neecutu sa simayndi ndudzu yaha nacuhui cutu nee chihy taacaa qhu vacuhui yoodzatihui vacuhui yoonacani neecutu ssā nitasitnonindi ndehe dzava yaha ndudzu nicachi mayña nitacusi nduhu pᵒ de la Cruz alldes barᵐᵉ de velasco Regᵒʳ testigo. barᵐᵉ de velasco. Juᵒ bautista nissācondaa tutu testamento vitna ssā ñeni domingo en .22. de mayo de 1633 aᵒs nitaa nduhu nanindi— [rubric & sign of the cross]

Andres
de Xeres [rubric]
escriuano [rubric]

[fol. 26] Memoria nee cutu dzama yuhua cuitu yuhua ticachi ndiye nani Lucia her̄z ñuquihui siqui dzu ñoo vitna domingo en 26 de Junio de 1633 aᵒs

<u>v</u> yuhua cuitu yuhua yaha ydza ndeye — 10 lᵃˢ
<u>v</u> yuhua ticachi ndaa yuhua ticachi ndayu — 7 lᵃˢ 8ᵒs
Memoria ndeye nisihy ñu cani Andrea
cá maa sitna pedronilla dzaya pasqual sachez —
<u>v</u> yuhua cuitu yondaa yaha — 6 — lᵃˢ
<u>v</u> yuhua ticachi ndaa yuhua ticachi ndayu — 4 lᵃˢ 8ᵒs
<u>v</u> uni paño vaha .1. paño yadzi — 4 paño
<u>v</u> 1 dzoo dziyu 2 .1. dzoo dziyo .1. 1. camissa 3
<u>v</u> calçone ticachi tuhu — 1
<u>v</u> 1. dzoo ticachi ndaa — 1
<u>v</u> 1. dziyo nicōo noo yuhua yaha 1
<u>v</u> .1. dzico caa yuhua ndahui .1. dziyo ticachi seal — 2
<u>v</u> .3. dziyo ticachi nuu quachi ssa saa 3

v̲ yño cuilo 2 balona 6

v̲ ninatuhui tucu .1. dzicō ndico .1. dzico cuissi cuca dzoo caa yuhua
ndahui 3

v̲ uhui ca paño ninatuhui tucu 2

v̲ uni pedaço tapita quãa 3

[fol. 26v] v̲ uhui Jompon .1. dzoo tuhu 3

v̲ chindu cascabela 42

v̲ yuhua ninatuhui tucu yuhua ticachi ndaa ninatuhui tucu 4 l^{as}

v̲ 1 libra yuhua cuitu 1 l^{as}

v̲ tumenes ninatuhui vitna domingo en 26 de Junio de 1633 a^{os}

v̲ usi dzico pos caa ndodzo uni p^{os} cadza uvi 200 — 3p^{os} — 2 t^{os}
tomines

v̲ ysabel delcado yonay vaha hoho
dzico p^{os} 100 – p^{os}

v̲ yca ninassino cano ssã ho [uni] dzico
p^{os} caa ndodzo uni p^{os} uhui t^{os}—

v̲ saha tumines ndiye nani andrea
camañe dzaya andres cahui dzunina caa ndodzo ta Justia yyo
hoho dzico ssã ho uni p^{os} dza vhui p^{os} quisi cuhui yño dzico p^{os} 118. p^{os}

v̲ ninatuhui tucu nisiyo nay huaha
ma ñu tnoo oco hoho p^{os} tumines

may pasqual sanchez — 25 p^{os} 446 pesos

Translation

1 Thus I declare [that] I am named Lucía Hernández Ñuquihui of this
ñuu siqui [named] Dzumañuu, my ñuu siqui. In the name of God the father,
God the son, and God the holy spirit, let it be done in the name of Jesus.

2 Let all the officials see this document of mine, Lucía Hernández
Ñuquihui, of this ñuu siqui [named] Dzumañoo, the ñuu siqui Dzumañuu
to which I belong, [in] this *yuhuitayu* of San Pedro y San Pablo (Teposcolula) to which I belong. Today, I make a testament for today it is certain that I am suffering the punishment and affliction of our Lord God.
Although I am sick, I am clear of heart (mind). I have loved our lord God.
I do not know for certain if I will live or die, so now I will speak truthfully
about my will that is to be written on this paper because nobody should
contradict, nobody should obstruct, anything which I declare today.

3 First, I believe in the only true deity, God the father [who is] one person, God the son [who is] one person, [and] God the holy spirit, three persons but only one true deity God. And I believe all that my precious holy mother Church of Rome believes. First I declare that I offer my soul to our Lord God, the lord (*yya*) who created me, and I leave my body to the earth and worms whence it came. Also, I declare that when I have died, I request that my precious father [the priest] say a high (*terno*) mass.[11] I offer three *pesos* to my precious lord father to say a mass for the benefit of my soul when my body dies; [I also offer] one peso for the vigil [and] four *tomines* to pay the cantors. I pay twelve tomines for these services that I request. I request that my body be buried inside the church, at the foot of the altar of the holy sacrament, next to Santa Inés; [for which] I pay four pesos. I request a gold *cruzmanga* (a cloth adornment that covers part of a cross); [for which] I pay four tomines. I pay four tomines for the ringing of the bells. I request a few candles [from] the [confraternity of the] Holy Cross [and] a few candles [from] the [confraternity of the] black Santa María when my body dies. Also, I declare that my precious father say a sung (*cantada*) mass for me nine days after my body has died, and I also request that a mass be done before [the image of] San Miguel; [for which] I offer to pay one peso.[12]

4 And also I declare that my precious father should receive money to say a mass in the church twenty-nine days after I have died. I request a high mass, [for which] I offer three pesos; one peso [for] the vigil; four *tomines* to pay the cantors. I offer a half peso before Santa María, a half peso before San Pedro, a half peso before San Pablo, a half peso before San Diego. I offer a half peso for the souls in purgatory. And this is what I declare concerning obligations on behalf of my soul.

5 And also I declare that my oldest child named Pascual Sánchez will have eighty pesos that I have because three of his father's mules were sold; [but] I spent part of the money when I was sick, so that [Pascual] will have the twenty pesos that remain. And I have a cultivated field that the deceased Ana García sold to me; I order that my oldest child Pascual Sánchez have it [to pay] for the tribute of our lord king. And I also order that masses be said for my soul on the feast days of saints, that masses be requested for the benefit of my soul.

6 I give to my child, Pascual Sánchez, a field [in the place named] Dzinisaha, and my child Pascual will have a field [in the place named]

Yuhuyahy. Pascual and my [grand]child Pedro should divide the land between them.

7 Also I declare that my grandchild, Pedro Sánchez, the child of my child, Pascual Sánchez, will have sixty pesos and thirty magueys and a field [in the place named] Tadzahua, a field that the deceased Domingo Sisa sold, and a field [in the place named] Yodzohuaya that Francisco García sold for ten pesos.

8 Also I declare that my child, the woman named Petronilla Sánchez, will have sixty pesos and a field [in the place named] Yuhundiye, and a field [in the place named] Yodzoyuhusichi, and a field that Juan Bautista sold for five pesos, and a field that Diego Camaa sold, and also a house that is located above [the field] is hers.

9 Also I declare that my two children, Clemente Ramírez and his child, the girl named Juana Ramírez, are to have five houses, a steam bath (*temascal*), and the patrimonial land in back of the houses. The magueys that are on the [following] four lands are to be sold [to pay] for masses for my soul: a field [in the place named] Sahayucundaa, and a field [in the place named] Cahuacundi, and a field [in the place named] Nduhuaychi, and also [in the place named] Dzahuayaha. And my child named Juana should not allow them [the lands] to be sold. As to my child, Clemente Ramírez, this is all I give him because he already has spent eighty pesos; I wasted eighty pesos when he stabbed [a person named] Juan [from] the coast, for the crime that he committed. This is all that I have to give to my children; they should not dispute it.

10 Also, here is written an inventory of the money that is owed to me. María López has (owes me) twenty-two pesos; Lorenzo de Chávez [owes me] fourteen pesos; Juan Gómez [owes me] three pesos; Francisca Conchi has two pesos [of mine]; María Nacusi [owes me] six pesos; Sebastián Qhñoo from the ñuu of San Juan [owes me] two pesos; and so my executors will take care of that which is mine and arrange masses for my soul.

11 Thus, this document attends now to the business [of naming my executors]: I command, I give power [of attorney] to Pedro Mariscal [and] Dionisio Delgado, that these two lords (*toho*) will bear the burden of obligations on behalf of my soul, that these lords will guard the money of the church [for] the priest to say masses, that you will make certain that my children receive everything that I have given them. Thus you two will be my executors, you will take care of all my possessions, and all these words of mine will be done, will be realized. Nobody should obstruct, nobody should impede anything that I have declared. And thus I have heard these words that she has spoken: Pedro de la Cruz, *alcalde*, Bartolomé de Velasco, *regidor*, the witnesses Bartolomé de Velasco and Juan Bautista. The testament was written today, in the afternoon of Sunday, on May 22, of the year 1633. I wrote my name, Andrés de Jeréz, *escribano*.

Inventory of all the cloth, cotton yarn, and wool yarn of the deceased named Lucía Hernández Ñuquihui, of the *siqui* Dzumañuu. Today, Sunday, on 26 of June of [the year] 1633.
- Ten pounds of [white] cotton yarn and cloth. 10 lbs.
- Seven pounds and eight ounces of blue and black wool yarn. 7 lbs. 8 ounces

Goods of the deceased Andrea Camaa, grandmother of Petronilla, who is the child of Pascual Sánchez.
- Six pounds of cotton yarn. 6 lbs.
- Four pounds and eight ounces of blue and black wool yarn. 4 lbs. 8 ounces
- Three fine cloths, 1 maguey cloth. 4 cloth
- Two cloaks and one shirt. 3
- Used woolen trousers. 1
- A blue woolen cloak. 1
- One skirt made from cloth here. 1
- One *huipil* of poor cloth; one woolen *sayal* skirt. 2
- Three small, new woolen skirts. 3
- Six collars and one large collar. 6
- There were also one *huipil*, one white *huipil*, a cloak of poor cloth. 3
- There were also two woolen cloths. 2
- Three pieces of yellow taffeta. 3
- Three doublets and one cloak. 3
- Forty-two *cascabeles* (little bells). 42
- There was also blue woolen cloth. 4 lbs.
- One pound of white cotton cloth. 1 lb.

Money that was presented today, Sunday, on June 26, 1633.
- 202 pesos and two *tomines*.
- Isabel Delgado has 100 pesos.

- That makes 303 pesos and 2 *tomines*.
- The money of the deceased person named Andrea Camañe, child of Andrés Cahui, which amounts to 118 pesos.
- Also the 25 pesos that María [of] Tilantongo has, which belong to Pascual Sánchez.

Total = 446 pesos

Notes

1. This has been recataloged as Civil legajo 10, expediente 25. I thank the former and present archivists of the AHJ in Oaxaca, Gonzalo Rojo Martínez and Israel Garrido Esquivel, respectively, for their invaluable work in the archive and their equally valuable assistance in facilitating our research. I would also like to thank Barry David Sell for his work with me on a very preliminary transcription and translation of this document in 1992, when he showed an interest in learning Mixtec in addition to Nahuatl.
2. The Nahuatl terms *calpolli* and *tlaxilacalli* refer to constituent parts of the larger *altepetl*. The latter term is actually more commonly attested in the record, but both seem to refer to the same semi-independent subgroup of the *altepetl*. See Lockhart 1992, 16 for a concise treatment of these terms.
3. Ñudzahui is a commonly attested form of the word in native-language writings from the colonial period, even though some friars who studied the language and who attempted to develop and promote a standardized orthography in the Mixteca Alta distinguished *vui* from *hui* and wrote *dzavui* instead of *dzahui*, for reasons described in the section on language in this chapter. I have found that many (if not most) native writers from the Mixteca Alta, however, wrote *dzahui* for "rain" or the "rain deity." In any case, this term, spelled and pronounced many different ways, is still used by many Mixtecan speakers in reference to themselves, as it was in the colonial period.
4. Spaniards introduced a currency based on gold and silver in the sixteenth century. The rapid adoption of coin in native society suggests a familiarity with the concept of exchange value. Both Mesoamerican and European societies had well-developed market systems and trading traditions, but preconquest Mesoamerica did not rely on precious metals as an exclusive means of exchange. More important, currencies had supplemented the bartering of goods before the arrival of the Europeans. The main indigenous currency used in the early sixteenth century was cacao. Woven goods were also a major tribute and trade item in Mesoamerica, and especially in the Mixteca.
5. See Terraciano 2001, 238–248 for a discussion of the cloth trade and long-distance trade in the Mixteca. See also Romero Frizzi 1990, 185—187 for the decline of this trade.

6. For a fuller treatment of the language as it was written in the colonial period, see Terraciano 2001, 66–101; see also p. 322 for references to *dzaha ñudzahui*.
7. Similarly, there was a great deal of ambiguity in Nahuatl orthographies that did not distinguish between long and short vowels and did not record glottal stops.
8. Note that the phonetic value of Spanish *ll* changed in the course of the colonial period, approaching [y] by the eighteenth century (hence the entry "cocodrillo" in Alvarado's *vocabulario* of 1593, cited in the previous note). Originally, no Mixtec equivalent corresponded to *ll*.
9. "Crocodile" appears as *coo yechi* in the vocabulario (Alvarado, fol. 135, under *lagarto cocodrillo*) and as *quevui* in the older calendrical vocabulary (Terraciano 2001, 152). The *ñ* in *ñuquihui* represents an alveopalatal nasal and is very common in colonial Mixtec texts.
10. Numbers in bold preceding each paragraph of the transcribed testament correspond to sections marked by *item* (written as "<u>v</u>") in the original document. The Mixtec-language text in the numbered paragraphs of the transcription corresponds to the English-language text in the numbered paragraphs of the translation. I have not numbered the entries of the separate inventory, however. In the transcription, brackets indicate illegible letters in the original document that are obscured by paper damage or the margins of the document; letters in the brackets represent my approximation based on what I can see or what I think should have been written. In the translation, words that are implied but not stated in the original text are placed in brackets to help make sense of the translation. Finally, words in parentheses in the translation are meant to clarify the preceding word or words, sometimes drawing attention to the precise Mixtec term used.
11. Hernández Ñuquihui requests a "missa [d]e terno," a type of high mass involving a priest and two ministers or servers, and referring to their particular vestments for the mass.
12. Here and elsewhere in the testament, Hernández Ñuquihui requests masses to be said and gives alms "before" (*nana*) a saint, as if she were standing in front of the actual image of a saint in the church.

References

Alvarado, fray Francisco de. 1962 [1593]. *Vocabulario en lengua mixteca*. Edited by Wigberto Jiménez Moreno. Mexico City: Instituto Nacional de Antropología e Historia.

Josserand, J. Kathryn. 1983. "Mixtec Dialect History: Proto-Mixtec and Modern Mixtec Text." Ph.D. dissertation, Department of Anthropology, Tulane University.

Lockhart, James. 1992. *Nahuas After the Conquest: A Social and Cultural History of the Indians of Central Mexico, Sixteenth through Eighteenth Centuries*. Stanford, Calif.: Stanford University Press.

Reyes, fray Antonio de los. 1976 [1593]. *Arte en lengua mixteca*. Publications in Anthropology no. 14. Nashville, Tenn.: Vanderbilt University.

Romero Frizzi, María de los Ángeles. 1990. *Economía y vida de los españoles en la Mixteca Alta, 1519–1720*. Mexico City: Instituto Nacional de Antropología e Historia.

Terraciano, Kevin. 2001. *The Mixtecs of Colonial Oaxaca: Ñudzahui Writing and History, Sixteenth through Eighteenth Centuries*. Stanford, Calif.: Stanford University Press.

PART 2

Gulf of
Mexico

Ixil, Yucatan,
Mexico

Xochimilco,
Mexico

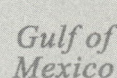

Rabinal,
Guatemala

South

Pacific

Ocean

Galapagos Islands

Strategies of the Elite

This section focuses on strategies used by members of the indigenous elite to maintain their position in a constantly shifting colonial environment. At times they individually petitioned the Spanish court; at others they worked as members of a family, and occasionally their responsibilities to the public served to justify their place within a community. All three chapters build on the historiography of studies focused on elite, or noble, indigenous rule during the colonial period. Works such as "A Battle of Wills: Inventing Chiefly Legitimacy in the Colonial North Andes" (Powers 1998), *Indigenous Rulers: An Ethnohistory of Town Government in Colonial Cuernavaca* (Haskett 1991), and *After Moctezuma: Indigenous Politics and Self-Government in Mexico City, 1524–1730* (Connell 2011) illustrate some of the themes in these chapters by examining the actions taken by native elites to maintain their prominence in indigenous government and society immediately following European contact and throughout the colonial period.

Richard Conway's chapter, "Accessories to Inheritance: Nahua Pictorial Documents and Testaments in Early Colonial Central Mexico," examines legal cases presented by elite Nahuas, such as doña Josepha Cerón Cortés y Alvarado, to defend their estate inheritances. His examination of these documents shows how the testamentary tradition of Spain and indigenous pictorial documents, or *pinturas*, became intertwined to lend additional legitimacy to landowning indigenous elites' petitions to preserve their estates.

In "The Spoils of the Pech Conquistadors," Mark Christensen employs more than 100 wills to trace the sociopolitical and economic positions of the descendants of Ah Dzulub Pech of Ixil, who assisted Spanish conquistadors in subduing other Maya communities and in establishing Catholicism. For this he and his descendants obtained noble *hidalgo* status in perpetuity. Using a collection of eighteenth-century wills, Christensen demonstrates that in terms of wealth, marriages, and political positions, the

Pech still maintained prominence in their community, though other elites were starting to make inroads.

The role of community leaders in the testamentary process comes to the forefront in Owen Jones's chapter, "'One or Two of My Living Words': K'iche' Testaments from Guatemala in the Seventeenth and Eighteenth Centuries." In creating a K'iche' testament, notaries in Rab'inal made the process a community affair. As such, some testaments contain the voices of community leaders as well as the testator's. As readers we are given the rare opportunity to "hear" the process as the leaders entered the homes of the deceased and announced their presence. Their role was such that if a community member died intestate, the community came together and generated a will for the deceased posthumously.

Collectively the three chapters in this section provide a glimpse of how elite natives maintained a place for themselves in the evolving colonial world. Individuals fought for their inheritance through joint use of the Spanish legal system and precontact *pinturas*; members of a lineage worked collectively to maintain their prominent position in the town hierarchy and the colonial system; and leaders played an official role in the funerary rituals of their community.

References

Connell, William F. 2011. *After Moctezuma: Indigenous Politics and Self-Government in Mexico City, 1524–1730*. Norman: University of Oklahoma Press.

Haskett, Robert. 1991. *Indigenous Rulers: An Ethnohistory of Town Government in Colonial Cuernavaca*. Albuquerque: University of New Mexico Press.

Powers, Karen Vieira. 1998. "A Battle of Wills: Inventing Chiefly Legitimacy in the Colonial North Andes." In *Dead Giveaways: Indigenous Testaments of Colonial Mesoamerica and the Andes*, edited by Susan Kellogg and Matthew Restall, 182–213. Salt Lake City: University of Utah Press.

CHAPTER 5

Accessories to Inheritance

Nahua Pictorial Documents and Testaments in Early Colonial Central Mexico

RICHARD CONWAY

In 1686 a Nahua noblewoman named doña Josepha Cerón Cortés y Alvarado appeared before the viceroy of New Spain clutching a bundle of papers. The documents supported her petition to inherit a landed estate in the central Mexican *altepetl* (ethnic state) of Xochimilco. Much depended on the viceroy's ruling. Doña Josepha stood to gain considerable wealth, the estate consisting of valuable urban properties and extensive tracts of land, including many of the fertile aquatic gardens known as *chinampas* for which Xochimilco is famed. Inheritance would have further given her the superior social standing of a *cacica*, the female equivalent of an indigenous ruler. Unfortunately, doña Josepha's chances of success were slim at best: although distant ancestors had once traced their prestigious lineage back to Acamapichtli, the Mexica forebear of the emperor Moteuhcçoma Xocoyotzin (r. 1502–1520), by the time of her petition the direct line of descent had broken. Doña Josepha was but the illegitimate daughter of the previous estate holder's nephew (Cline 1991). That the estate records had come into her possession thus mattered a great deal. Doña Josepha presumably hoped the papers might offset the weakness of her case, as if they could somehow surmount her awkward status. Intriguingly, though, and despite having many other kinds of sources—including legal papers and testaments—she chose to bolster her claim by drawing the authorities' attention to her Nahuatl pictorial documents, or *pinturas*. Why, in particular, did she ask to be granted the inheritance in accordance with these "maps and paintings" (AGN, Vínculos y Mayorazgos 279, 1; AGN, Indios 29, 249:201v—202v)? Why did they apparently matter so much?

Doña Josepha's pictorial records included house plans, maps, and cadastrals (land registers). Art historians have classified these and other sources—tribute records, censuses, genealogies, and inventories of possessions—as economic or practical documents in order to distinguish them from other Mesoamerican manuscripts, such as the famous books of fate, or divinatory codices, which fulfilled markedly different purposes (Glass 1975; Boone 1998).[1] As a whole, the indigenous manuscripts stood apart from their European counterparts in the ways they recorded and transmitted information: the *pinturas* were not supposed to replicate spoken language, as with alphabetic script; instead, they made use of glyphs and other pictorial conventions to impart information visually.[2] These differences made doña Josepha's emphasis on the pictorial sources surprising, especially given that the tradition of making *pinturas* had all but come to an end by the 1680s.[3] Conceivably, it would have been difficult for Spanish authorities, including the officials whom doña Josepha approached, to make complete sense of them. Fortunately for us, the *pinturas* in doña Josepha's possession were accompanied by alphabetic texts written in Spanish and Nahuatl. By examining the two kinds of sources in light of each other, we can glimpse some of the meaning of the pictorial sources, discern how Nahuas used them, and gain a sense of why doña Josepha attached so much importance to them.

The pictorial documents formed a crucial part of Nahua efforts to preserve property and pass it on to future generations. In this the *pinturas* came to be closely connected with last wills and testaments. The two types of sources reinforced one another, serving as valuable evidence to verify the legitimate owners of houses and land. The testaments and the pictorials, as evidentiary allies, lay at the heart of the Nahuas' legal strategies before the courts, especially those of the elite. That doña Josepha's estate records covered a span of some 150 years, and were rare for having been kept together so well, attests to her ancestors' considerable success in maintaining their holdings and, by extension, their elevated social and economic position (Gibson 1964, 157).

Over the years, and as the pictorial documents were handed down from one generation to the next, they were repeatedly brought out and examined by officials of the city council, or *cabildo*. Scribes altered the pictorials' appearance as they were updated, annotated, and modified to reflect changing circumstances and new ways of recording information. The sources' meaning and functions thus changed under new judicial and bureaucratic influences. Eventually, the pictorial sources and testaments began to converge as documentary genres. In testaments, Nahuas bequeathed the paperwork, including pictorials, that pertained to their property. Heirs in turn presented their *pinturas* to be examined alongside testaments in probate sessions. And during these proceedings, notaries inserted information from testaments and other sources into the pictorial documents themselves. The pictorial records thus came to have a history of their own, one that can be reconstructed from doña Josepha's papers.

Land and Record Keeping in Postconquest Mexico

The *pinturas* formed part of a long-standing tradition of record keeping in central Mexico. Before the arrival of Europeans, painters of books, known as *tlacuiloque*, had specialized in the making of maps, land cadastrals, and other practical documents.[4] Although colonial-era scribes gradually replaced the painters of books, the making of pictorial documents did not, as some scholars once maintained, come to an abrupt end.[5] Nor were the *pinturas* supplanted by alphabetic texts in a simple, linear fashion (Cline 1993, 10–11). Rather, during the early colonial period the two types of source overlapped and coexisted. This coincidence meant that some Nahuas were conversant with both ways of recording information. Among others, one of Xochimilco's notaries, Mateo Ceverino de Arellano, would have likely been familiar with both writing systems. He received training at the Franciscan Colegio de Santa Cruz in Tlatelolco, where he also worked with fray Bernardino de Sahagún on the *Florentine Codex*, the remarkable ethnographic account of Nahua history and culture that combined alphabetic texts with images (Lockhart 1992, 472).[6] Similarly, a noble from Xochimilco named don Esteban de Guzmán—one of the most influential Nahua political figures in the sixteenth century—was evidently familiar with the different kinds of records. In 1553, while serving as Xochimilco's governor, he supervised the drafting of a new set of written regulations, set down in Spanish script, for the *cabildo*. When later serving as the governor of Mexico-Tenochtitlan, don Esteban was involved in the making of the *Codex Osuna*, which contained painted testimony for a lawsuit.[7]

The indigenous documentary tradition further survived alongside its European counterpart because the *pinturas* catered so well to the needs of Spaniards. The art historian Elizabeth Boone has persuasively shown that Spanish authorities served as patrons for the continued production of pictorial documents. On the one hand, the *pinturas* provided information vital to governing newly conquered territories. Hence, when the first viceroy, don Antonio de Mendoza (r. 1535–1550), sent a councilman from Xochimilco to investigate a boundary dispute, he asked explicitly for a *pintura* to accompany the written report.[8] On the other hand, because Spaniards accepted the pictorial records as evidence admissible before the courts, indigenous people such as doña Josepha presented them when submitting petitions or otherwise dealing with the authorities (Boone 1998). In 1550 Nahua officials approached Viceroy Mendoza to request that the center of Xochimilco be reconfigured to accommodate a new marketplace and to conform to the Spanish-style *traza*, or grid, layout. The representatives presented a *pintura* to make the proposed changes visually comprehensible and their request all the more compelling. (Alas, the *pintura* is not preserved with the petition, AGN, Mercedes 3, 397, 144.)

Nahuas also relied on pictorials for the internal administrative needs of their *altepetl*. Communities preserved in their archives *pinturas* containing various kinds of information, from census figures to tribute payments, as well as details essential for determining land ownership.[9] This basic function underpinned several of doña Josepha's documents, which distinguished land owned by members of the Cerón y Alvarado family from that of their neighbors (AGN, Vínculos y Mayorazgos 279, 1:48, 77v, 116). The sources further helped the authorities reckon with the tremendous complexity of land tenure in the *chinampa* districts, where there were thousands of the small raised gardens.[10] Nahuas owned some of these outright, but others were held under communal, usufruct rights. Further complicating the situation, households might have access to many garden plots, which, in order to minimize risk, were not necessarily contiguous but instead scattered across different locations.[11] In a 1577 testament, included in doña Josepha's bundle of papers, doña Ana de Guzmán bequeathed nearly 400 *chinampas* to a dozen individuals, all of them in the same area (AGN, Vínculos y Mayorazgos 279, 1:19–21v). In a single place, then, *chinampas* could be owned by many different households. Cadastral records were used to keep track of this. One such cadastral showed five individuals—

identified by glyphs of heads that appeared in profile—who shared fifteen *chinampas* that were possibly classified under four types of land tenure, as indicated by the use of color (AGN, Tierras 1525, 5:3).[12]

In addition to sorting out the complexities of land distribution, the pictorials also helped government officials resolve disputes. While the threat of land alienation extended back to Aztec times, new sources of conflict over property emerged during the colonial period (Gibson 1964, 271; Lockhart 1992, 141–163). The influx of Spanish or other non-native settlers could engender conflicts. Demographic decline also brought upheaval. Residents sometimes argued over the reallocation of land that had fallen vacant. On other occasions, the viceregal government exacerbated these disputes by redistributing land to commoners in order to obtain tribute payments in exchange for the usufruct rights.[13] Beyond these sources of conflict, transfers of title also afforded opportunities for rivals to contest property rights. Occasionally such challenges accompanied sales of property. More often, though, and arguably more perilously, challenges might follow an individual's death, especially if there were any questions about testamentary bequests. The reconstitution of families, with widows remarrying and having offspring with new partners, could compound such problems.[14] Arguably no situation was more susceptible to disagreement than an individual's intestate demise, as was the case with one of doña Josepha's ancestors. The existence of a flawed testament was scarcely less problematic. Aggrieved heirs could quarrel over provisions, in some circumstances even asking that testaments be annulled. In 1586 the overturning of a testament also affected one of doña Josepha's relatives, and the ensuing quarrel inspired numerous protracted lawsuits. Six decades later, in 1649, relatives were still fending off plaintiffs (AGN, Vínculos y Mayorazgos 279, 1:121–125, 131v). Because of the very real possibility of disputes, Nahua testators took care to pass on the pictorial records to their heirs so that they could verify their property rights and, if necessary, surmount legal challenges.

Pictorials and the Defense of Property

Pictorial records constituted an important part of the evidence Nahuas presented before the courts because, on a fundamental level, they served as certificates of title. Doña Josepha argued as much in 1687 when she insisted that having the *pinturas* and other sources conferred rights to the inheritance, as though the possession of *pinturas* and property were one and the same. In this case doña Josepha sought to obtain property; for those who already had property and faced challenges to their holdings, the *pinturas* served as essential proof of ownership. In 1568 a Nahua noblewoman named doña María de Mendoza argued that a set of *chinampas* belonged to her. In response, the current occupant, Martín Iuctli, presented a pictorial to establish that he held them legitimately. Martín explained that the *pintura* came into his possession when he was awarded the *chinampas* as part of a viceregal inspection that had taken place a decade earlier. Then, the viceroy had appointed a Nahua official to redistribute lands that had fallen vacant. Martín explained how he came into possession of both the *chinampas* and the *pintura*. His document not only served as a property title but also as proof of the existence of other documentation supporting his claim (AGN, Tierras 1525, 5).

As with Martín Iuctli, Nahuas did not rely on their pictorial records solely to defend their rights. They also used *pinturas* to generate supplementary documentation to further secure their ownership. In 1591, Magdalena Tlaco received an inheritance of a house and its plot of land (*solar*) from her father. To verify the legitimacy and accuracy of the testament, and to obtain from Spanish authorities a confirmation of her possession, Magdalena presented a pictorial document. To further protect her inheritance, Magdalena also sought an *amparo*, or judicial order, which made interference illegal (AGN, Indios 5, 564:156v).[15] In this case, Magdalena surrounded her father's testament with the protective shield of other legal and administrative records, and in this the *pintura* served as a key piece of the overall evidence.

In other cases, instead of corroborating information, the *pinturas* could reveal errors in testaments. In 1572 the notary Mateo Ceverino de Arellano set down the last will and testament of a merchant named Constantino de San Felipe (AGN, Tierras 1525, 3). When the merchant passed away, his widow and mother fought over some of the testament's provisions. The mother, Juliana Tlaco, triumphed because she presented three pictorial documents to support her case. The pictorials—a genealogy as well as two inventories of possessions—showed discrepancies between their content and that of the testament. The pictorials established to the satisfaction of a judge that Constantino had bequeathed property that did not, in fact, belong to him. The accompanying pictorial materials thus enabled Juliana to expose and resolve mistakes in the testament (NL, Ayer 1901, 1902; Goupil 1891).[16]

Recognizing their evidentiary value, Nahuas obtained pictorials when they came into possession of new property. Members of the Cerón y Alvarado family did so after acquiring land in Xaxalpan following the intestate demise of don Pedro de Sotomayor in 1582. A noble who had a long career in local government, don Pedro had enjoyed rights of access to a set of *chinampas*. Political commitments, though, meant that he had not actually cultivated the fields himself. Instead, he relied on dependent laborers, called *terrazgueros*, to do so as part of the perquisites of high social status.[17] The *terrazgueros* exploited the opportunity of don Pedro's demise to seize control of the *chinampas*. In response, his widow, doña Juana de Guzmán, turned to don Martín Cerón y Alvarado, the governor, for help. For indigenous nobles in central Mexico—as with their Maya counterparts in the Yucatan, for instance, the Pech dynasty discussed by Mark Christensen in this volume—the control of political office was vital to the maintenance of high social status. On this occasion, don Martín succeeded in evicting the *terrazgueros* because the *chinampas* were classified as communal lands, and, as governor, he could reallocate them with the approval of the *cabildo* over which he presided (AGN, Vínculos y Mayorazgos 279, 1:76–78v).

While the governor returned some of the *chinampas* to doña Juana de Guzmán, others became the property of his son, don Martín Cerón Villafañez. The circumstances behind this transfer were not captured in the documentary record. Maybe doña Juana did not need or want all of the *chinampas*; after all, she might have been leery about dealing with recalcitrant *terrazgueros*. Alternatively, she may have given them to the Cerón y Alvarado family as a gesture of thanks or as a payment for the family's assistance. Either way, don Martín Villafañez petitioned the *cabildo* for title to some *chinampas*. To this end, he presented a *pintura* (Figure 5.1).

The *cabildo* granted and confirmed the transfer. A scribe then updated the pictorial image so that it displayed the names of don Martín Villafañez and his neighbors in alphabetic script. The *chinampas* and the pictorial record of them now became part of the family estate, and both were handed down to successive generations of heirs.

To secure the smooth transmission of property, Nahuas took the precaution of passing on the relevant paperwork to their heirs. In turn, heirs such as doña Francisca Cerón, the wife of don Martín Villafañez, presented pictorial documents before the *cabildo* to secure their inheritance. In 1582, after learning that her mother was ill and had asked to set down her testament, Nahua officials dispatched a scribe along with a couple of

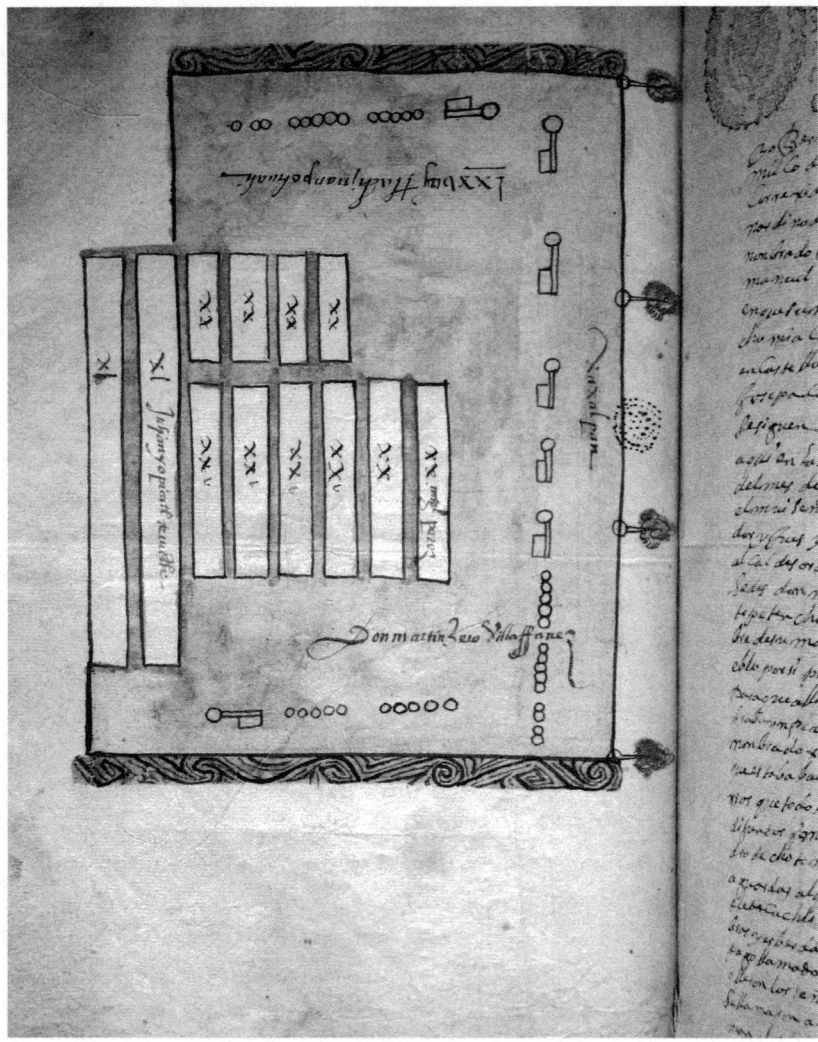

FIGURE 5.1. *Chinampas* in Xaxalpan belonging to don Martín Cerón Villafañez. (AGN, Vínculos y Mayorazgos 279, 1:77v.)

councilmen to serve as witnesses. The scribe then brought the testament to the *cabildo* for ratification. The authorities held an audience, presided over by the governor, don Martín Cerón y Alvarado (doña Francisca's father-in-law), with the interested parties in attendance. Much as the community was often involved in the making of notarial records, as Owen Jones notes in this volume, so probate and other hearings were held before a public audience (see also Restall 1997, 57). In keeping with Nahua traditions of oral recitation—before the conquest, specialists trained in deciphering the glyphs in pictorial records had explained their meaning to audiences in oral performances—officials read testaments and other sources out loud (Boone 1998, 158; Leibsohn 1994). On this occasion, the assembled residents and interested parties were asked to state their satisfaction with the mother's will. The *cabildo* then issued a confirmation and forbade anyone from interfering with the inheritance.[18]

Leaving nothing to chance, when her mother died, doña Francisca moved swiftly to secure her new estate. She brought the relevant paperwork, including pictorial records, before the *cabildo*. Its officers examined the papers and called upon doña Francisca to explain them. Again revealing the oral, performative dimensions of Nahua discourse, the scribe set down her testimony, allowing us to hear the voice of a grieving but no less forthright and independent young lady asserting her rights and demanding that her mother's last wishes be honored. She also acted on her brother's behalf. Her testimony affords us the rare privilege of listening to someone actually interpreting, in Nahuatl, a pictorial document. One excerpt reads in translation: "I demand justice be done and that my older brother don Francisco Axayacatl be given the house facing the hills and also the land in Cintemalpan and Xalpan as well as the *chinampas* in Tlilapan, all of which are shown here painted in yellow" (AGN, Vínculos y Mayorazgos 279, 1:84). Satisfied by doña Francisca's explanation, the governor confirmed her inheritance and issued new titles. *Cabildo* officials and community elders then accompanied doña Francisca to her new properties, where she performed the customary rituals of taking possession—for instance, crossing thresholds and throwing stones in the four cardinal directions (AGN, Vínculos y Mayorazgos 279, 1:82–88v).

In a few, rarely documented instances testators ensured their heirs received the relevant documentation by listing them in wills. The last holder of the family estate, who also happened to be named don Martín Cerón y Alvarado, wrote a testament in which he identified plots of land and their corresponding papers. Don Martín specified that "there are papers for the land located in a place called Xaxalpan Moyotepec" (AGN, Vínculos y Mayorazgos 279, 1:10). He might well have been referring to a *pintura*, perhaps even the cadastral in figure 5.1, which depicts a place with the same name.

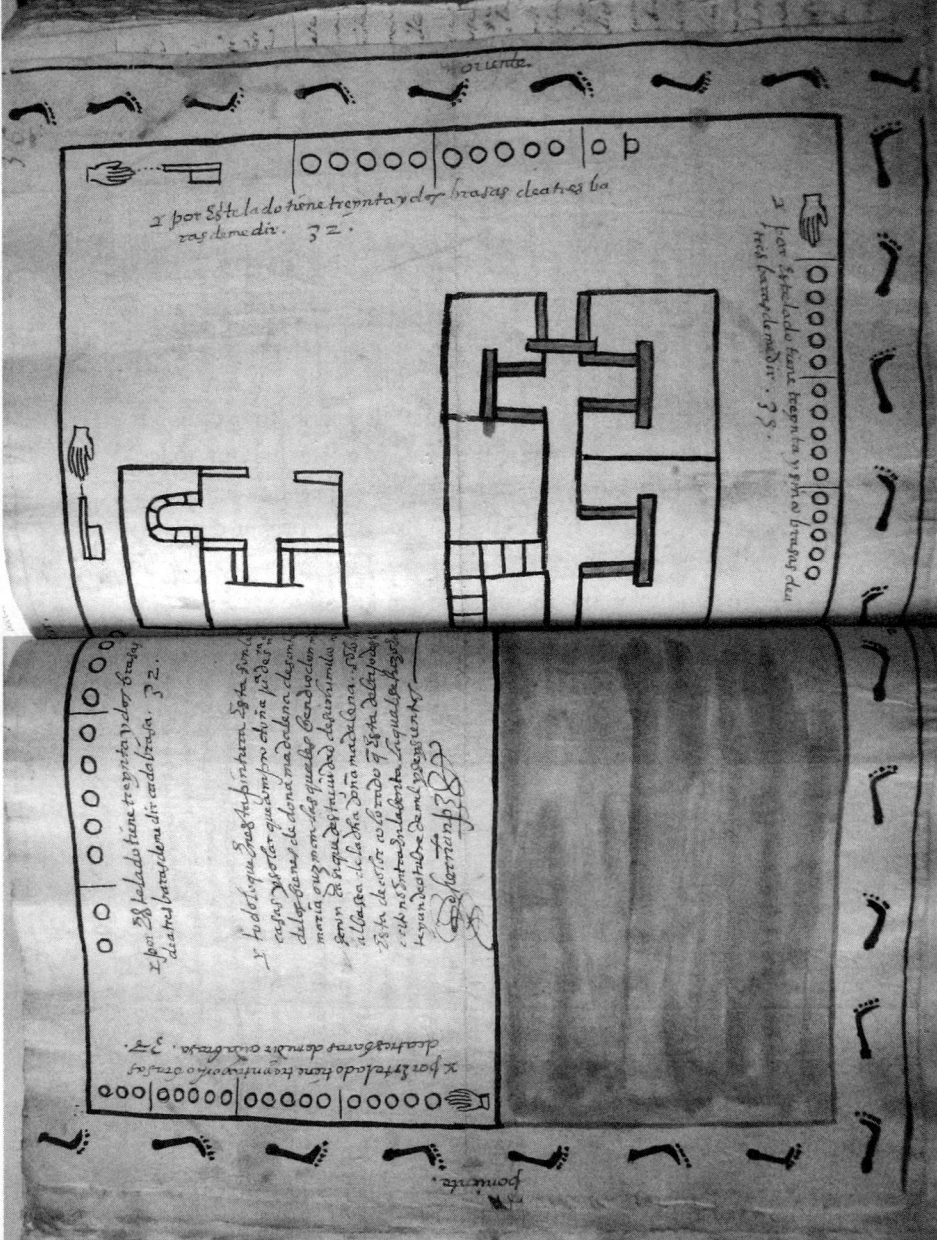

FIGURE 5.2. House plan, Xochimilco. (AGN, Vínculos y Mayorazgos 279, 1:36.)

Changes in the Pictorial Documents

Over the years, as Nahuas passed them down from one generation to the next, the appearance of the pictorial documents gradually changed. Scribes, for instance, added the names of new owners of land, as we have seen with don Martín Villafañez and the *chinampas* in Xaxalpan. The impetus behind many of these changes lay in scribes and judges examining the *pinturas* and modifying them for administrative or judicial purposes. Spanish law and legal practice, as Susan Kellogg has convincingly shown, fostered cultural change among the Nahuas, and the *pinturas* illustrate this process of cultural adaptation (Kellogg 1995, 37).

The pictorial documents did not change solely under the influence of the courts. Nahuas adopted European paper even as they continued to use its indigenous equivalent, *amatl*. They also made use of new kinds of ink and began painting with brushstrokes. Some postconquest manuscripts employed European perspective and portraiture styles as opposed to the indigenous tradition of depicting people in profile, and the *pinturas* displayed new features of the landscape, with churches serving as emblems of communities (Mundy 1996). Conversely, some of the older artistic conventions gradually fell into disuse. Dozens of cadastrals from Mexico City and its environs show that glyphs disappeared from the sources, although the rates of obsolescence varied for different types of glyphs.[19] Numeric glyphs, such as those used in measurements, seem to have endured longer than did others, such as glyphs that art historians have described as sociological because they identified an individual's gender, age, and—with other artistic embellishments—marital and social status (Williams 1984). Other artistic conventions, however, remained consistent features of the *pinturas*. Footprints still indicated paths and roads, while swirls of blue ink showed streams and rivers, and, in a map from 1654, channels that flowed through the lake (AGN, Tierras 1631, 1, 11:96).

Alphabetic glosses amounted to the most conspicuous changes in the pictorial documents. Some of these annotations translated the meaning of glyphs—for instance, writing out measurements. Others provided alternative information that had less to do with the content of the pictorial documents than with the circumstances of local administration and litigation. This can be seen in a pictorial image of a house brought before Xochimilco's *cabildo* in 1600 (figure 5.2).

Don Martín Cerón y Alvarado presented the house plan in his capacity as an executor charged with selling the house. Doña Juana de Santa María y Guzmán, who happened to be the decedent's daughter, purchased it. On completion of the transfer, a scribe updated the house plan so that it now included an annotation explaining what had happened: the gloss inserted doña Juana's name as the new owner, explained how she obtained title via a testament and then a bill of sale, identified the participants in the transaction, provided its date, and translated the measurement glyphs into Spanish. The official attested to the authenticity of this synopsis by adding his signature (AGN, Vínculos y Mayorazgos 279, 1:31–39v). The addition of the alphabetic script not only altered the appearance of the house plan but also effectively changed its function. Whereas previously the house plan had served as a property title, now it also became a documentary summary, compiling relevant details from other sources.

A few of the *pinturas* became something like judicial synopses. A lawsuit in 1627 required evidence of prior ownership of some land. At the judge's request, details from other documents, including a bill of sale and a testament, were added to a cadastral. Prices and dates of transactions were also recorded, along with the names of the previous owners and the witnesses (AGN, Vínculos y Mayorazgos, 279, 1:43–49). In addition to being a certificate of title, the land map now functioned as a summary of the land's recent history. And in its exposition of other sources, the pictorial laid out the evidence and precedents that informed the judge's decision.

Other pictorials, in effect, became legal instruments. Some even resembled certified notarial sources. In 1574 the prominent politician don Esteban de Guzmán wrote a testament in which he gave his daughter, doña Ana, a house in Mexico City. This bequest annoyed don Esteban's wife, who had devoted time and effort to the house's maintenance. To avoid a quarrel, and with the intercession of fray Alonso de Escalona, doña Ana agreed to cede part of the inheritance to her mother. The two noblewomen devised a contract, which the notary set down on paper, in which they agreed to divide the house between them. The *cabildo* then examined the contract, together with the testament and the accompanying house plan, and ratified the transaction. The scribe then transferred the details of the testament and the contract to the pictorial document. Having summarized the details of the case, the scribe turned the *pintura* into a kind of official record. It concluded with the formulaic phrase "done before me" and the scribe's signature (AGN, Vínculos y Mayorazgos 279, 1:91–97v). The document was arguably transformed into an approximation of a notarial instrument that set down, under the confirmation of a signature, the details of a contract, and thereafter it became an important part of the family's paperwork. Three years later, doña Ana included her part of the house in a testamentary bequest.

As pictorial documents changed over time, they came to serve more than one purpose. *Pinturas* were updated to identify new owners. They specified the terms and conditions by which these new owners came into the possession of property, be it through a contract, a bill of sale, or a testament. In providing a synopsis, the pictorials either signaled the existence of other corroborating documentation, including testaments, or they incorporated salient details from them into the *pintura*. In this sense, the *pinturas* were transformed from property titles into more complex, composite sources. As compilations, the *pinturas* were turned into quasilegal documents akin to affidavits. The sources became more bureaucratic, if not legalistic, precisely because they were so important in safeguarding property before colonial institutions.

Conclusions

In 1686 doña Josepha Cerón Cortés y Alvarado was able to petition for the rights to the family estate because her ancestors had so assiduously preserved their holdings and their paperwork. The decline of the family's fortunes owed less to its property dealings than it did to appallingly high mortality rates. The last holder of the estate added a codicil to his testament in 1650 because of a lack of direct heirs, and it was to the friary that he sent the proceeds from his property. The money was to be spent on behalf of the souls of deceased family members (AGN, Vínculos y Mayorazgos 279, 1:12–13v; INAH, Fondo Franciscano 48:7, 19–19v).

The Cerón y Alvarado family managed to hold on to its estate for so long and in spite of many challenges because family members harnessed the venerable tradition of recording information pictorially to preserve their holdings. The pictorial records had been integral to efforts to retain and, at times, even augment the estate, as shown in the case of the *chinampas* in Xaxalpan and the pictorial record of them. The *pinturas*, moreover, complemented other kinds of documentation, especially testaments. Nahuas deployed the pictorial records to confirm, corroborate, and clarify the information contained in other sources. In so doing, plaintiffs secured favorable verdicts before the *cabildo* and the courts. The *pinturas* thus remained sufficiently important that Nahuas passed them on to their heirs. The last estate holder took the added precaution of explicitly mentioning the paperwork in his testament. And the very insertion of the word *testament* in the pictorial images serves as a compelling reminder of the enduring link between the different documentary genres.

The *pinturas* retained their value long into the colonial period. Their longevity meant that their appearance and content changed as Nahuas presented them for inspection in probate proceedings and in notarial transactions. While some preconquest artistic styles gradually disappeared, the documents continued to retain much of their communicative currency. The *pinturas* were not displaced quickly by alphabetic texts. Rather, alphabetic texts were incorporated into the *pinturas* and complemented and supplemented the information conveyed by visual means. The pictorial records thus became hybrid texts in two senses: in their inclusion of information from multiple sources, and in the blending of different documentary traditions.[20] Examples of cultural mixtures, as with doña Josepha's pictorials, have often been studied in terms of survivals from the earlier, prehispanic past. As such, the identification of hybrid cultural forms has often been about discerning the markers of cultural differences as well as the asymmetrical relationships of colonialism (Dean and Leibsohn 2003, 6–8, 21–23).[21] In the case of doña Josepha's records, the majority of the *pinturas* were modified not by Spanish courts but by the *cabildo*. Nahua officials and scribes, some of whom were evidently conversant with both Mesoamerican and European forms of communication, were the ones who added the alphabetic glosses to the sources. Thus, rather than viewing alphabetic writing as simply the imposition of a foreign culture, the pictorial records reveal that much as the Nahuas used the imported practice of writing last wills and testaments, so they likewise incorporated a new communicative medium into the repertoire of Nahua expression.

Ultimately, the estate records provide us with insights into the ongoing diverse, expressive richness of Nahua culture. Nahuas continued to produce graphic forms of record keeping, including the use of glyphs. At the same time they produced alphabetic documents in Spanish and Nahuatl, including testaments. We can hear, preserved in these sources, a young noblewoman, doña Francisca, asserting her claims to testamentary bequests and ensuring that pictorial records and the property they represented were securely held and able to be passed on to the next generation. Eventually the pictorial documents were listed in testaments. Thanks to the testaments and their associated pictorial sources, as late as 1686 doña Josepha was able to present paperwork to the courts in her bid to inherit the family's estate.

Last Will and Testament of don Martín Cerón y Alvarado, n.d. (but before 1650)

Transcription

(AGN, Vínculos y Mayorazgos 279, 1:10–10v)

<u>y</u> yca yn itocatzin Santissima trinidad Dios tetatzin Dios tepiltzin Dios Espū Santo nicpehualtia yn nomemoria testamento yn nehuatl niquitohua ca nican nichane yn ipan çiudad Xochimilco Nitlatohuani notoca Don mīn ceron alvarado auh nipohui nicavecera yn ipan tlaxilacalli tepetenchi niquitohua yn axcan ca huel ninococohua yn notlallo yn noçoquio auh yn noyolia yn nanima Caquen catqui ca çan pactica auh yeçe Ca ye nicchixtica yn miquiztli yn niman ayac yxpampa yehua motlatia Auh ca huel achtopa yc nipehua yn noyolia yn nanima yn iquac tzonquiçaz yn tlalticpac nonemiliz ca huel icenmactzinco nocontlalia yn notlaçotatzin Dios ma quihualmaniliz ma quimoceliliz canel ytlachihualtzin ytlamaquixtiltzin yca yn itlaçoeçotzin auh niquitohua ca onpa nitocoz yn tohueyteopa San ber^no de Jesus ynin huel oncan yn nocapilla yn oncan moetztica notlaçotatzin S. Diego ynic oncan moteochihuaz yn noceportura yhuan niquitohua ynic niquimiliuhtaz ca yehuatl yn itlaçotlaquentzin yn totlaçomahuiztatzin S fran^co yn iabitotzin____

   <u>y</u> ynic çentlamantli niquitohua yn iquac ye onechmopolhui yn Dios ynic palehuiloz y nanima yn ixpantzinco Dios ynic amo Onpa huecahuaz techipahualoyan purga^o monamacaz calli onpa manic tepepa yhuan tlalli manic S. matheo ytocayocan tlacatecpan huel huey tlalli centzonmecatl auh matlactin yn quitequichihua tequitque auh quixtlahuazque yn tlalaneyoni cenpohualli onmatlactli pesos nanima yc palehuiloz missa yc nopan mochihuaz yhuan Cequi yc nitocoz____ 30 . p^os

   <u>y</u> ynic ontlamantli niquitohua yn ixquich tlalli yn nican nictenehua yn ipan notestamento . Atle monamacaz ca yn quenin Onictetlaneuhtiaya

çan iuh yez auh yc nipehua tlalli manic San lorenço tlatzintla ycçotitla
. emecatl ça ye no onca . onmecatl temic otenco yc maCuilmecatl . auh
ynic tetlaneuhtiloz cecenxiuhtica Onpohualli yhuan macuilli pesos ynin
tomin yc missa mochihuaz____ 45 . p°s

- yhuan tlalli manic ytocayocan xaxalpan moyotepec tlalmilli
Oncatqui yn iamayo auh ynic tetlaneuhtiloz y ce xihuitl cenpohualli
pesos ynin yc missa mochihuaz____ 20 . p°s

- niman tlalli manic ytocayocan calquapan emecatl . onca yyamayo
quimocohuita Çihuapilli Doña fran^ca ypatiuh mochiuh napohualli peso
ynin quitlanehuizque yn tequitque quixtlauhtazque y ceçenxiuhtica
onpohualli onmatlactli pesos ynin missa yc mochihuaz____ 50 . p°s

- tlalli manic xochitepec quitlanehuizque yn quichihua
quixtlauhtazque y cecenxiuhtica çan ixquich chicuey peso missa yc
mochihuaz____ 8 . p°s

- tlalli manic ytocayocan hecatepec san hieronimo ynin quimocohuita
yn notlaçotatzin yn Dios oquimohuiquili Don mīn ceron alvarado Onca
yyamayo auh ymactzinco tlacohualli padre guar^an fr. hieronimo de
mendieta ynin ayemo mota yn quezqui yc motlanehuiz____

v yniquetlamantli niquitohua monamacaz yn tlalli nican nictenehua
tlalli manic tecomic ynic ocan tlalli manic tiçatepec auh tlaco
onicnamacac ypatiuh omochiuh matlactli omome peso auh yn oc tlaco
ypatiuh quixtlahuaz español ytoca Joseph ximenez tolyahualco chane ca
yehuatl quimati yn quezqui quixtlahuaz yniquexcan tlalmilli manic San
andres tepepatlachco monamacaz huel quimati yn onpa tlaca yehuanti
quineltilizque auh yn ipatiuh mochihuaz ca mochi teopan calaquiz missa
yc mochihuaz____

v ynic nauhtlamantli niquitohua yn tecpancalli yn manic Olac ycal
catca Don fran^co omacatzin auh ca ye oxixitin Ca ça tecalli monamacaz
huel imania____

- yhuan monamacaz xolar manic ycaltepotzco . Juana chocolatera
yhuan agustin perez yhuan juan perez monamacaz . ytech pohuiz missa
yn Doña mag^na yn iquac ye omonamacac____

- yhuan xolar manic ycaltepotzco gabriel Domingo çapatero
notlacohual niquincohuili hipolito yhuan miguel acmomatitzin ynin ca
onca yyamayo monamacaz nanima ytech pohuiz____

- yhuan çan no xolar manic Ospital quiyahuac ytech hualehua
teopan calnacaztli cōcepcion ytech hualaçi y yaocalli tlamelahua

Ospital caltepotzco toquaxochnamiqui español fran^co belazquez ynin
monamacaz ytech pohuiz Don mīn Cordes yhuan Doña Ana ynin ca
onca yn iyamayo____

v ynic macuillamantli niquitohua yn nocal yn onca Oninotlacatili
monamacaz huel imaniyan quihuicaz yn ixolalo Onpa hualehua yn itech
yaocalli ytech hualaçi yn itech calnacaztli yn mexicopa auh tlamelahua yn
tonatiuh yquiçayanpa ytech onaçi yn acalotli auh yn quauhtlacopa [*verso*]
yehuatl quaxochtli yn ahuehuetl____

- yhuan monamacaz centetl caltentli huey quihuicaz yn puerta huey
yn ipatiuh mochihuaz yc [missa] chihuililoz yn notatzin Don ceron____

v ynic chiquacentlamantli niquitohua monamacaz libros nicpia oncan
ca huehuey caxtolli niman tepitoton matlactli ynin mochi patiyo yn iquac
omonamacac yn ipatiuh ca yc missa mochihuaz____

v ynic chicontlamantli niquitohua yn niquinnopielia Santome
cetzin niño Jesus hueytzintli huel mahuizticatzintli yhuan Omentzitzin
tepitzitzin niño Jesus yhuan Santo xp̄os heyntzitzin yhuan cetzin ecce
homo lienço niman Omentzitzin totlaçonantzin lienço yhuan cetzin
totlaçonantzin tepitzin yhuan oncan quinmotlaqualtili apostoles
yhuan San Joseph lienço yhuan San nicolas lienço ynin amo [çan]
tlapic Canpa mohuicazque huel motaz yn quenin mochihuaz yntla
monamacatzinozque ca mo[chi] missa yc mochihuaz____

v yhuan niquitohua y yehuatzin S . san nicolas lienço hueytzintli
teopan mocalaquiz ynahuactzinco [mo]yetztaz yn San diego ypantzinco
tlatozque yn Confradias____

v ynic chicuetlamantli niquitohua monamacaz Ome cama . ce huey .
ce tepiton yhuan tlacuilotlatecoma chicome nahui huehuey ey . tepitoton
yhuan ce huey xicalli oncan nematequilo yhuan centetl cuezcomatl yhuan
ce caxa michhuacayotl yancuic tzacayo yhuan ytic moyetzticate maje
ome [lamina] auh yn iquac monamacaz mochi yc missa mochihuaz____

- Ahuin oc çe caxa çan no michhuacayotl ca nehuatl nicmati yn aquin
nicmacatehuaz ayac ytech [tlatoz] auh çan no yuhqui mocahua . yn
tohueytlatocatzin ixiptlatzin yhuan ychpotzin____

v ynic nican nictlamiltia ynin testamento onicchiuh axcan ca miac oc
nicpia tlalli yhuan ama[tl] yn amo niquelnamiqui Ca yn iquac neçiz Ca
oc ce memoria nicchihuaz____

- Ca ye yxquich yn niquitohua yn notestamento y huel
nocenquizcatlanequiliz ca huel yehuatl neltiz [mo]chihuaz . y

yeyca ca ye notzonquiçalizpantlanequiliz ca çenca Oninopechtecac
Oninomanepano yxpantzinco notlaçomahuiztatzin teoyotica
tlatohuani nr̄o padre fr alonso de la lima Difinidor canel noconfesortzin
omochiuhtzino ca onicnixpantili yn ixquich yeyca canel totepach[ocauh]
toguar^antzin totemachticatzin Omoyetzticatca ypampa ca yn ixquich
noneyolcuitilizpa onicquixpantili ca ye mochi quimaçicamachiltitica
ypanpa yn axcan noalvaceatzin nicnochihuilito ca yehuatzin
quimoyectililiz quimochipahuiliz yn quenin huel oquimaçicamachilti
cayac aquin oncan tlatoz anoço oncan mayahuiz yn manel guar^anes
anoço temachtianime yn manel arçobispo anoço Justiçia ca niman
ayac ytlatohuayan yez ca ça huel yehuatzin quimocenc[hipa]huiliz auh
quimopalehuiliz y yehuatzin Señor Diego hernandez español yhuinin y
niquitohua auh ynic nicneltilia yn notestamento ca nican ce cruz ytech
niquetza yn notoca y nofirma ymixpan testigos españoles nican chaneque
ypan inin altepetl ciudad xuchimilco – mathias fran^co de molina yhuan
yehuatzin alonso de chabez yhuan bar^me Dominguez Samodio yhuan
andres de ordega omocencauh yn notestamento yhuan oquitlalique yn
itocatzin yhuan ynfirmas

     don mīn ceron   matias fran^co
     Bar^me Dominguez   de molina
     Samudio
       Andres de ordega
   Al^o de chaves
   Nixpan omochiuh
   pedro fran^co
   escri^o Sta yglesia

Translation

v In the name of the most Holy Trinity, God the father, God the child, and
God the Holy Spirit, I begin my memorandum of testament. I say that I am
a citizen here in the city of Xochimilco, I am a dynastic ruler, and my name
is don Martín Cerón Alvarado. I belong and am ruler in the *tlaxilacalli* of
Tepetenchi. I say that I am now very sick in my earthly body. There is nothing wrong with my spirit and soul, but it is sound. I am nevertheless awaiting death, from which no one can hide. I begin first of all with my spirit
and soul. When my life on earth comes to an end I place it entirely in the
hands of my precious father God; may he come take and receive it because

it is his creation, redeemed by his precious blood. I say that I will be buried in our main church of San Bernardino de Jesús right in my chapel where my precious father San Diego is, and there my grave is to be blessed. I say that I am to be wrapped in the precious raiment and habit of our precious revered father San Francisco.

v̲ First, I say that when God has effaced me, in order to help my soul before God, and not to spend a long time in purgatory, the place of cleansing, a house that is in Tepepan is to be sold. And as for the land in San Matheo at the place called Tlacatecpan, which is a very large plot of land 400 *mecatl* in size, ten do tribute duties and are tributaries; they are to pay a [rent] of 30 pesos; with it my soul is to be helped, with it a mass is to be held for me, and some of the money is to be used to bury me. 30 pesos.

v̲ Second, I say that none of the land I mention here in my testament is to be sold; it is to stay the same way as I have been renting it out. I begin with the land in San Lorenzo, in the lower part, in Icçotitlan, which measures 3 *mecatl*, and there are also 2 *mecatl* on the edge of the road, with which it is 5 mecatl. It is to be rented for 45 pesos per year, with which masses are to be held. 45 pesos.

- And there are papers for the land located in a place called Xaxalpan Moyotepec, cultivated fields that are to be rented for 20 pesos per year; with this masses are to be held. 20 pesos.

- Then there is land in the place named Calquapan, 3 *mecatl*, for which there are papers, and which the noblewoman doña Francisca purchased for the price of 80 pesos; it is to be rented to tributaries who will pay each year 50 pesos, with which masses are to be held. 50 pesos.

- Those who are working the land that is in Xochitepec will pay only 8 pesos each year, with which masses are to be held. 8 pesos.

- There is land in the place called San Gerónimo Ecatepec that my precious father don Martín Cerón Alvarado, whom God took, purchased, and for which there are papers. It was purchased with the help of the father guardian fray Gerónimo de Mendieta. It has not yet been looked into how much the land is to be rented for.

v̲ Third, I say that the land I mention here is to be sold: the land is in Tecomic and in a second place, Tiçatepec. I sold half of it for the price of 12 pesos. The price of the other half is to be paid by a Spaniard named Josef Jiménez, who is a resident of Tolyahualco. He can decide how much he will pay. A third field in San Andrés Tepepa Tepepantlachco is to be sold. The people there fully understand how to carry this out; the price it makes is all to be delivered to the church and with it masses are to be held.

v̲ Fourth, I say that the palace in Olac, which was the house of don Francisco Omacatzin, has collapsed. Just the stone is to be sold.

- And the *solar* (house lot) behind the houses of Juana the chocolate seller, Agustín Pérez, and Juan Pérez, is to be sold, and is to be dedicated to holding a mass for doña Magdalena when it has been sold.

- And the house lot behind the house of shoemaker Gabriel Domingo, which I bought from Hipólito and Miguel Acmomatitzin, and for which there are papers, is to be sold and be dedicated to my soul.

v̲ Likewise the house lot located outside the hospital, coming from the corner of the church of Concepción, reaching as far as the house of war and goes straight behind the hospital where it borders on the [house] belonging to the Spaniard Francisco Velásquez. The house lot is to be sold for masses on behalf of don Martín Cortés and doña Ana, and there are papers for it.

v̲ Fifth, I say that my house, where I was born, is to be sold as it is. It is to include the lot accompanying the house, which comes from beside the house of war and reaches as far as the corner facing Mexico City. It goes straight to the east where it arrives at the canal and to the south a cypress tree is the border.

- And a large entryway is to be sold; it is to include a large door; with the price that comes from it a mass is to be held for my father don Martín Cerón.

v̲ Sixth, I say that the books I have are to be sold; there are 15 large ones and 10 small ones; all of this is to be sold; when it has been sold, masses are to be held with its price.

v̲ Seventh, I say that I have saints: a Niño Jesús that is rather large and very splendid, as well as two small ones, three [small?] Santo Cristos, one *ecce homo* painting, two paintings of our precious mother, one small one of our precious mother, one in which [Jesus] fed the apostles, and a painting of San Josef and one of San Nicolás. They are not to be taken somewhere frivolously; what is to be done is to be considered well; if they should be sold, masses are to be held with all of it.

v̲ And I say that the rather large painting of San Nicolás is to be delivered to the church and be near San Diego. The *cofrades* are to be in charge of it.

ⴸ Eighth, I say that to be sold are two beds, one large and one small, seven painted cups, of which four are large and three small, and one large gourd vessel for washing hands. Also to be sold are a grain bin and a new chest made in the Michoacan style,[22] with a lock, and inside it are images, two illustrations. When it is sold, masses are to be held with all of it.

- As to another chest, likewise in Michoacan style, I have decided to whom I will give it on dying. No one is to make objections about it. An image of our great ruler and his daughter are being left in the same way.

ⴸ Here I finish this testament that I have done today. I have many other lands and papers that I do not remember. When they are found I will make another memorandum.

- That is all I say in my testament, which is truly my entire will. It is to be realized and carried out because it is made as my last will, for I have greatly bowed down and folded my hands in prayer before my precious revered father, the ruler in holy matters, our father fray Alonso de la Lima, chair of the order chapter, because he has been constituted my confessor. I have presented everything to him because he has been our governor, our father guardian, our preacher, so I have informed him of everything in my confession, and he is entirely aware of all of it. Therefore now I have made him my executor. He will fix and clear up (everything, matters, the testament) according to his full understanding of it. No one is to say anything about it or intervene, whether it be the guardian fathers, preachers, the archbishop, or officers of the law; no one else at all is to have anything to say about it, for he alone is to clear it all up. Señor Diego Hernández, a Spaniard, is to help him. This is what I say. I verify my testament by making a cross here next to my name and rubric. Before Spanish witnesses who are resident here in this *altepetl* and city of Xochimilco, Matías Francisco de Molina, Alonso de Chaves, Bartolomé Domínguez Zamudio, and Andrés de Ortega, my testament was prepared, and they set down their names and signatures

[signatures]

Done before me, Pedro Francisco, notary of the holy church

Notes

I would like to thank James Lockhart for his kind assistance in translating the testament; any mistakes are mine.

1. Scholars who have examined the economic documents include Boone (1998); Lockhart (1992, 331–335); Harvey (1991); Williams and Harvey (1988,

1997); Williams (1980, 1984); Offner (1984); H. Cline (1966); and S. L. Cline (1986, 130–131).

2. The content and meaning of the Mesoamerican pictorial manuscripts are now better understood thanks to recent advances in the scholarly literature. Some recent works include Yannakakis 2011; Boornazian Diel 2008, 2011; Leibsohn 2009; Williams 2009; Asselbergs 2008; Carrasco and Sessions 2007; Boone 2000, 2007; and Mundy 1996. For a survey of scholarship on Mixtec codices, see Terraciano 2001, 6–7.

3. With the notable exception of the genre of documents known as primordial titles (Wood 1998a, 1998b, 2003).

4. See the observations of Fernando de Alva Ixtlilxochitl, Alonso de Zorita, and fray Juan de Torquemada mentioned in Kagan 2000, 48–49; and Boone 1998, 172, 174.

5. Glass 1975, 4; Robertson 1994, 1; Kubler 1964.

6. A Nahua named Juan Badianus provides another example. He wrote a beautiful herbal full of pictures of plants, some of which contained glyphs representing soil varieties, accompanied by Nahuatl and Latin texts (Gibson 1964, 300, 382).

7. LC, Krauss Ms 140:436–451v; Boone 1998, 168–169; Chávez Orozco 1947; NL, Ayer 1121:211–211v, 348–352; AGN, Mercedes 3, 91:44; Mercedes 4, 118:35v; Mercedes 5–6, 1a:134–134v; Chimalpahin Quauhtlehuanitzin 1997, 1:177, 2:41. See also Lockhart 1992, 34; Pérez Zevallos 2002, 1:61, 63); and Connell 2011, 36–38, 49–50.

8. AGN, Mercedes 1, 82:44v–45.

9. See, for instance, the *Códice Santa María Asunción* (Williams and Harvey 1997).

10. Lockhart 1992, 170–176; Gibson 1964, 263–267.

11. Horn 1997, 116–120. Cline (1986, 88), has estimated that individuals would need access to at least seven *chinampas* to be able to sustain themselves.

12. Cadastrals from the Cerón y Alvarado estate also show the same interspersed pattern of ownership. AGN, Vínculos y Mayorazgos 279, 1:48, 77v.

13. Gibson 1964, 274–282; Owensby 2008, 18; Horn 1997, 144–200; Tutino 1976.

14. AGN, Vínculos y Mayorazgos 279, 1:51–57v; AGN, Tierras 2959, 109:275–276; AGN, Tierras 35, 6:230–322; Cline 1986, 70–71.

15. Owensby 2008, 20, 51.

16. The testament has been translated in Karttunen and Lockhart 1976, 93–97; and discussed in Lockhart 1992, 193. Other examples of inventories of belongings can be found in NL, Ayer 1900; Goupil 1891. The pictorial documents can be seen online at http://publications.newberry.org/aztecs/section_4_home.html.

17. AGN, Vínculos y Mayorazgos 279, 1:91–95.

18. AGN, Vínculos y Mayorazgos 279, 1:82–83v.

19. The cadastrals are reproduced in Reyes García et al. 1996 and Rojas Rabiela et al. 1999–2004.

20. Boone and Mignolo 1994; Rappaport and Cummins 2011.
21. See also Young 1995 and de la Cadena 2005.
22. The "Michoacan" style apparently refers to the regionally distinctive crafts of Michoacan, in western Mexico, such as items of furniture (Salazar Simarro 2005, 240).

References

Asselbergs, Florine G. L. 2008. *Conquered Conquistadors: The Lienzo de Quauh-quechollan: A Nahua Vision of the Conquest of Guatemala*. Boulder: University Press of Colorado.

Berdan, Frances F., and Patricia Rieff Anawalt, eds. 1997. *The Essential Codex Mendoza*. Berkeley and Los Angeles: University of California Press.

Boone, Elizabeth Hill. 1998. "Pictorial Documents and Visual Thinking in Postconquest Mexico." In *Native Traditions in the Postconquest World*, edited by Elizabeth Boone and Tom Cummins, 149–199. Washington, D.C.: Dumbarton Oaks.

———. 2000. *Stories in Red and Black: Pictorial Histories of the Aztecs and Mixtecs*. Austin: University of Texas Press.

———. 2007. *Cycles of Time and Meaning in the Mexican Books of Fate*. Austin: University of Texas Press.

Boone, Elizabeth Hill, and Walter D. Mignolo, eds. 1994. *Writing without Words: Alternative Literacies in Mesoamerica and the Andes*. Durham, N.C.: Duke University Press.

Boornazian Diel, Lori. 2008. *The Tira de Tepechpan: Negotiating Place under Aztec and Spanish Rule*. Austin: University of Texas Press.

———. 2011 "Manuscrito del aperreamiento (Manuscript of the Dogging): A 'Dogging' and Its Implications for Early Colonial Cholula." *Ethnohistory* 58(4): 585–611.

Carrasco, David, and Scott Sessions. 2007. *Cave, City, and Eagle's Nest: An Interpretive Journey through the Mapa de Cuauhtinchan No. 2*. Albuquerque: University of New Mexico Press.

Chávez Orozco, Luis, ed. 1947. *Códice Osuna*. Mexico City: Ediciones del Instituto Indigenista Interamericano.

Chimalpahin Quauhtlehuanitzin, Don Domingo de San Antón Muñón. 1997. *Codex Chimalpahin: Society and Politics in Mexico Tenochtitlan, Tlatelolco, Texcoco, Culhuacan, and other Nahua Altepetl in Central Mexico*, edited by Arthur J. O. Anderson and Susan Schroeder. 2 vols. Norman: University of Oklahoma Press.

Cline, Howard F. 1966. "The Oztoticpac Lands Map of Texcoco, 1540." *Quarterly Journal of the Library of Congress* 23: 77–115.

Cline, S. L. 1986. *Colonial Culhuacan, 1580–1600: A Social History of an Aztec Town*. Albuquerque: University of New Mexico Press.

———. 1991. "A *Cacicazgo* in the Seventeenth Century: The Case of Xochimilco." In *Land and Politics in the Valley of Mexico: A Two-Thousand Year Perspective*, edited by H. R. Harvey, 265–274. Albuquerque: University of New Mexico Press.

———, ed. 1993. *The Book of Tributes: Early Sixteenth-century Nahuatl Censuses from Morelos*. Los Angeles: UCLA Latin American Center Publications.

Connell, William F. 2011. *After Moctezuma: Indigenous Politics and Self-Government in Mexico City, 1524–1730*. Norman: University of Oklahoma Press.

Dean, Carolyn, and Dana Leibsohn. 2003. "Hybridity and Its Discontents: Considering Visual Culture in Colonial Spanish America." *Colonial Latin American Review* 12(1): 5–35.

de la Cadena, Marisol. 2005. "Are Mestizos Hybrids? The Conceptual Politics of Andean Identities." *Journal of Latin American Studies* 37(2): 259–284.

Gibson, Charles. 1964. *The Aztecs under Spanish Rule: A History of the Indians of the Valley of Mexico, 1519–1810*. Stanford, Calif.: Stanford University Press.

Glass, John B. 1975. "A Survey of Native Middle American Pictorial Manuscripts." In *The Handbook of Middle American Indians: Guide to Ethnohistorical Sources*, pt. 3, vol. 14, edited by Howard F. Cline, 3–80. Austin: University of Texas Press.

Goupil, E. Eugène. 1891. *Documents pour servir à l'histoire du Mexique*. Paris: E. Leroux.

Harvey, H. R. 1991. "The Oztotocpac Lands Map: A Reexamination." In *Land and Politics in the Valley of Mexico: A Two-Thousand Year Perspective*, edited by H. R. Harvey, 163–185. Albuquerque: University of New Mexico Press.

Haskett, Robert. 1991. *Indigenous Rulers: An Ethnohistory of Town Government in Colonial Cuernavaca*. Albuquerque: University of New Mexico Press.

Horn, Rebecca. 1997. *Postconquest Coyoacan: Nahua-Spanish Relations in Central Mexico, 1519–1650*. Stanford, Calif.: Stanford University Press.

Kagan, Richard L. 2000. *Urban Images of the Hispanic World, 1493–1793*. New Haven, Conn.: Yale University Press.

Karttunen, Frances. 1983. *An Analytical Dictionary of Nahuatl*. Austin: University of Texas Press.

Karttunen, Frances, and James Lockhart. 1976. *Nahuatl in the Middle Years: Language Contact Phenomena in Texts of the Colonial Period*. Berkeley and Los Angeles: University of California Press.

Kellogg, Susan. 1995. *Law and the Transformation of Aztec Culture, 1500–1700*. Norman: University of Oklahoma Press.

———. 1998. "Indigenous Testaments of Early-colonial Mexico City: Testifying to Gender Differences." In *Dead Giveaways: Indigenous Testaments of Colonial Mesoamerica and the Andes*, edited by Susan Kellogg and Matthew Restall, 37–58. Salt Lake City: University of Utah Press.

Kubler, George. 1964. "On the Colonial Extinction of the Motifs of Pre-Columbian Art." In *Essays in Pre-Columbian Art and Archaeology*, edited by S. K. Lothrop, 14–34. Cambridge, Mass.: Harvard University Press.

Leibsohn, Dana. 1994. "Primers for Memory: Cartographic Histories and Nahua Identity." In *Writing without Words: Alternative Literacies in Mesoamerica and the Andes,* edited by Elizabeth Hill Boone and Walter Mignolo, 161–187. Durham, N.C.: Duke University Press.

———. 2009. *Script and Glyph: Pre-Hispanic History, Colonial Bookmaking, and the Historia Tolteca-Chichimeca.* Washington, D.C.: Dumbarton Oaks.

Lockhart, James. 1991. "The Testimony of Don Juan." In *Nahuas and Spaniards: Postconquest Central Mexican History and Philology,* 75–87. Stanford, Calif.: Stanford University Press; Los Angeles: UCLA Latin American Center Publications.

———. 1992. *The Nahuas After the Conquest: A Social and Cultural History of the Indians of Central Mexico, Sixteenth Through Eighteenth Century.* Stanford, Calif.: Stanford University Press.

Mundy, Barbara E. 1996. *The Mapping of New Spain: Indigenous Cartography and the Maps of the Relaciones Geográficas.* Chicago: University of Chicago Press.

Offner, Jerome A. 1984. "Household Organization in the Texcocan Heartland: The Evidence in the Codex Vergara." In *Explorations in Ethnohistory: Indians of Central Mexico in the Sixteenth Century,* edited by H. R. Harvey and Hanns J. Prem, 127–146. Albuquerque: University of New Mexico Press.

Owensby, Brian P. 2008. *Empire of Law and Indian Justice in Colonial Mexico.* Stanford, Calif.: Stanford University Press.

Pérez Zevallos, Juan Manuel. 2002–2003. *Xochimilco Ayer.* 3 vols. Mexico City: Instituto Mora, Gobierno del Distrito Federal, Delegación Xochimilco.

Rappaport, Joanne, and Tom Cummins. 2011. *Beyond the Lettered City: Indigenous Literacies in the Andes.* Durham, N.C.: Duke University Press.

Restall, Matthew. 1997. *The Maya World: Yucatec Culture and Society, 1550–1850.* Stanford, Calif.: Stanford University Press.

Reyes García, Luis, Eustaquio Celestino Solís, Armando Valencia Ríos, Constantino Medina Lima, and Gregorio Guerrero Díaz, eds. 1996. *Documentos nahuas de la Ciudad de Mexico del siglo XVI.* Mexico City: CIESAS y Archivo General de la Nación.

Robertson, Donald. 1994. *Mexican Manuscript Painting of the Early Colonial Period: The Metropolitan Schools.* Norman: University of Oklahoma Press.

Rojas Rabiela, Teresa, Elsa Leticia Rea López, Enrique Nieto, Mercedes de los Santos Ortega, and Constantino Medina Lima. 1999–2004. *Vidas y bienes olvidados.* 5 vols. Mexico City: Centro de Investigaciones y Estudios Superiores en Antropología Social, Consejo Nacional de Ciencia y Tecnología.

Salazar Simarro, Nuria. 2005. "Los monasterios femeninos." In *Historia de la vida cotidiana en México,* vol. 2, *La ciudad barroca,* edited by Pilar Gonzalbo Aizpuru, 221–259. Mexico City: El Colegio de México, Fondo de Cultura Económica.

Terraciano, Kevin. 2001. *The Mixtecs of Colonial Oaxaca: Ñudzahui History, Sixteenth through Eighteenth Centuries.* Stanford, Calif.: Stanford University Press.

Tutino, John M. 1976. "Creole Mexico: Spanish Elites, Haciendas, and Indian Towns, 1750–1810." Ph.D. dissertation, University of Texas, Austin.

Williams, Barbara J. 1980. "Pictorial Representations of Soils in the Valley of Mexico: Evidence from the Codex Vergara." *Geoscience and Man* 21: 51–62.

———. 1984. "Mexican Pictorial Cadastral Registers: An Analysis of the Códice de Santa María Asunción and the Codex Vergara." In *Explorations in Ethnohistory: Indians of Central Mexico in the Sixteenth Century*, edited by H. R. Harvey and Hanns J. Prem, 103–125. Albuquerque: University of New Mexico Press.

———. 1991. "The Lands and Political Organization of a Rural Tlaxilacalli in Tepetlaoztoc, c. A.D. 1540." In *Land and Politics in the Valley of Mexico: A Two-Thousand Year Perspective*, edited by H. R. Harvey, 187–208. Albuquerque: University of New Mexico Press.

Williams, Barbara J., and H. R. Harvey. 1988. "Content, Provenience, and Significance of the Codex Vergara and the Códice de Santa Maria Asunción." *American Antiquity* 53(2): 337–351.

———, eds. 1997. *The Códice de Santa Maria Asunción: Facsimile and Commentary: Households and Lands in Sixteenth-century Tepetlaoztoc*. Salt Lake City: University of Utah Press.

Williams, Robert Lloyd. 2009. *Lord Eight Wind of Suchixtlan and the Heroes of Ancient Oaxaca: Reading History in the Codex Zouche-Nuttall*. Austin: University of Texas Press.

Wood, Stephanie. 1998a. "The Social versus Legal Context of Nahua Títulos." In *Native Traditions in the Postconquest World*, edited by Elizabeth Boone and Tom Cummins, 201–231. Washington, D.C.: Dumbarton Oaks.

———. 1998b. "Testaments and Títulos: Conflict and Coincidence of Cacique and Community Interests in Central Mexico." In *Dead Giveaways: Indigenous Testaments of Colonial Mesoamerica and the Andes*, edited by Susan Kellogg and Matthew Restall, 85–111. Salt Lake City: University of Utah Press.

———. 2003. *Transcending Conquest: Nahua Views of Spanish Colonial Mexico*. Norman: University of Oklahoma Press.

Yannakakis, Yanna. "Allies or Servants? The Journey of Indian Conquistadors in the Lienzo of Analco." *Ethnohistory* 58(4): 653–682.

Young, Robert J. C. 1995. *Colonial Desire: Hybridity in Theory, Culture, and Race*. London: Routledge.

CHAPTER 6

The Spoils of the Pech Conquistadors

MARK CHRISTENSEN

I who am Macan Pech,
the first noble conquistador here in this land.

—*Title of Yaxkukul* (1769)[1]

An eighteenth-century document written in Yucatec Maya recounts the how Macan Pech and his town of Yaxkukul provided aid to the Spanish conquistadors—and their religion—in the sixteenth century. Aside from participating in the military submission of uncooperative Maya towns and assisting the Spaniards in establishing Catholicism, Macan also offered tribute. Other Maya nobles accompanied him, including Ah Dzulub Pech of Ixil. According to Macan, "These were the first to pay tribute to the foreigners, and this status (the noble status of *hidalgo*) was given to them through God and the reigning king to all of their descendents until their days are gone" (Restall 1998b, 112–113).[2]

For his assistance and loyalty to the Spaniards, Ah Dzulub Pech of Ixil and his descendants received *hidalgo* status in perpetuity. Such status not only exempted them from paying tribute, but also secured a sociopolitical legitimacy that gave them access to political offices and material benefits.[3] Although Ah Dzulub Pech secured these benefits in the early sixteenth century, one wonders if, and how, he and his lineage maintained such spoils. This chapter employs more than 100 eighteenth-century wills from Ah Dzulub's town of Ixil to examine if his spoils continued to benefit his Pech decedents. A brief overview of the Pech and Ixil leads to an exploration of the Pech position in Ixil through the items they bequeathed, the people they married, and the positions they held. As a result of the wills the Pech left behind, we are able to glimpse whether or not the spoils of the Pech conquistadors truly benefited "all of their descendents until their days are gone" (Restall 1998b, 113)—or at least until the eighteenth century. More generally, this study contributes to our understanding of Maya nobles' attempts to maintain their positions of authority and privilege in colonial Yucatan.[4]

The Pech and Ixil

Colonial documents trace the Pech *chibal* (patronym group [plural *chibalob*]) back to the founding of Mayapan. The city reportedly dominated the Yucatan Peninsula from the thirteenth to mid-fifteenth centuries and represented a conglomerate of the most powerful dynasties in the region, including the Chel, Cocom, Xiu, Canul, Canche, and Pech. When Mayapan fell in the 1440s, the noble *chibalob* claimed various districts of the Yucatan Peninsula as their own, with the Pech taking a section of the northwestern tip commonly referred to as "Ceh Pech" (Landa [1566] 1975).

Upon the arrival of the Spaniards to Yucatan in 1528, the Pech made efforts to solidify their status and position within the new colonial system. To do so, they made political and military alliances with the Spaniards— a technique practiced by various Nahua communities in central Mexico upon the arrival of Cortés (Restall 2003; Chamberlain 1966, 132–149; Cogolludo 1688, 123–132; Matthew and Oudijk 2007; Matthew 2012). In return for their political and military support, the Pech received accolades from the Spaniards, including exemption from tribute payment and labor service, and the right to use the noble title *don*.[5] The previously mentioned *Title of Yaxkukul* states that in 1541 the *adelantado* (licensed conqueror) Francisco de Montejo ("el mozo" [the son]) met with a delegation of Pech nobles that included Ah Macan Pech, *batab* (Maya governor) of Yaxkukul; Nakuk Pech, *batab* of Chicxulub; and Ixkil-Itzam Pech, *batab* of Conkal. The Pech offered both gifts and their service to Montejo and his accompanying Spaniards. This assistance was repeated a number of times and no doubt aided the Spaniards in establishing the capital of Merida—founded just south of Pech territory (Restall 1998b, 107–128; Quezada 1993, 32–38). To further solidify their alliance, the Pech reportedly embraced Christianity; the names they adopted after baptism provide clear examples of their acceptance of both the Spaniards and their religion. For example, Naum

Pech–*batab* of the most influential *cah* (Maya sociopolitical unit or town [plural *cahob*]) in the Ceh Pech territory, Motul–was baptized as don Francisco de Montejo Pech.

Fragmentary evidence from both Spanish and Maya accounts confirms the success of the Pech in solidifying a dominant position for themselves in sixteenth-century Yucatecan society. Indeed, the Ceh Pech region included some twenty-five *cahob*, and the Pech ruled as *batabs* in twenty-one of them by 1567 (Quezada 1993, 157–168). Moreover, in 1567 various Maya nobles composed ten letters originating from the Maní, Ceh Pech, Ah Kin Chel, and Champotón provinces and sent them to the King of Spain after fray Diego de Landa's brutal campaign against idolatry; the Pech represent 49 percent of all signatories.[6] And by the 1580s the Pech still governed in many of the *cahob* in the Ceh Pech region, including Ixil.[7]

Located 20 miles northeast of Merida, Ixil remained a town of modest size throughout the eighteenth century. In a 1700 census of more than 130 Maya towns in Yucatan, Ixil reported 729 tributaries, and twenty-one years later the reported number of adult Mayas was 715 (AGI, México 1035; Patch 1993, 60). Ixil's size enabled it to have its own indigenous *cabildo* (town council), which included a Maya governor, council members, and a notary. The town's distance from Merida and the *camino real* (the primary road linking Campeche and Merida) protected it from becoming inundated with Spanish settlers and influence. In the end, eighteenth-century Ixil was content to continue governing its own internal affairs through prominent Maya figures who sat on the *cabildo* and to remain a place that some Spaniards might have heard of but few ever visited.

Yet eighteenth-century Ixil was not without its own challenges. Epochs of famine and disease swept through the town between 1747 and 1760, resulting in many deaths.[8] According to procedure, when a Maya in Ixil felt death approaching, he summoned the *cabildo* to record his last words. Here, the notary played a prominent role in formulating the will's preamble—an introduction that included formulaic religious statements—and recording the testator's bequeathed items and requests. Upon completion, the notary recorded the names of the *cabildo* members and added the will to the town's book of testaments.

Over time, many of these books were lost or destroyed; however, in the early 1990s, Matthew Restall located a corpus of Ixil wills dating between 1765 and 1768. He also located three additional wills removed from Ixil's

TABLE 6.1. Number of Ixil wills and codicils per corpus and year

	1738	'48	'55	'60	'65	'66	'67	'68	'69	'73	'77	'79	Total
Christensen corpus		34	1	3									38
Restall corpus					5	34	24	2		1	2		68
Individual wills	1								1			1	3

Sources: Data from AHAY, "Oficios, 1748–1749, 1801–1884," vol. 1, "Peten Itza"; Restall, *Ixil Testaments*.

book of testaments and used as evidence in a lawsuit over a plot of land. In his analysis of the wills, he claimed the Pech as the dominant *chibal* in Ixil (Restall 1995, 6–7). In 2007, I (re)discovered an additional corpus of thirty-four Ixil wills and four codicils from 1747–1760.[9] The combined corpus consists of more than 100 wills from between 1738 and 1779 and is the largest collection of substantive Maya testaments extant today (see Table 6.1).[10] As such, this expanded collection of Ixil wills provides valuable information on the culture and society of Ixil. But more particular for this study, the collective corpus of Ixil wills provides a detailed and nuanced view of the Pech's socioeconomic standing in eighteenth-century Ixil.

The Pech in Eighteenth-Century Ixil

As mentioned, the Pech earned the status of *hidalgo* and the right to affix *don* to their names due to their support of the Spaniards during the conquest. This honor continued in eighteenth-century Ixil, as throughout the corpus many Pech appear with *don* affixed to their names. Some are testators; others are relatives or acquaintances mentioned in the wills. The only other appearances of *don* outside the Pech lineage occur in relation to the former and current *batabs* of Ixil, who in deference to the office were allowed to use and retain the honorific title. In short, the Pech represented the only *chibal* with *hidalgo* status in Ixil.

Yet evidence of the Pech's ability to benefit from their spoils as conquistadors goes beyond the use of *don*. The items bequeathed in their wills, the lineages they chose to marry into, and the offices they held all support their position as the dominant *chibal* in Ixil. Recording the items a testator bequeaths is an important, and usually the lengthiest, part of each will. Items in Ixil varied widely from house doors to shotguns, planting sticks to *kax* (plots of land [plural *kaxob*]), and colored yarn to metal spoons. Anything and everything was eligible for bequeathment. Spoons, shirts, belts, jars, and other objects considered ephemeral by today's standards fill the pages of Ixil's wills. Much like today, the objects Ixil testators possessed often accurately reflected their status and wealth.

For example, the will of a poor Maya in Ixil might include some articles of clothing and maybe a tool of some kind, if anything at all. The average testator would add to this list a *kax* or two and perhaps a mule. Wealthier Mayas typically bequeathed similar items but in greater numbers or of finer material, such as a silver spoon or a gold chain. In addition, the wills of wealthy testators often included a wider variety of goods and/or evidence of an increased involvement with the Spanish economy as producers of honey, wax, or other goods. When examining the surviving wills of five Pech who died in Ixil, the goods they left behind illustrate their wealth according to this pattern.[11]

Bequeathed Items

The Ixil corpus provides evidence of only two male Pech deaths between 1748 and 1768. The first, Ignasio Pech (1748), best represents the *chibal's* status through wealth.[12] Ignasio divides between his three sons and one daughter two house plots with wells, three *kaxob*, two mules, seven horses, three house doors, two silver spoons, two fur blankets, numerous clothing items and household possessions, and two shotguns—forbidden items given that the Maya were generally prohibited from owning firearms. Although Diego Chan kept more livestock—a donkey, five mules, nine horses, and five cows—and Miguel Tun owned more land—two house plots, three wells, and four forests—no other testator can boast the variety of wealth Ignasio possessed. The other male Pech, don Pedro (1779), left a peculiar will. For someone of his standing, the will is extremely short, bequeathing only two *kaxob*. The document is an anomaly among other Pech wills, leaving us to wonder about its brevity and his lack of possessions. Although don Pedro's economic status in the *cah* might be difficult to discern through wealth, however, the title of *don* informs the reader of his noble position.

Similar to men, Maya women both owned and bequeathed property; however, the Ixil wills expose general patterns in land and material holdings among the Maya that break along the contours of gender roles.[13] Generally speaking, men labored in the *kax* away from the *solar* (house plot), while women toiled within the *solar*. The possessions each gender bequeathed reflect these roles. Women possessed lengths of cloth and looms, while men claimed axes, machetes, house doors, and shotguns. In an analysis of the possessions bequeathed by Ixil women, Pech women emerge as prominent.

The earliest recorded death of a Pech in the Ixil corpus is that of Viviana Pech, who died in 1738. Although her testament is uncommonly brief for someone of her status, she does leave her sons Pedro (seen above as don Pedro Pech) and Felipe Pech six *kaxob*; no other resident of Ixil, male or female, bequeathed such an amount. In fact, the second largest bequest of *kaxob* from a female comes from Bernarda and Luisa Tec, who both left two *kaxob* for their children. As the Tec were a powerful *chibal* in Ixil ranking just below the Pech, the holdings of Bernarda and Luisa conform to the social hierarchy.

In 1748 two other Pech women died: Phelipa and Martha. Among the seven children she left behind, Phelipa divided three petticoats, two dresses, a chest, a length of blond yarn, a house plot with its accompanying well, and a *kax* she was to inherit from her father (who evidently outlived her). Martha, whose will is translated below, also had significant holdings that she divided among her four children and, interestingly, her husband, thus emphasizing Maya women's ability to hold property as individuals. Her bequeathed property included eight horses (four mares, two geldings, and two colts), two cows, a petticoat, and a dress. Livestock typically fell into the hands of Maya men, so Martha's possession of eight horses and two cows is impressive. Indeed, out of the three other women who bequeathed livestock, the next largest number comes from Luisa Tec, who owned two mules and a horse. A final Pech woman appears in Ixil's records in a statement to the *cabildo*, not in a will. In 1760, Lorensa Pech testified that she gave her son, Mateo Coba, a red mamey orchard and some money to dig a well.

In general, although an analysis of bequeathed items is insightful, it is also limited to those who died. Of more than 100 wills, only five represent the Pech. To be sure, the bequeathed items in these wills alone support the Pech's dominant position in Ixil. Yet wills from other *chibalob*—the Tec, Matu, Tun, Chan, and Yam—bequeath items also suggesting wealth equal to or even surpassing that of the Pech. Thus, to attain a more comprehensive view of the Pech's standing, we must also consider their patterns of marriage and office holding.

Exame de
alianza
(matri mo
niale

Marriage Patterns

Wills from Ixil are unique among the existing testamentary corpora in that each testator identifies his parents.[14] This allows for a clear view of marriage patterns in Ixil, which, upon examination, suggest the dominant role of the Pech *chibal*. As is common throughout most cultures, nobility tend to marry nobility to strengthen social, economic, and political alliances. As mentioned, the Tec occupied second place in socioeconomic status; however, other *chibalob* such as the Cante, Cime, Coba, Uetz, Yam, Tun, and Huchim also held noble status. When marrying, the Pech chose from this pool of nobles.

Yet they also chose from among their own ranks. Traditionally, scholars claimed that endogamy was a taboo practice among the Maya (Tozzer 1941, 99–100). More recently, Philip Thompson's study of Tekanto (1999) offered a more nuanced interpretation. He suggests that "one could not marry members of one's immediate lineage but could marry members of other lineages of the same surname" (Thompson 1999, 210). This is particularly the case when dealing with a large *chibal*, such as the Pech in Ixil. Restall also suggested that nobles were allowed some exception to the rule (Restall 1997, 397 n29). Both elements appear to have played a role in Ixil, with the Pech marrying other noble *chibalob*—including the Yam, Cime, Coba, Uetz, and Cante— but also other Pech.

For example, although Alonso Pech married Ursula Cime, their daughter, Viviana Pech, married Agustin Pech. This happened again with the parents of Phelipa Pech, Francisco and Maria Pech, and again with Martha Pech, whose previous husband was from the Cime *chibal*, but whose current husband was Phelipe Pech. If one were to draw conclusions from the available testaments, it seems that the Pech preferred to marry within their own *chibal* 33 percent of the time. The only other occurrence of intra-*chibal* marriage comes from the will of Lorensa Yam (1767), whose noble parents were Antonio and Petrona Yam. Additional data from Ixil's baptismal records confirms the Pech's tendency toward endogamous marriages and indicates that this tendency only increased over time. Out of 101 records of baptized Pech children from 1786 to 1885, an astonishing 54 (53 percent) of these children had both parents in the Pech *chibal* (LDS Archives, 2012)![15] A record search in other Yucatecan towns revealed that although endogamous unions between the Pech occasionally occurred in various other *cahob*, the numbers are nowhere near those seen in Ixil. Nor did my searches suggest that any other *chibalob* routinely illustrated such marriage practices, at least nowhere near the degree exhibited by the Pech.[16]

Clearly the Pech increasingly chose to marry other Pech; but why? Two possibilities are likely. Because Mayas seldom married outside their resident *cah*, the dominance of the Pech *chibal* of the Ceh Pech region would make intra-*chibal* marriage an increasing necessity, particularly in the small *cah* of Ixil where the Pech abounded. The second is not exclusive of the first and would reflect the Pech struggling to maintain its landholdings and political dominance within Ixil.[17] As the native population of Yucatan began to rebound, and as Spaniards increasingly encroached upon native towns, the demand on land increased. Thompson's study of Tekanto again provides an illustrative example. Here, by the mid-eighteenth century increasing native populations coupled with an increase in Spanish residents eager to acquire land placed pressure on noble landholdings.[18] Whereas Ixil did not have the same Spanish presence as Tekanto, the increasing native population, particularly among other noble *chibalob*, surely placed pressure on the Pech to maintain their dominance of the land and the *cabildo*, and, perhaps, led to an increased inclination toward endogamy.

Office Holdings

Finally, patterns of office holding illustrate the Pech's ability to maintain their conquistador spoils. Prior to the arrival of the Spaniards, each Maya *cah* managed everyday affairs through their respective municipal councils. Officers in these councils derived from the *cah*'s *almehen* (nobility), who relied on such positions to maintain their sociopolitical status. During colonial rule, these preexisting councils adapted to the Spanish *cabildo* model which, in Ixil, included a *gobernador* (governor), *teniente* (lieutenant, usually serving as an assistant batab), *alcaldes* (judges), *regidors* (councilmen), and an *escribano* (notary). The *batab* became the *gobernador*, Mayas knowledgeable in record keeping became *escribanos*, and preexisting offices such as the *ah cuch cab* could become those of the *alcalde* and *regidor* (Restall 1997, 61–83; Thompson 1999, 221–304).

Applied in a colonial Maya setting, the *cabildo* allowed the Maya nobility to reinforce their sociopolitical status. Yet the Maya modified the positions within the Spanish *cabildo* to accommodate preexisting standards of importance and representation. For example, in a Spanish *cabildo* the *escribano* was not necessarily of noble rank, nor did he advance to become a *cabildo* officer with voting rights. In Maya *cahob*, however, only nobles of high rank filled the office of *escribano*, which also served as a stepping stone to the higher offices of *teniente* and *batab*. In general, the offices within Ixil's *cabildo* could be ranked in importance from *batab* to *teniente*, *escribano*, *alcalde*, and *regidor*.

A noble *chibal* in Ixil with a high position on the social ladder, such as the Pech, probably occupied a variety of *cabildo* offices, but especially those of *batab*, *teniente*, or *escribano*. Likewise, nobles toward the lower rung of the ladder primarily held the offices of *regidor* and, occasionally, *alcalde*. Fortunately, every will from Ixil was notarized by the indigenous *cabildo*, thus providing an indication of which *chibalob* held which positions. Moreover, unlike data regarding bequeathed items and marriage alliances, which are limited to those Pech who died, the *cabildo* appears on every will regardless of the testator, thus providing the most comprehensive representation of the Pech's socioeconomic status. In short, if the Pech maintained their status into the eighteenth century, their positions in the *cabildo* should demonstrate as much.

Tables 6.2 and 6.3 verify the Pech's ability to maintain their status through office holding. They not only held positions as *batab* and *teniente* but also were well represented in the *alcalde* and *regidor* offices. In the *cabildo* offices recorded in the testaments, the Pech occupied the most seats, holding nineteen between 1738 and 1807 (see Table 6.3). Other prominent *chibalob* such as the Tec, Yam, Coba, Cob, and Canul also demonstrated their ability to reinforce their noble status through the *cabildo*. Restall originally argued that the holding of *cabildo* offices corresponded directly to land holding and wealth. Analysis of the expanded Ixil corpus confirms his argument, with the Pech, Tec, Yam, Coba, and Cob *chibalob* owning the most wealth in Ixil.

In general, the wills suggest that the Ixil *cabildo* allowed the Pech and other prominent *chibalob* to maintain their positions of dominance and nobility. Although colonial ordinances required that *cabildo* members rotate in annual elections, this was not the case in Ixil—or at least no record of such elections is known.[19] Instead, it appears that the noble *chibalob* of Ixil rotated positions and drew new candidates from the ranks of wealthy and politically powerful *chibalob*. This rotation allowed Joseph Pech to operate as *alcalde* in 1766 and *regidor* in 1773, and Gaspar Yam to serve as *alcalde*

TABLE 6.2. Pech seats on the *cabildo*, 1738–1807

1738	'48	'55	'60	'65	'66	'67	'68	'69	'73	'77	'79	?	1807
3	1	2	2	2	2	0	0	1	3	0	0	3	0
B	A	B	R	A	A			A	A			T	
A		R	R	R	R				R			A	
R									R			A	

Sources: Data from AHAY, "Oficios, 1748–1749, 1801–1884," vol. 1, "Peten Itza"; Restall, *Ixil Testaments*.
Note: B = *batab*; T = *teniente*; A = *alcalde*; R = *regidor*.

TABLE 6.3. *Chibal* office holding according to annual rotations, 1738–1807

	Batab	Teniente	Escribano	Alcalde	Regidor	Total
Pech	2	1	0	8	8	19
Coba	0	3	1	4	7	15
Tec	5	1	2	2	2	12
Yam	0	1	1	3	5	10
Cob	2	0	4	0	2	8
Canche	0	2	0	0	4	6
Canul	1	0	0	1	3	5
Chim	0	0	2	1	2	5
Couoh	0	0	0	2	2	4

Sources: Data from AHAY, "Oficios, 1748–1749, 1801–1884," vol. 1, "Peten Itza"; Restall, *Ixil Testaments*.
Note: Because a yearly rotation existed in Ixil, and because the same person could occupy the seat more than once, the numbers do not necessarily indicate separate individuals, only the number of rotations a *chibal* held a seat. For example, don Ignacio Tec was the only Tec to serve as *batab* but held the seat for five rotations.

in 1767, *regidor* in 1773, and then again as *alcalde* in 1777. Through this systematic rotation, dominant *chibalob*, particularly the Pech, employed the *cabildo* to maintain their positions within the *cah*.

Strangely, the wills fail to represent any Pech as holding the office of *escribano*, even though the position is represented in nearly all other high-ranking *chibalob*, particularly the Cob. As mentioned, being an *escribano* was helpful in attaining a future position as *batab* or *teniente*. For example, Joseph Cob served as *escribano* in 1760 and 1765 before he became *batab* in 1773 and again in 1777. Other *chibalob* such as the Yam, Coba, and Chim seem to have been awaiting their chance at the *batab*-ship by climbing the social ladder and occupying the position of *escribano*. (Indeed, if the documentation existed, it would likely illustrate *batabob* from such *chibalob*.)

Perhaps some of the Pech were *escribanos* and we simply lack the documentation. Or, perhaps the Pech's *hidalgo* status allowed them to skip the *escribano* stepping stone to the *batab*-ship.

Another possibility is that the Pech might have been losing their political grip as the eighteenth century progressed. Although they controlled the highest number of *cabildo* seats, most of those represented the *alcalde* and *regidor* offices. Indeed, when examining which *chibal* appears most often as *batab, teniente*, or *escribano*—offices that wielded the most sociopolitical clout—the Tec emerge as dominant, with the Coba and Cob close behind (see Table 6.4). In general, existing documentation suggests that by the latter half of the eighteenth century the Pech were increasingly made to share prestigious seats on the *cabildo* with other noble *chibalob*.

Conclusion

In the late nineteenth century, Yucatan's bishop, Crescencio Carrillo y Ancona, collected a variety of Maya documents. One codex in particular contained various religious tracts, zodiacs, almanacs, and medicinal commentaries—and it originated from Ixil. Later referred to as the Chilam Balam of Ixil, this eighteenth-century document fails to mention its author(s).[20] However, in Laura Caso Barrera's (2011) transcription and translation of the text, she uncovered an interesting find while attempting to identify the unnamed author(s). She notes that at the bottom of one of the pages, the following was written: "yo proveye junn yPolito Pech" (rubric), "I supplied the paper/book, Hipólito Pech." No other name is found within the codex. Hipólito Pech, no doubt, took pride in his role in the composition of the Chilam Balam, and he wanted all readers, present and future, to know of his contribution to an important manuscript for the town. By the eighteenth century, then, the Pech were continuing to secure their position in Ixil, and the wills from Ixil illustrate their efforts in detail.

Admittedly, even an expanded corpus of wills provides a limited glimpse of the past. Yet, generally speaking, an examination of bequeathed property, marriage patterns, and office holding among testators illustrate that the Pech maintained a dominant sociopolitical and economic position in eighteenth-century Ixil. Pech testators consistently bequeathed items in numbers and of value that indicate their prosperity. Similarly, the Pech *chibal* maintained high standards regarding marriage, choosing only noble *chibalob*, or their own. The Pech also occupied the most positions within

TABLE 6.4. *Chibal*-held *cabildo* offices, Ixil, 1738–1807

Batab	Teniente	Escribano	Alcalde	Regidor
don Francisco Pech, '38	don Pasqual Pech*		Ignacio Pech, '38	Mateo Pech, '38
don Pedro Pech, '55			Bartolome Pech, '48	Pasqual Pech, '55, '65
			Andrés Pech, '65	Francisco Pech, '60
			Joseph Pech, '66	Jacinto Pech, '60
			Juan Pech, '69	Antonio Pech, '66
			Gaspar Pech, '73	Bartolome Pech, '73
			don Antonio Pech*	Joseph Pech, '73
			don Manuel Pech*	
don Ignacio Tec, '60, '65-'69	Andres Tec, '67	Pablo Tec, '66, '68	Francisco Tec, '98	Antonio Tec, '66
			Manuel Tec, '98	Leonardo Tec, '98
	Sebastian Yam, '60	Esteban Yam, '98	Gaspar Yam, '67, '77	Agustin Yam, '38
			Francisco Yam, '86	Sebastian Yam, '48
				Gaspar Yam, '73
				Pasqual Yam, '77
				Alexandro Yam, '86
	Ignacio Coba, '48, '55	Salvador Coba, '48	Bernardino Coba, '38	Pasqual Coba, '55, '65, '98
	Gaspar Coba, '66		Salvador Coba, '55, '68	Gaspar Coba, '60
	Francisco Coba, '98		Ignacio Coba, '60	Juan Coba, '68, 86
				Pedro Coba, '79
don Joseph Cob, '73, '77		Joseph Cob, '60, '65		Bonifacio Cob, '55
		Alonso Cob, '69		Gaspar Cob, '79
		Ysidro Cob, 1807		

Sources: Data from AHAY, "Oficios, 1748–1749, 1801–1884," vol. 1, "Peten Itza"; Restall, *Ixil Testaments*; Restall, *Maya World*, app. C.

* These individuals appear as witnesses in a 1779 testament by name and former *cabildo* position, although they did not sit on the *cabildo* at that time.

the *cabildo* of any other *chibalob*. All such strategies contributed to creating what Laura Matthew (2012, 6–11) termed a social memory that validated the Pech's position in Ixil.

The expanded corpus of wills also suggests, however, that the Pech's spoils were under threat from other noble *chibalob*. Although they bequeathed the most valuable and varied material possessions, the Tec, Yam, and Huchim bequeathed more land, and the Tun and Chan *chibalob* more livestock. Although the Pech married into noble families, they also engaged in intra-*chibal* relationships that perhaps represent an effort to maintain their wealth and position of authority. And although the Pech occupied more *cabildo* seats than any other *chibal*, the testaments in this corpus suggest that most of those seats were for the offices of *alcalde* and *regidor*, while other *chibalob* increasingly claimed the more prominent offices of *batab*, *teniente*, and *escribano*.

Additional colonial documentation also supports the possibility of a threat to the dominance of the Pech in the Ceh Pech region—or at least of their having to share their spoils. For example, the Pech ruled Cacalchen prior to the arrival of the Spaniards and exhibited subsequent influence throughout the sixteenth century (AGI, México 367, 62; *Relaciones* 1983, 338). However, testaments from Cacalchen reveal that between 1646 and 1656, not one Pech governed as *batab*, and only two appear as *cabildo* members. Likewise, Pech *batabs* were absent in the towns of Mococha and Baca in 1785, but were found as a *teniente* and *alcalde* in Motul in 1762 (AHAY, Visita Pastorales 1782–1785, "Visita de Mococha"; ANEY 1796–1797, 205).[21] And in modern-day Ixil, of the twenty-seven *presidentes municipales* appointed between 1941 and 2012, the Pech, although nominated more frequently than any *chibalob*, only held the office three times, sharing the position with the Tec, Tun, Canche, May, Matu, and, increasingly, individuals with Spanish surnames (Gobierno del Estado de Yucatán 2011).[22]

When compared with other native nobility throughout Latin America, the Pech display similarities and differences. Similarities include the Pech's strategies of creating a historical memory that allies their lineage with the first conquistadors, political maneuvering within Ixil's *cabildo*, marriage alliances, and distinctions of wealth to maintain their nobility. Yet the Pech's increasing inclination toward endogamous marriages and their ability to maintain their position (however tenuous) as the dominant *chibal* within Ixil into the late eighteenth century is notable. By the eighteenth century, much of the native nobility throughout Latin America, while maintaining their distinction from lower classes, increasingly found their socioeconomic status challenged by a growing native and Spanish population, and a political economy that alienated natives more and more (Gibson 1964; Lockhart 1992; Restall 1997; Terraciano 2001; Thomson 2002; Connell 2011). This is not to say that the native nobility disappeared completely or that they all shared the same homogenous fate, but rather that the lines demarcating their status became increasingly blurred.

The Pech of Ixil, however, suggest that nobles in the peripheries fared better than their metropolitan counterparts, at least initially. To be sure, although the Pech would eventually face challenges generally similar to other native nobles, their location in peripheral Ixil seems to have delayed such change somewhat.[23] For example, the growing population of *castas* (mixed-race people) that increasingly occupied ruling positions in other, larger towns with stronger Spanish influence did not have a noticeable presence in Ixil until well into the nineteenth century.[24] Instead, the eighteenth-century Pech's greatest threat seemed internal, deriving from the growing population of their noble peers.[25]

In the end, the efforts of sixteenth-century Ah Dzulub Pech of Ixil in accompanying Macan Pech to pay tribute to the Spanish conquistadors seems to have paid off. The Pech became *hidalgos* whose economic and sociopolitical spoils are evident in the testaments of eighteenth-century Ixil. According to Macan Pech, God had given them their spoils "until their days are gone." By the nineteenth century (and even the twenty-first!) the Pech were still enjoying their spoils, although they were increasingly learning how to share.

Last Will and Testament of Martha Pech, 1748

Transcription
(AHAY, Oficios 1748–1749, 1801–1884, vol. 1, "Peten Itza," fol. 13r)
Martha pech Cimi en 17 de ablil de 1748 anōs

Tu kaba dios yumbil y dios mehen y dios espiritu santo oxtul personas huntulili dios uchuc tumen tusinil maix pimobi lai bin in ylabae u hunil yn thokyahthan tin testamento hibicil tenil Martha pech u yx mehen marcos pech u yalen Juana uetz Bacacix cimil yn cah lae tohuol tin pucsikal y tin nat uetsihcie Baixan u olah mucul yn cucutil ychil yotoch ca

ku na lae Baixan Cin uoktic ynba ti ca pixanil yum padre guardian ca
yalab hunpeɔ missa yokol in pixan ca antabac tu numyail anima
purgatorio y ca u masen tu payalchi ychil u missa lae Bayxan bin ɔabae u
limosnyl oxpel tostones y Capel tumin helusalen lae ___ _

   Baixan Capok yeua tzimin y hunpok capon tzimin y hunpok uacax cin
ɔaic tin u al marcos cime = Baixan hunpok ye ua tzimin y hunpok podro
tzimin y hunpel pic cin ɔaic tin u al man^la cime = Baixan hunpok yeua
tzimin y hunpel pic cin ɔaic tin u al aguitina pech = Baixan hunpel ipil

   cin ɔai tin u al pasguala pech = Baixan hunpok yeua tzimin y hunpok
podro y hunpok capon tzimin y hunpok uacax cin ɔaic tin u icham
phelipe pech = Baixan he cen bal cubin u ɔa ten in u icham Cabin cime
lae ɔae tin u al marcos cime lae halibe matheᵒ tec abaseas

ygnasio coba theᵉ	Dⁿ gaspar canul	gaspaʳ tun
Batolme pech aᵈᵉ	Batab	Diego mitz
Sebastian uh aᵈᵉ	Saruador Coba esⁿᵒ	antᵒ Juchim
		Sebastian yam
		Regidoresob

   Cumpliose este funeral se le canto una missa como la pidio el difunto
y lo firme

   Fr. Joseph Villamil

Translation

Martha Pech died on the 17th of April, 1748.

   In the name of God the Father and God the Son and God the Holy
Spirit, three persons one God almighty. The document of my final words
in my testament will be seen, insomuch as I who am Martha Pech, the
daughter of Marcos Pech, the child of Juana Uetz. Although I am dying,
well is my heart and my understanding is as it should be. Likewise, I wish
my body to be buried inside the home of our temple (church). Likewise, I
supplicate our blessed father, Padre Guardian, to say one mass to help my
soul in the suffering of souls in purgatory, and that a prayer be said for me
in that mass. Likewise, it will be given in alms three *tostons* and two *tomin*
for Jerusalem.

   Likewise, two mares and one gelding and one cow I give to my child,
Marcos Cime. Likewise, one mare and one colt and one petticoat I give to
my child, Manuela Cime. Likewise one mare and one petticoat I give to
my child, Agustina Pech. Likewise, one dress I give to my child, Pasquala

Pech. Likewise, one mare and one colt and one gelding and one cow I give
to my husband, Phelipe Pech. Likewise, all that my husband gives me when
he dies will be given to my child Marcos Cime. There is no more. Mateo
Tec, executor.

Ignasio Coba, lieutenant	don Gaspar Canul	Gaspar Tun
Bartolome Pech, *alcalde*	*Batab*	Diego Mitz
Sebastian Uh, *alcalde*	Salvador Coba, notary	Antonio Huchim
		Sebastian Yam
		Regidors

This funeral was carried out, a mass was sung as the deceased requested,
and I signed it.
fray Joseph Villamil

Notes

I am grateful for the comments I received on this study from the Second Annual
Yucatan/PA Roundtable held at Pennsylvania State University. I also thank Matthew Restall, Spencer Delbridge, and Jonathan Truitt for their suggestions.

1. The *Title of Yaxkukul* can be found in Tulane University's Latin American
   Library. My translations derive from Matthew Restall's (1998b, 107–128)
   translation of the document.
2. In fact, the Pech were not the first to assist the Spanish conquistadors; many
   others, including the Pat and Chel, had already given their aid (see Chamberlain 1966, 45–66).
3. The scholarship on Indian conquistadors is impressive and continues to grow,
   illustrating how native efforts to secure benefits in colonial society through
   conquest were met with varying degrees of success. For an overview of the
   scholarship see Matthew and Oudijk 2007.
4. The erroneous assumption that the Spanish conquest reduced all natives to
   the status of commoners has long been refuted. Regarding the Pech and their
   ability to maintain positions of status, see Restall 1997, 87–97; 1998b. See also
   Quezada 1993.
5. For a detailed study on Maya *hidalgos* in Tekanto see Thompson 1999, 155–171.
6. Data taken from Restall's (1998b, 151–168) analysis of the letters; in particular,
   see note 4.
7. The Pech are mentioned frequently throughout the *Relaciones* (1983).
8. The four extant corpora of Maya testaments from Cacalchen, Tekanto, Ebtun,
   and Ixil nearly all reflect epochs of famine and/or epidemics. For more on the
   effects of famine and disease in Tekanto and Ixil, see Bricker and Hill 2009.
9. In her *Maya Society*, Farriss (1984, 450 n44) notes a corpora of testaments
   that were misfiled in the AHAY. This is surely that same corpora.

10. At 412 wills, the Tekanto corpus is, admittedly, larger; however, only 56 wills contain information on bequeathed items. My fortunate discovery of the additional Ixil corpus occurred in the AHAY while searching through the box "Oficios 1748–1749, 1801–1884, vol. 1." Written in pencil on the first testament are the words "oraciones-Maya." Restall's and my forthcoming *Return to Ixil* provides a more detailed examination of the newly expanded corpus.

11. For more on the material world of the Maya see Restall 1997, 98–109.

12. A transcription and translation of this will can be found in Christensen 2013, 279–281.

13. For more on the gender patterns of bequeathed items see Restall 1997, 124–130. The appendix tables D.7–D.12 are particularly relevant.

14. Wills from Tekanto and Cacalchen only mention the testator, not his parents, unless included as recipients of bequeathed items.

15. This is not a case of the woman adopting the man's patronym upon marriage, as this was not done in Maya society, although the children would inherit the appellative mark of their father. See Restall 1997, 42–43.

16. The Church of Jesus Christ of Latter-day Saints has made significant efforts to convert their extensive microfilm collection of worldwide genealogical data into an online database available at familysearch.org. This website made possible my search of many parish archives throughout Yucatan to retrieve the data presented here. The ever-increasing access to marriage and death records will no doubt continually expand our understanding of intra-*chibal* marriage patterns.

17. The work of Paola Peniche Moreno (2007, 175–178) also recognizes the Pech's practice of endogamy in Ixil and views this as a way to maintain material and social benefits.

18. Restall (1997, 220–25) also provides evidence from various *cahob* on the Spanish purchase of land from Maya nobles.

19. Elections did occur in other *cahob*. See Thompson 1999, 51–53.

20. *Chilam Balams* refer to colonial, Maya-authored texts recording myriad information originating from both Maya and Spanish culture deemed important by the individual *cah*. Most of the nine examples that exist today are eighteenth-century copies of earlier originals. Interestingly, the Pech's connection to the Chilam Balams originates in precontact times; colonial documents state that Nahau Pech, a *chilam balam* (priest), predicted the coming of Christianity prior to the Spaniards' arrival (Cogolludo 1688, bk. 2, chap. 11). An edition of Nahau Pech's prophecy is found in the Chilam Balam of Chumayel (see Edmonson 1986, 69–70).

21. Restall (1998a, 157–162) provides a transcription and translation of Juan Cutz's testament.

22. A link to this report can be found at http://www.yucatan.gob.mx/estado /municipios/ver_municipio.php?id=39. The common Spanish surnames of the *presidentes* reflect the impact that Spaniards and their *casta* descendants would eventually come to have on Ixil's *cabildo*.

23. Increasingly, scholars are noticing the varying effects of colonialism on those populating the peripheries. For an example concerning the production of wills, see Jones's chapter in this volume; also Christensen 2013; Pizzigoni 2012. For an example of another lineage of nobles attempting to resist the pressures of the eighteenth century, see Villella 2012.
24. For examples illustrating the increase in non-Indian rulership, see Haskett 1991, 138; Yannakakis 2008; Villella 2012.
25. Although the threat would come in the nineteenth century, when birth records suggest a more significant presence of a mixed-race population in Ixil.

References

Barrera, Laura Caso. 2011. *Chilam Balam de Ixil: Facsmiliar y estudio de un libro maya inédito*. Mexico City: Artes de México y del Mundo.

Bricker, Victoria R., and Rebecca E. Hill. 2009. "Climatic Signatures in Yucatecan Wills and Death Records." *Ethnohistory* 56:227–268.

Chamberlain, Robert S. 1966. *The Conquest and Colonization of Yucatan, 1517–1550*. New York: Octagon.

Christensen, Mark Z. 2013. *Nahua and Maya Catholicisms: Texts and Religion in Colonial Central Mexico and Yucatan*. Stanford: Stanford University Press.

Cogolludo, Diego López de. 1688. *Historia de Yucatán*. Madrid: J. García Infanzón.

Connell, William. 2011. *After Moctezuma: Indigenous Politics and Self-Government in Mexico City, 1524–1730*. Norman: University of Oklahoma Press.

Edmonson, Munro S. 1986. *Heaven Born Mérida and Its Destiny: The Book of Chilam Balam of Chumayel*. Austin: University of Texas Press.

Farriss, Nancy M. 1984. *Maya Society Under Colonial Rule: The Collective Enterprise of Survival*. Princeton: Princeton University Press.

Gibson, Charles. 1964. *The Aztecs Under Spanish Rule: A History of the Indians of the Valley of Mexico, 1519–1810*. Stanford, Calif.: Stanford University Press.

Gobierno del Estado de Yucatán. http://www.yucatan.gob.mx/estado/municipios /ver_municipio.jsp?id=39.

Haskett, Robert. 1991. *Indigenous Rulers: An Ethnohistory of Town Government in Colonial Cuernavaca*. Albuquerque: University of New Mexico Press.

Kellogg, Susan, and Mathew Restall. 1998. *Dead Giveaways: Indigenous Testaments of Colonial Mesoamerica and the Andes*. Salt Lake City: University of Utah Press.

Landa, fray Diego de. 1975. *Landa's Relación de las cosas de Yucatan: A Translation*. Translated by Alfred M. Tozzer. Papers of the Peabody Museum vol. 18. Cambridge: Harvard University, the Peabody Museum, 1941. Reprint, Millwood, N.Y.: Kraus Reprint Company.

Lockhart, James. 1992. *The Nahuas After the Conquest: A Social and Cultural History of the Indians of Central Mexico, Sixteenth Through Eighteenth Centuries*. Stanford, Calif.: Stanford University Press.

Matthew, Laura E. 2012. *Memories of Conquest: Becoming Mexicano in Colonial Guatemala*. Chapel Hill: University of North Carolina Press.

Matthew, Laura E., and Michel R. Oudijk, eds. 2007. *Indian Conquistadors: Indigenous Allies in the Conquest of Mesoamerica*. Norman: University of Oklahoma Press.

Patch, Robert W. 1993. *Maya and Spaniard in Yucatan, 1648–1812*. Stanford, Calif.: Stanford University Press.

Peniche Moreno, Paola. 2007. *Ámbitos del parentesco: La sociedad maya en tiempos de la Colonia*. Mexico City: CIESAS.

Pizzigoni, Caterina. 2012. *The Life Within: Local Indigenous Society in Mexico's Toluca Valley, 1650–1800*. Stanford: Stanford University Press.

Quezada, Sergio. 1993. *Pueblos y Caciques Yucatecos, 1550–1580*. Mexico City: El Colegio de México.

Relaciones histórico-geográficas de la gobernación de Yucatán, vol. 1, *Mérida, Valladolid y Tabasco*. 1983. Mexico City: Universidad Nacional Autónoma de México.

Restall, Matthew. 1995. *Life and Death in a Maya Community: The Ixil Testaments of the 1760s*. Lancaster, Calif.: Labyrinthos.

———. 1997. *The Maya World: Yucatec Culture and Society, 1550–1850*. Stanford, Calif.: Stanford University Press.

———. 1998a. "Interculturation and the Indigenous Testament in Colonial Yucatan." In *Dead Giveaways: Indigenous Testaments of Colonial Mesoamerica and the Andes*, edited by Susan Kellogg and Matthew Restall, 141–162. Salt Lake City: University of Utah Press.

———. 1998b. *Maya Conquistador*. Boston: Beacon Press.

———. 2003. *Seven Myths of the Spanish Conquest*. New York: Oxford University Press.

Terraciano, Kevin. 2001. *The Mixtecs of Colonial Oaxaca: Ñudzahui History, Sixteenth through Eighteenth Centuries*. Stanford, Calif.: Stanford University Press.

Thompson, Philip C. 1999. *Tekanto, a Maya Town in Colonial Yucatan*. New Orleans: Tulane University Middle American Research Institute.

Thomson, Sinclair. 2002. *We Alone Will Rule: Native Andean Politics in the Age of Insurgency*. Madison: University of Wisconsin Press.

Villella, Peter. 2012. "Indian Lords, Hispanic Gentlemen: The Salazars of Colonial Tlaxcala." *The Americas* 69(1): 1–36.

Yannakakis, Yanna. 2008. *The Art of Being In-between: Native Intermediaries, Indian Identity, and Local Rule in Colonial Oaxaca*. Durham, N.C.: Duke University Press.

CHAPTER 7

"One or Two of My Living Words"

Seventeenth- and Eighteenth-Century K'iche' Testaments from Guatemala

OWEN H. JONES

In the eighteenth century the Achí (Maya) of the Guatemalan town of Rab'inal declared their final testaments upon their deathbeds and transmitted what they humbly called "only one or two of [their] *casliquil tzih*" or "living words." They declared orally in the presence of witnesses and community leaders their last wishes for the repartition of their property and bequeathed all of their earthly possessions to their immediate kin. The scribe of the municipal council wrote down their living words in their own language.[1] On March 12, 1768, the scribe in Rab'inal, Lucas Tauico, wrote in the will of Diego Macha': "We are witnesses. We are hearers of one or two of his words of his testament, indeed, living words. This, well, his first word of his testament is only for his own memory because we are only mortals" (TULAL, 497.281, Q6d2).[2] As this testament suggests, each will became a script for the dying to relate a final message of "living words" or "words of counsel" to their family members.

The sick and dying—young and old, male and female, relatively rich and dismally poor—all made last testaments. Some K'iche', like the elites of Xelajú and San Miguel Totonicapán, well before they became terminally ill, chose to have their wills recorded with the public scribe, a Spanish official who acted as notary in specific pueblos that had Spanish colonial administrators (Luján Muñoz 2011, 4). He drafted their testaments in Spanish using an official interpreter if necessary. The K'iche' elites of Xelajú were bilingual in K'iche' and Spanish, but the elites of San Miguel Totonicapán needed a general interpreter to help produce their wills. Upper-class

K'iche' made their testaments with the public scribe because his signature carried greater legal and political clout than that of the indigenous municipal council's scribe. In some instances the Spanish magistrate required the public scribe to produce the testament in Spanish so that an accounting could be made of the individual's acquired wealth. For example, the will of Balthazar Guicol from San Miguel Totonicapán had an accounting of 72,143 pesos and 5 reales, a small fortune that the colonial magistrate wanted to account for to hedge against later conflicts (AGCA, A.1, 1500, 9988). Indigenous scribes, as bilingual indigenous leaders, often participated as witnesses in the drafting of these wills and strategically transferred the formulaic language used by public scribes into the production of their own testaments in K'iche'.

There are two corpora of fifty-nine wills and sundry papers written in K'iche' from the *cabildo* book of Rab'inal, two small corpora of wills from the towns of San Miguel Totonicapán and Espíritu Santo Xelajú de la Real Corona (or Quetzaltenango), and one will from San Cristobal Totonicapán. The San Miguel corpus contains seven wills and the Xelajú corpus five that span the late seventeenth to the late eighteenth centuries. Four corpora of wills from three K'iche'-speaking communities allow us to examine the differences in the drafting of testaments and their literary conventions. The contextualization of these corpora of K'iche'-language wills demonstrates indigenous innovation in testament making in some cases and the reproduction of Spanish legal norms in others (Hanks 2010, 21).

Function and Structure of K'iche' Testaments

The indigenous leadership shaped the structure of the testaments that they produced. The greatest influence in testament composition emanated from the training of the scribe. Continuity in testamentary organization is consistent from testament to testament and was transmitted from scribal teacher to student. Scribal schools defined the formulae in which wills would be written as teachers taught students the conventions of community record keeping.

Testaments from some communities contain the voice of community leaders—the municipal council and the *chinamit* (ward of the indigenous township)—as well as the testator's.[3] There were several *chinamit* in a single community, as well as various leaders called *chinamitales*. The K'iche' referred to them as *tz'aqal chinamital*, "advocates and lineage heads" (Christenson, n.d.).[4] *Chinamitales* assisted and advocated for their *ral cual*, "child of a mother, child of a father," a descriptor of the non-elite who lived within their *chinamit*. Thus, for the K'iche', the inclusion of the *chinamit* in a will seemed logical as it followed precontact traditions of community configuration that hinged on the familial structure.

Justices present at the write-up of a will could include first and second *alcaldes*, an indigenous governor, a scribe (who was paid by the testator), an indigenous *fiscal* (priest's assistant), any number of aldermen, and many of the *chinamitales* of the community's different wards. Besides municipal leaders and the testator, witnesses and family members were also in attendance. Not all of the justices had to be present; for some wills only *chinamitales* and the scribe presided over the event, as was the case in the will of Manuel Xpattaq' (included below). Production of a will was a complicated and important community action that included the participation of a large number of societal leaders who not only helped to guide the words of the testator but also aided in relieving community strife through their witness to the dying person's spoken words. They identified themselves as the *taol*, "the hearers" of the "living words" of the testator, and they used the testament as a document that confirmed the restructuring of land and the bequeathal of personal property.

Production of a K'iche' testament had several stages. In the initial creation of the will, the testator related the *casliquil tzij* (living words) or *pixab tzij* (words of counsel) that would express his or her wishes. The second stage of the testament was the probate proceedings, in which Rab'inal's municipal leaders, who called themselves the *jachol* (disseminators), partitioned the deceased's assets to the intended family members. The last stage of a will could include any and all contestations to the bequeathal of property, for which the community leaders could consult the will of the testator and also those of his or her ancestors. Some of the Rab'inal wills are not the testator's first testament but *suculiquil* (a correction) to the first will.

Not all testaments written in K'iche' contain the testator's "living words" or "words of counsel." If someone died intestate, before they could leave a last will, the community leaders from the municipal council or the *chinamit* attempted to reconstruct the individual's probable wishes. The creation of a testator's probable wishes is unique to indigenous language testaments. It involved gathering the family members together to make the appropriate repartition of assets and property. The community leaders from Rab'inal called themselves "we the *banol*"—the doers, makers, or creators of the words of the deceased. These testaments still had the same literary conventions as wills produced from the "living words" of the testator: a dialogue still takes place within the document between the deceased testator and the community leaders. The will then proceeds to follow the same conventions as those in which the testator is dictating his or her wishes to the community leaders. Whether this dialogue was the product of divination is not entirely clear but is clearly implied. What is certain is that the will was a community document that involved the communal leadership of the *tinamit amaq'*, the town and nation.

Community leaders advocated for the deceased as *jachol*, disseminators of the bequeathed goods or executors of the testator's wishes. The documents they created related directly to testaments and recorded the process of the repartition of property, similar to probate proceedings. Often in their role as *jachol*, community leaders dispensed justice, with the testator threatening community intervention at the end of testaments. In some wills, testators beseeched town council members, lineage elders, or *chinamitales* to resolve disputes that might arise between their family members. Still, in other wills testators threatened that the community leaders would punish their family members with lashes if their heirs ignored their wishes. The standard was sixty lashes, to be witnessed by the community elders themselves. In some probate proceedings, which occurred after the testator died, the community elders dispensed justice on those family members who did not cooperate with their mandates (AGCA, A1.20, 1784, 55535, Testament of Pedro Gomes Xiquitzal).

Provenance

As Robert Hill II (1998) similarly notes for Kaqchiquel wills, K'iche' testaments, at least from Rab'inal, do not stress the provenance of the testator but rather focus on the testator's affiliation with his or her *chinamit*, the ward or neighborhood in which the testator resided. It is perplexing that in the Rab'inal wills the scribe did not include the names of the *chinamit*. In fact, for the Rab'inal wills, the only instance in which a testator's provenance is mentioned is when they were foreign to the *tinamit amaq'* in which the testator made the will. The same cannot be said for wills from *tinamit amaq'* where the leadership links themselves to Spanish precedents, as in Xelajú and San Miguel Totonicapán, and the testators announce their towns of origin, stating that they are a *natural* of said town.

One reference to a *tinamit amaq'* is Josepha Lucas's statement that she is *ah Zalama*, "she [of the town] of Salamá," a township adjacent to Rab'inal.[5] The identification of town of origin is a concept originating from Spanish legalism and became general practice in the testaments of K'iche' *tinamit amaq'* in which the indigenous inhabitants had frequent contact with the public scribe. The names in the Rab'inal testaments can be compared to other documentation from Rab'inal, and the references to local areas prove that the wills originated there. Connections to people within the community rather than to place seem more prevalent in Rab'inal wills.

Q'a Chuch Q'ahau

In Rab'inal testaments, community leaders held a title reserved for diviners and day keepers in modern K'iche' communities in Guatemala. In his testament, Sebastian Gotierres describes them using an uncommon term: "First, well, his word in the name of God the Father, God the Son, and God the Holy Ghost with my lady Mary. And may there be, well, someone to help him, to say one or two of my words before them, these, my mothers my day keepers" (TULAL, 497.281, Q6d2). It is unusual in Rab'inal testaments for the scribe or testator to consider the town council elders as "my mothers, my day keepers." Usually the expression is *q'a chuch q'ahau* (our mothers, our fathers) (Tedlock 1982). Although unusual, it is not strange that the scribe, Lucas Tauico, chose to use the phrase "these, my mothers, my day keepers" to describe the council members. Barbara Tedlock asserts that "the mothers, fathers" are first *ah q'ij* (day keepers) before they become diviners. They function as counters of the days, keepers of time, and as redistributors of space and land. They become intercessors between the gods, even the Christian gods, which include the trinity, and because of the quadripartite nature of K'iche' thought in reference to time and space may include the Virgin Mary as a fourth deity.

The dying had the reassurance that their words continued on long after they had passed away and that their wills would be consulted if there were any contest or infighting among their heirs. They believed that the words of the dead could speak from the mouths of those who had access to the voices of the ancestors, *q'a chuch q'ahau*. Their duties included knowledge of the proper days on which to perform rituals and ceremonies to receive inspiration and messages from departed ancestors, especially those who held their same leadership position in life. The title "mothers, fathers" in the seventeenth and eighteenth centuries was one that every member of the indigenous *cabildo* held and one that every *chinamital* (ward lineage head) also possessed. In K'iche' ideology, the deceased community leaders had what they would consider to be better sight: an understanding of the past and a vision for the future that could aid contemporary leaders in making important decisions that would affect the community's well-being.

Fray Francisco Ximénez, translator of the *Popol Vuh* and a resident priest in the head town of Rab'inal, alludes to this practice related to death and dying. He states that when the dying were terminally ill, the K'iche' used herbal medicine and then called in the magician, the necromancer, or augury specialist to prescribe sacrifices to cure the sick (Ximénez 1929, 99).

In the correction of the last testament of Mateo Q'onibel in Rab'inal in 1776, the town council acted as diviners and summoned up the words of the testator's deceased grandfather. Scribe Lucas Tauico wrote, "he says well his word of this our grandfather Mateo Q'alah God received me. With their mother every one of you come together in common and do a mass with our mother."[6] The first words here are those of a man who was already dead. He was advising his family that he did not need a mass said for him because he was already in the presence of God. The town council channeled his wishes from beyond the grave, proclaiming that the family needed to arrange for a mass for their mother (Jones 2009, 183).

Dialogocentrism

Many of the wills from separate scribal schools contain the same literary conventions, suggesting the strong influence of the scribes in using the proper formulae. These elements coincide with the access that scribes and other community leaders had to Spanish legal customs through their interactions with public notaries. The wills from San Miguel Totonicapán and Quetzaltenango, for example, are much closer to Spanish testaments than are wills from Rab'inal. Scribes appear to have had a fair bit of artistic license in writing testaments given that they did not include every element of Spanish-language wills made by public notaries; instead they improvised, making the testaments coincide with K'iche' customs.

Most Spanish wills from the same period represent only the testator's monologue of individual bequeathals of property and effects, but the

Rab'inal wills are written in a narrative style that cuts in and out of the third and first persons as if it were a dialogue between the testator and the community's leaders. This style is similar to the way that the K'iche' tell stories and betrays an oral tradition that follows a K'iche' and a larger Mesoamerican method. The dialogue of the testament reveals the wishes of the testator in the first person, but reveals the intervention of the municipal council and *chinamitales* as third-person narrators.

Matthew Restall refers to this notarial style in Yucatec Maya testaments as the "dialogocentric" nature of Maya thought (Restall 1997, 242).[7] Dialogocentrism appears only in the K'iche' language wills from Rab'inal. The 1762 testament of Sebastian Pio states, "This is the first of his words thus this for my mass to help my soul before God."[8] The community leaders are the third-person narrators, and Sebastian Pio's voice is in the first person. This dialogocentrism is also present in the *Popol Vuh* and in K'iche' dance dramas such as the *Tum Teleche* and *Rab'inal Achí*, and is an indicator that last wills and testaments were a form of ritual performance: a script for the dying (Jones 2009, 262).

The Xelajú and Totonicapán testaments lack the strong dialogocentric format of the wills from Rab'inal. The community leaders did not usually assert their primacy in these testaments, nor act in defining the desires of the individuals involved. The wills were not made in the testators' homes but rather *pa ja tzib* (in the house of the scribe). The invocations include a much longer and more detailed statement of faith, and the wills include the same sorts of conventions found in Spanish-language wills, such as the testator claiming that witnesses were "within [their] five senses" (AGCA, A1.20, 1504, 9981, 208, Testament of Anttonio Marin). They also tend to name the missionary friar as the benefactor of the last rites, which included the Eucharist and the unction of holy oil.

The fact that the testaments from Xelajú and Totonicapán are not dialogocentric does not mean that community leaders were not involved in their production. K'iche' leaders in Xelajú enjoyed a privileged relationship with the regional magistrate and other Spaniards who lived in their *tinamit* because of their elite status and recognition as *indios ladinos* (latinized Indians) bilingual in Castilian and K'iche' (AGI, Escribania 356B). The strong connection between *indios ladinos* and Spanish colonial leadership profoundly influenced the production of wills in the *tinamit amaq'* of Xelajú.

Despite more Spanish legal influence, these testaments are also typically K'iche' in the preoccupations of the testators. The testaments from Totonicapán and Xelajú both reveal the need to express *pixab tzih* (words of council) even if the testator, as in the example of doña Anna Siqih, had nothing to bequeath to one of her children (AGCA, A1.20, 1500, 9977, fol. 6). Doña Anna's will confirms that a piece of property in Xepettak was inherited by her young daughter, Cathalina, from her mother, that she received it before her mother's death because of some necessity, and that she had sold the property to Nicolas Xuruq y Borena before her mother had made out her will. Not only did the land destined for her inheritance become the property of Nicolas Xuruq, but the house on that land "with the door facing east" and all of the portable goods that doña Anna had intended for Cathalina.

Why would the K'iche' place emphasis on a land sale in which the intended inheritance of one party was purchased by another—a transaction that had transpired before the production of the final testament? The will became a statement of intent to enact future obligations or to record past actions, a forum for council and advice, as well as a legal document that represented bequeathed inheritance. The town council thus ensured that the property in question would be respected as the property of Nicolas Xuruq and not as the inheritance of Cathalina Siqih. Both individual testators and the town council used wills for this purpose, representing both an individual and a collective voice (Jones 2009, 285). The preoccupation in some wills was to prevent future conflicts within the community. Testaments were preventative judiciary documents that bound family members to the words of a patriarch or matriarch after they had passed on to the next life. The K'iche', like other Mesoamerican groups, held, and still hold, a strong connection to an unseen world of ancestors who float in and out of their quotidian world.

Each corpus of wills has its own expressions that are particular to a scribal school in each community and became part of the formula in producing mundane notarial documentation. Formulaic expressions are used repeatedly in each document. A particular scribal style often defined the conventions that formulaic expressions would take, including not only phrases from Spanish colonial exemplars (expressions that are routinely part of the Spanish record-keeping tradition), but also indigenous expressions as part of a formulaic adaptation in testament writing.

Many of the formulaic expressions found sprinkled throughout the wills prepared by K'iche' scribes are illustrative of Mesoamerican concepts and ideologies, and highly metaphoric. For example, one formulaic phrase found in wills from San Miguel Totonicapán, *chi be q'ij chi be saq*, means "in the road of the day/sun, in the white road [the road of the dawn]." The phrase relates to the pan-Maya concept of the road that the sun travels daily across the sky, which is also symbolic of the road that the dead take to the flowery afterworld of happiness, and that the spirits of the ancestors use to return to advise the living. Francisco Ximénez (1929, 101) also spoke of the road of the dead as a white or flowery road. It was an expression used to convey the concepts of eternity and forever, comparing time to a journey. This phrase appears in Totonicapán's early titles, such as the *Title of Yax*, written in approximately 1560, and was used exclusively among the scribes of San Miguel Totonicapán up until the 1783 testament of Pedro Gomes Xiquitzal (Carmack and Mondloch 1989, 93 n32).[9] The phrase does not appear in notarial documents in other K'iche' *tinamit amaq'* but does appear in several eighteenth-century wills in the Kaqchiquel-dominated town of Sololá as *ti be q'ih ti be sak*.[10] It is illustrative of archaic formulae and forms of speech that remained significant after the Spanish conquest to the K'iche' in San Miguel and to the Kaqchiquel of Sololá who live along the road connecting these two towns.

Like other Mesoamerican peoples, the K'iche' used language as a vehicle to express multiple concepts. Mesoamerican languages use terms that have multiple meanings and can be used to evoke several significances within a single phrase. Each community seems to have had its own scribal style. Formulaic expressions within the wills of Rab'inal, Totonicapán, and Xelajú each reflect their unique scribal schools.

Wills in K'iche' communities evidence a concern for exactness and reverence in protecting the words of the dying—those who were soon to become part of the multitude of ancestors of the *tinamit amaq'*. Some testaments in areas with a closer connection to colonial leadership seemed to adapt Spanish conventions, such as a first-person narrative style; nevertheless, they retained indigenous concepts. Indigenous peoples used wills for more than merely preemptive extralegal documentation. They adopted the legalist tendencies of the Spaniards into their conceptualizations of jurisprudence, providing evidence of judicial adaptation and a conscientious legal strategy.

The Xelajú leadership used Spanish legalist formulae, but rather than give their traditions and practices away in K'iche'-language testaments, they kept their rites in secret. A visit in 1744 to Quetzaltenango (Xelajú) and the larger highland region by the archbishop of Guatemala and the Verapazes, Pedro Cortés y Larraz, provoked these comments:

> [I]t is true that there are fortune tellers, healers and enchanters, but you cannot convince [the K'iche'] with witnesses, nor even do some want to believe it, but that as proof the calendar that they use for their government was delivered to me.... This is the almanac that is used in all of the parishes of the Kaqchikel, the K'iche' and in the Mam, and it is the same, but written in their own languages...; and I am persuaded that it is the same that they had in their paganism.... (Cortés y Larraz 1958, 156–157).

Further reflections denounce the use of the calendar, and the day count associated with it, claiming it was responsible for the spiritual transgressions not only of the K'iche' community in Quetzaltenango but of all other ethnicities in the town (Spaniards, mestizos, mulattoes, and Africans).

K'iche' testaments provide evidence that leaders used divination to provide them with direction, including the last "living words" or "words of counsel" from their community's elders. The style, form, rhetoric, and formulae may differ depending upon which community produced the testament, but the use of K'iche' infused each will with cultural significance innately embedded in the language.

The Testament of Manuel Xpattaq'

Transcription

En 12 de Mayo del año 1766 a.o xculun ui pa rochoch Man.l Xpattaq' oh chinamital oh taol rech hun caib u testamento tzih casliquil tzih chupam u bi D.s Q'ahox.l, D.s caholax.l ruc D.s Espiritu S.to q'aloq'olah chuch S.ta M.a cacha cut u tzih uae Alcd.es co chic chupam u yabil are cut uae hun ha e oxib ual cual pu ui Miguel P.o Pablo u achi cut qui Dios xaui = E qui huhun quech chiquihunal are uae Migl. Hun Q'ahaual rech P.o xaui q'i hun q'ahaual rech uae qui chaq' Pablo caib chutiq' tiox rech ecseomo xaui ru hun niño = uae chi cut qui zolar xaui E qui e oxib pu vi hu nam hach chi sucul chuach Dios Maui huñ he chel rech = uae chi cut uleu

chaq'ih uleu ox rabah xaui q'i hutaq' rabah quech chiqui huhunal are uae
Mig.l hu rabah rech ca cha culbat Andres Alvar.o, uae P.o hu rabah rech
co chu culbat Antt.o Garcia – xaui uae Pablo xaui q'i hu rabah rech co chu
culbat Pablo Q'ohom cha q'a be pa cux quehe cut mix Q'a ban Q'a pattan
oh ui chinamital chi rech u ha chic squetaq' qui zolar xaui ruc squitaq'
culeu= fuera loq'om uleu, hun abir hach chi sucul – chuach D.s Mauihun
chuban ch'aoh chiquech ca cha u tzih Man.l quehe cut ca tzibax q'umal
o chinamital fran.co tzullen Nicolas Garnica Diego Raxcoco cuc caib
Q'anauinaq' Pablo Gon.s Man.l Gon.s quehe caq'a tzibah ui Juan Tauico
Man.l Tzullen

Translation

On the 12th of May of the year 1766, we the lineage leaders sat here in the
house of Manuel Xpattaq', we the hearers of one or two of his testament
words, living words. In the name of God the Father, God the Son, with
God the Holy Spirit and our sacred mother Saint Mary he says, well, his
word. This *alcalde* is here in his infirmity. There is, well, one house and
there are three of my children who own it, Miguel, Pedro, and Pablo. And
now, well, there are their gods also for every one of them and to be shared
between them. There is for this Miguel one Our Father and for Pedro simply theirs one Our Father. For this their younger brother Pablo two small
saints of the *Excelentisimo* also with one *Niño*. This other, well, their *solar*
is also theirs; the three own it equally. It is disseminated in truth before
God and no one can forcefully take it from them. This other, well, land,
dry land of three measures is theirs held between all of them. This Miguel,
one measure is for him. It is at the border marker of Andres Alvarado. This
Pedro, one measure is for him. It is at the border marker of Antonio Garcia.
Also, this Pablo, there is also a measure for him. It is at the border marker
of Pablo Q'ohom. So that it shall go into their hearts, thus it is. We shall
do work and our service, we of their lineage to disseminate their humble
goods, their *solar*, also with their humble goods of their land that would
have been purchased, a year ago, it was disseminated in truth before God.
Not one of them shall fight between them says the word of Manuel. Thus
it is. It is written by us, we the lineage leaders, Francisco Tzullen, Nicolas
Garnica, Diego Raxcaco with they the two witnesses Pablo Gonsales and
Manuel Gonsales. Hence we write it here Juan Tavico and Manuel Tzullen.

Notes

1. The Achí Maya today speak a newer Mayan language that they call Achí instead of the eastern K'iche' that they spoke in the sixteenth through the eighteenth centuries. The language has morphed over time and has become distinct to the department of Baja Verapaz, Guatemala.

2. This derives from "Memoria of Diego Macha" in Tulane's Latin American Library, William Gates Collection, *A Collection of Wills and Other Legal Papers in Quiché, 1752–1778.*

3. The colonial *chinamit*, defined as a ward or a moiety of the indigenous township, was a residual institution from precolonial K'iche' society. For more on the colonial *chinamit* see Hill 1989, 170–198.

4. My translation here derives from Christenson's online *K'iche'-English Dictionary* posted to the FAMSI website, http://www.famsi.org/mayawriting /dictionary/christenson/quidic_complete.pdf, entry *tzaqal tzih*, "interpreter, translator, lawyer." The term can be found in the testament of Sabastian Piox, November 8, 1762, and the testament of Domingo Leon Ernandez, February 11, 1768, in Tulane's Latin American Library, William Gates Collection, *A Collection of Wills and Other Legal Papers in Quiché, 1752–1778.*

5. For the assertion that these two corpora of wills are from Salamá see Sachse 2007, 14. For the assertion that Salamá was a Pipil town in the sixteenth to eighteenth centuries see Van Akkeren 2000. Hill (1998, 175) suggests that the K'iche' (Quiché) wills preserved in the Gates collection are from Quetzaltenango or environs. They are from Rab'inal. Not all the wills are short nor scant in their information, as Hill proclaims. Some are quite elaborate and lengthy, and bequeath a significant amount to the heirs, giving us the sense not all members of the K'iche' or Achi' community of Rab'inal were paupers. Some wills are shorter because the testator bequeathed fewer goods, revealing that there was a larger strata of society that made wills, not just the elite. Carmack (1973) correctly proveniences the town of origin of these wills.

6. Testament of Matteo Q'onibel, 1776, in Tulane's Latin American Library, William Gates Collection, *A Collection of Wills and Other Legal Papers in Quiché, 1752–1778.*

7. The use of the term *dialogocentric* comes from Burns (1991).

8. Testament of Sebastian Pio, November 8, 1762, in Tulane's Latin American Library, William Gates Collection, *A Collection of Wills and Other Legal Papers in Quiché, 1752–1778.*

9. See also AGCA, A1.20, 1784, 55535.

10. For example, see Jones 2009, 268–269; Testament of Juana Q'otuk, AGCA, A1.20, 38560, 4551, fols. 7–8; Testament of Juana Maqas, AGCA, A1.20, 28561, 4551, fol. 20; and Testament of Nicolas Mixixyacan, AGCA, A1.20, 38564, 4551, fols. 1–2.

References

Burns, Allan F. 1991. "The Language of Zuyua: Yucatec Maya Riddles and Their Interpretation." In *Past Present, and Future: Selected Papers on Latin American Indian Literatures*, edited by Mary H. Preuss, 35–40. Culver City, Calif.: Labyrinthos.

Carmack, Robert M. 1973. *Quichean Civilization: The Ethnohistoric, Ethnographic, and Archaeological Sources*. Berkeley: University of California Press.

Carmack, Robert M., and James L. Mondloch, trans. 1989. *El título de Yax y otros documentos Quichés de Totonicapán, Guatemala*. Mexico City: Universidad Nacional Autónoma de México.

Christenson, Alan J. n.d. *K'iche'-English Dictionary*. FAMSI. http://www.famsi .org/mayawriting/dictionary/christenson/quidic_complete.pdf

Cline, Sarah. 1998. "Fray Alonso de Molina's Model Testament and Antecedents to Indigenous Wills in Spanish America." In *Dead Giveaways: Indigenous Testaments of Colonial Mesoamerica and the Andes*, edited by Susan Kellogg and Matthew Restall, 13–33. Salt Lake City: University of Utah Press.

Cortés y Larraz, Pedro. 1958. *Descripción geográfico-moral de la diócesis de Goathemala*. Vol. 1. Biblioteca "Goathemala" de la Sociedad de Geografía e Historia de Guatemala, Volumen XX. Guatemala City: Sociedad de Geografía e Historia.

Hill, Robert M. 1989. "Social Organization by Decree in Colonial Highland Guatemala." *Ethnohistory* 36(2): 170–198.

———. "Land, Family, and Community in Highland Guatemala: Seventeenth Century Cakchiquel Maya Testaments." In *Dead Giveaways: Indigenous Testaments of Colonial Mesoamerica and the Andes*, edited by Susan Kellogg and Matthew Restall, 163–179. Salt Lake City: University of Utah Press.

Jones, Owen H. 2009. "Colonial K'iche' in Comparison with Yucatec Maya: Language, Adaptation, and Inter-Ethnic Contact." Ph.D. dissertation, University of California, Riverside.

López Marchán, Francisco. 2006. "Relación geográfica de la alcaldía mayor de Quetzaltenango, 1740 y 1743." In *Relaciones geográficas e históricas del siglo XVIII del reino de Guatemala*, vol. 1, *Relaciones geográficas e históricas de la década de 1740*, edited by Jorge Luján Muñoz, 113–163. Guatemala City: Universidad del Valle de Guatemala.

Preuss, Mary H., ed. 1991. *Past Present, and Future: Selected Papers on Latin American Indian Literatures*. Culver City, Calif.: Labyrinthos.

Restall, Matthew. 1997. *The Maya World: Yucatec Culture and Society, 1550–1850*. Stanford, Calif.: Stanford University Press.

Ricard, Robert. 1966. *The Spiritual Conquest of Mexico: An Essay on the Apostolate and the Evangelizing Methods of the Mendicant Orders in New Spain: 1523–72*. Translated by Lesley Byrd Simpson. Berkeley: University of California Press.

Sachse, Frauke. 2007. "Documentation of Colonial K'ichee' Dictionaries and Grammars." FAMSI Reports. http://www.famsi.org/reports/06009/06009 Sachse01.pdf

Tedlock, Barbara. 1982. *Time and the Highland Maya.* Albuquerque: University of New Mexico Press.

Terraciano, Kevin. 1998. "Native Expressions of Piety in Mixtec Testaments." In *Dead Giveaways: Indigenous Testaments of Colonial Mesoamerica and the Andes,* edited by Susan Kellogg and Matthew Restall, 115–140. Salt Lake City: University of Utah Press.

Van Akkeren, Ruud. 2000. *Place of the Lord's Daughter: Rab'inal, Its History, Its Dance-Drama.* Leiden, Netherlands: Leiden University, Research School, CNWS.

Ximénez, Fray Francisco. 1929. *Historia de la provincia de San Vicente de Chiapa y Guatemala de la orden de predicadores.* Vol. 1. Guatemala City: Tipografía Nacional.

PART 3

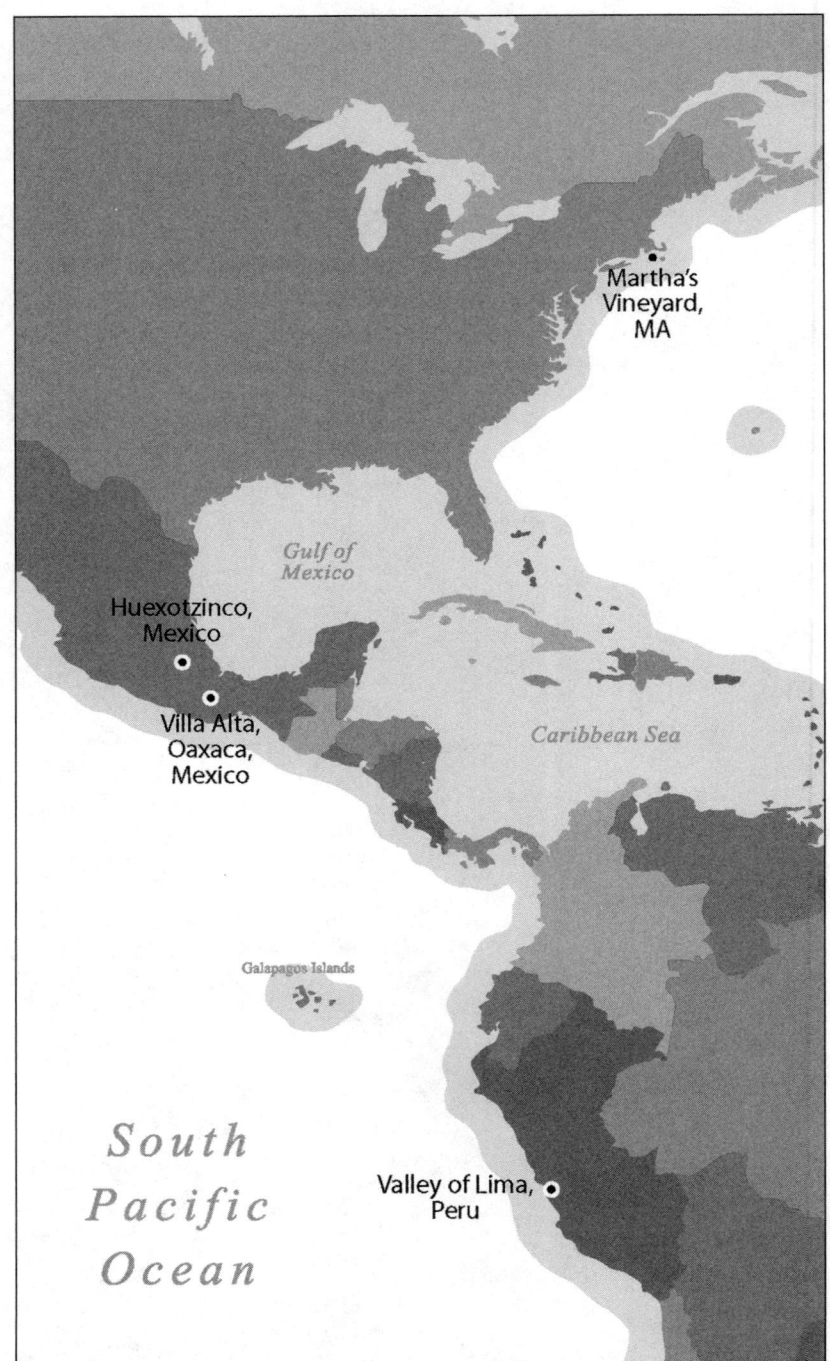

Martha's
Vineyard,
MA

Gulf of
Mexico

Huexotzinco,
Mexico

Villa Alta,
Oaxaca,
Mexico

Caribbean Sea

Galapagos Islands

South
Pacific
Ocean

Valley of Lima,
Peru

mapa
pin
scale

The Individual and Collective Nature of Death

The study of prehistoric peoples' concepts of death in the Americas has employed a wide range of sources, from religious plays (e.g., *Nahuatl Theater*, vol. 1, *Death and Life in Colonial Nahua Mexico* [Sell and Burkhart 2004]) to Inquisition cases focused on suicides ("Reading the [Dead] Body: Histories of Suicide in New Spain" [Tortorici 2011]). *Death and Conversion in the Andes: Lima and Cuzco, 1532–1670* (Ramos 2010) specifically uses wills to look at conversion, kinship, and colonial society. Ramos's work, alongside that of Eire (*From Madrid to Purgatory*, 1995), reminds scholars that at the time of death people are worried about much more than their afterlife. And it is in wills that familial ties, social networks, spirituality, and the care that testators have taken to provide for friends and family come to the forefront.

Kathleen Bragdon focuses on mortuary ritual in her chapter "Knowledge Production, Identity Formation, and Mortuary Ritual in Colonial Native New England: A View from Native-Language Documents." Her examination of testaments in southern New England suggests that new ideas and practices could exist alongside older customs and beliefs. Her chapter adds to the study of mortuary practice by incorporating wills into the burial and postburial rituals studied by anthropologists and archaeologists. By examining the context of mortuary practice, Bragdon highlights its role in defining native communities and their inhabitants in southern New England.

Lisa Sousa's work focuses on the Mixe of southern Mexico. Unlike other native groups who wrote testaments in their own languages or in Spanish, the Mixe opted to write testaments in what was a second language to them, Nahuatl. Sousa's corpus of documents runs from the sixteenth through eighteenth centuries and provides scholars the opportunity to see an indigenous language applied to represent foreign concepts and ideas, essentially placing Nahuatl in the same position as Spanish when applied to other native cultures.

Erika Hosselkus uses twenty-four testaments from Huexotzinco, in the Puebla-Tlaxcala Valley, to analyze the spiritual priorities of natives in the region. Despite being eclipsed in importance by Tlaxcala in the early 1560s, Huexotzinco went on to forge an active local Catholicism. Hosselkus's collection of wills is notable, in part, because indigenous notary Esteban de Coto recorded all twenty-four of them. Similar to the other wills discussed in this section, the Huexotzinco wills demonstrate an established social network that spread across the local community to include the resident friars as well. These networks proved essential for securing interment locations while alive and obtaining them after death. Ultimately, Hosselkus demonstrates that spiritual preparation for death among the Huexotzinco was prominent indeed.

Finally, in "'Networks of Trust': Debtors and Creditors in the Wills of Indian Nobles and Commoners in the Lima Valley, 1596–1607," Paul Charney examines how testaments reveal a world foreign to colonial-era Andeans, one of debtors and creditors that did not exist during the pre-Columbian period. This alien concept was not detested, however; instead, it was given its own cultural meaning. By creditors listing what was owed them and by whom, Andeans established "networks of trust." Although the networks were established during an individual's lifetime, the reciprocal nature of the exchange (a continuation from precontact times) was carried out even if the debtor or creditor in the relationship died.

While this part of the volume is the most spread out geographically, ranging from New England to the Andes, it highlights social networks that last wills and testaments helped to reinforce during periods of intense European colonialism. It should be noted that the resilience of the indigenous communities in each of these studies was not dependent on the introduction of the testaments; rather, the testaments have become an excellent tool for researchers in exploring and better understanding how Native Americans confronted and shaped European colonialism as it arrived on the shores of the Americas.

References

Eire, Carlos M. N. 1995. *From Madrid to Purgatory: The Art and Craft of Dying in Sixteenth-Century Spain*. Cambridge: Cambridge University Press.

Hanks, William F. 2010. *Converting Words: Maya in the Age of the Cross*. Berkeley: University of California Press.

Luján Muñoz, Jorge. 2011. *Ensayos de historia jurídica y del notariado en Guatemala*. Guatemala: Guatemala Academia de Geografía e Historia de Guatemala.

Ramos, Gabriela. 2010. *Death and Conversion in the Andes: Lima and Cuzco, 1532–1670*. Notre Dame, Ind.: University of Notre Dame Press.

Sell, Barry D., and Louise M. Burkhart. 2004. *Nahuatl Theater*, vol. 1, *Death and Life in Colonial Nahua Mexico*. Norman: University of Oklahoma Press.

Tortorici, Zeb. 2011. "Reading the (Dead) Body: Histories of Suicide in New Spain." In *Death and Dying in Colonial Spanish America*, edited by Martina Will de Chaparro and Miruna Achim, 53–77. Tucson: University of Arizona Press.

CHAPTER 8

Knowledge Production, Identity Formation, and Mortuary Ritual in Colonial Native New England

A View from Native-Language Documents

KATHLEEN J. BRAGDON

The Eastern Algonquian–speaking Massachusett and Wampanoag of southern New England became literate in their own languages in the mid-seventeenth century, and writings in those languages by native speakers were produced until the end of the eighteenth century. Native-language literacy was adopted in the context of the colonization of New England by English Puritan and Separatist settlers. Central to the adoption of literacy was the missionary effort initiated by John Eliot of Roxbury and Thomas Mayhew Jr. of Martha's Vineyard, and supported by the Society for the Propagation of the Gospel beginning in the 1640s (Goddard and Bragdon 1988; Bragdon 2009a). Among the manuscripts created and curated by native speakers and writers on Martha's Vineyard are three eighteenth-century wills, all associated with the Gay Head Christian Indian community. One will was written for Naomi Ommaush, the wife of native "preacher" Nehemiah Ommaush of Tucker's (Pasque) Island; another for Juday Chipnock, a *sachem's* (ruler's) daughter and heir; and the third for the Gay Head native preacher Peter Ohquanhut (Goddard and Bragdon 1988, docs. 7 and 48; Segel and Pierce 2003, 228).

While literacy and the acquisition of an English-influenced "legal consciousness" among the native people of southern New England has been interpreted principally using an acculturationist or a resistance framework (e.g., Wyss 2000), neither of these approaches is adequate for understanding the complex problems of cultural continuity, identity formation, and knowledge sharing in colonial native communities in New England that these native wills represent. For this purpose, ethnographic data on the adoption of Christianity and the associated transformation of ideas about personhood drawn from studies of chiefly societies[1] in other parts of the world, as well as evidence for earlier native mortuary customs in southern New England, should be consulted. These help to enrich our understanding of how and why will writing by native people in southern New England can be understood as part of a continuum of symbolic practices that functioned to maintain native communities during the colonial period. At the same time, the wills are exemplary of changes in the local language community of Gay Head, representing new language and legal models available to Christian Indians in the mid-seventeenth through eighteenth centuries. The native wills suggest that new ideas and practices could exist alongside older customs and beliefs.

A growing appreciation among social scientists for the complexity of identity formation and the construction of personhood is in part derived from ethnographic examples drawn from non-Western societies. In many of these, it has been argued that the person is socially constructed, emergent from a variable number of networks and social groups, which are themselves created through birth and marriage ties, and whose relationships are represented symbolically, particularly in the exchange of gifts. Marilyn Strathern's (1988, 13) study of Highland New Guinea society describes how people there "contain a generalized sociality within ... [which] persons are frequently constructed as the plural and composite site of the relationships that produce them" (see also Hess 2006).[2]

Although Strathern's conceptualization of personhood is sometimes characterized as idealized, there is support for her perspective in studies of funerary customs in other non-Western societies, both contemporary and archaeological (e.g., Brück 2006; Fowler 2005; Porter Poole 2010; Mosco 1992). Annette Weiner's research in Melanesia is in this genre and adds to Strathern's model the useful argument that gifts or prestations are better understood not as embodiments of reciprocal relationships, but as part of a multigenerational process of social reproduction (Weiner 1992). Through mortuary exchanges in particular, Weiner argues, people begin the process of replacing those who have died and, more important, replacing the social ties of which they were a part—ties that give structure to societies through time. This nuanced interpretation of personhood as not only social but generational causes some anthropologists to question the assumptions of Western social science that individuals can best be understood as "autonomous" persons (Comoroff and Comoroff 2010, 245).

Both the older models of mortuary exchange and those illuminated by feminist and reproductive perspectives highlight the centrality of mortuary rituals in structuring and reproducing social worlds. For anthropologists and many archaeologists, the burial itself and postburial rituals have attracted the most theoretical analysis. Less attention has been paid to practices preceding death, such as the writing of wills or other ways of passing on property or leadership responsibility. In fact, despite the revealing nature of wills for studies of personhood, few have been systematically analyzed for this purpose, and no analyses feature Native American wills.[3] This chapter attempts to incorporate Native American wills into the larger context of mortuary practices and their role in defining persons in native communities in southern New England.

Late Woodland Society in
Native Southern New England, AD 1000–1600

The native societies of coastal southern New England were chiefly societies with a subsistence base of arable land and a mixed woodland/wetland resource catchment area. Coastal groups relied on fish and other marine resources as well. At the time of the earliest European descriptions (ca. AD 1524) leadership was organized around elite hereditary *sachems* whose subjects owed tribute payments. Among other things, *sachems* allotted land, conducted diplomatic missions, and acted as military commanders. The native people of southern New England engaged in numerous kinds of property exchanges, including tribute payments, some of which resembled European-style barter and trade (what Roger Williams called "businesse" [1936, 159]); others were associated with life-cycle events such as marriage and death.

Social organization among southern New England's native people in the early contact period is poorly known. I have argued elsewhere (Bragdon 1999) for a lineage structure, based on ethnohistorical descriptions of sibling loyalty, descent of leadership, and kinship terminology. It is possible that native theory encompassed the notion of a superlineage system

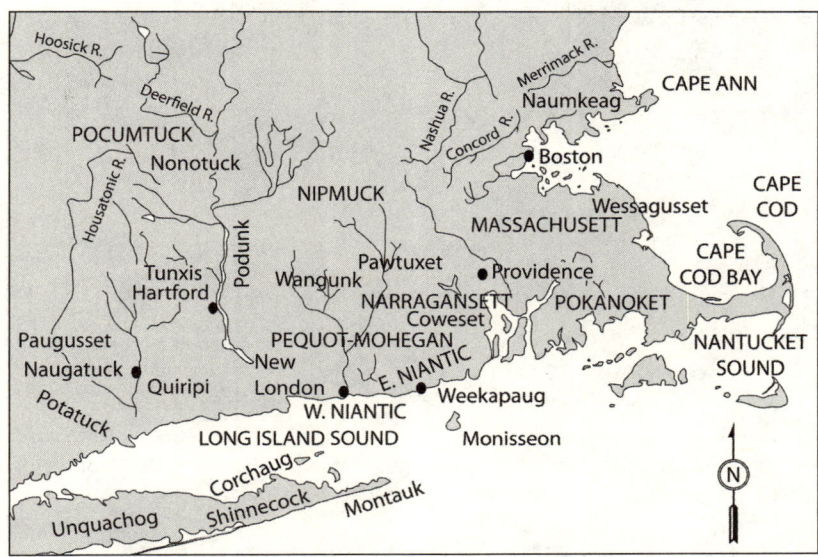

FIGURE 8.1 Tribes of southern New England. (Published with permission of the artist, Oliver Mueller-Heubach.)

or clan, as the English term *house* sometimes appears in contemporary translations of the term that also means "generation." In general, it appears that personal identity was closely bound to family and community membership, reinforced through marriage and gifts given then and perhaps for other life-cycle events, including mortuary rituals.

Southern New England Mortuary Customs in the Early Seventeenth Century

There is good evidence that wealth items and household goods were "given" or exchanged at death. Roger Williams, writing of the Narragansett, who were known to be particularly observant, described a mortuary ceremony led by a specialist known as Mockuttauce:

> One of chiefest esteeme, who winds up and buries the dead; commonly some wise, grave, and well-descended man hath that office. When they come to the Grave, they lay the dead by the Grave's mouth, and then all sit downe and lament; that I have seen teares run down the cheeks of stoutest Captaines, as well as little children in abundance; and after the dead is laid in Grave and sometimes (in

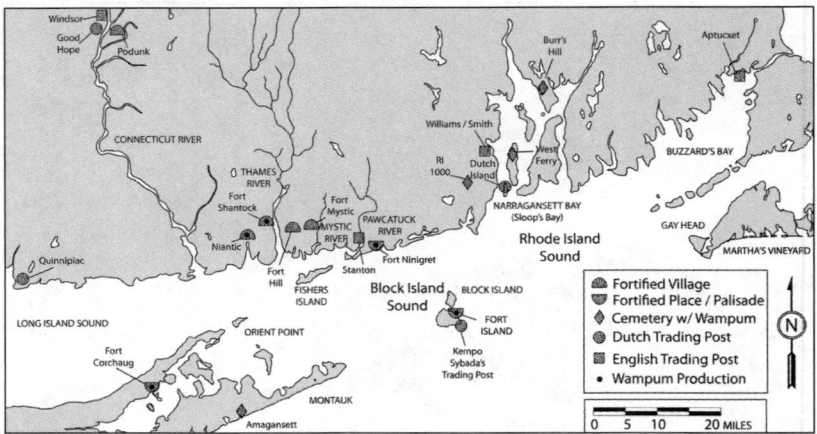

FIGURE 8.2. Location of contact-period cemeteries in southern New England. (Published with permission of the artist, Oliver Mueller-Heubach.)

some parts) some goods cast in with them, they have then a second lamentation, and upon the Grave is spread the Mat that the party died on, the Dish he eat in, and sometimes a faire Coat of skin hung upon the next tree to the Grave, which none will touch, but suffer it there to rot with the Dead. (Williams 1936, 161)

Although the early English descriptions, beginning in the 1620s, describe individual interments, there exists—particularly along the drainages of the Taunton River and near Narragansett Bay—a series of spectacular palisaded or otherwise enclosed native cemeteries that began to appear in the fifteenth century AD, and some were still in use in the early eighteenth century (Figures 8.2 and 8.3). Interments within these cemeteries were often accompanied by large numbers of grave goods, including wealth objects such as shell beads (wampum), trade goods of numerous kinds, and items of personal use such as pots, knives, points, pestles, and pipes (Gibson 1980; Robinson et al. 1985).

Archaeological investigations of several of these cemeteries revealed that grave goods found with the deceased were often linked to age, status, and gender (Zymroz 1997; Tuma 1985). Several accounts from the seventeenth century indicate that features such as color, directionality, and substance were part of the symbolism of mortuary ritual.

Wealth objects, tools, weapons, and containers of all materials were sometimes "killed" by being both broken and burned during the burial

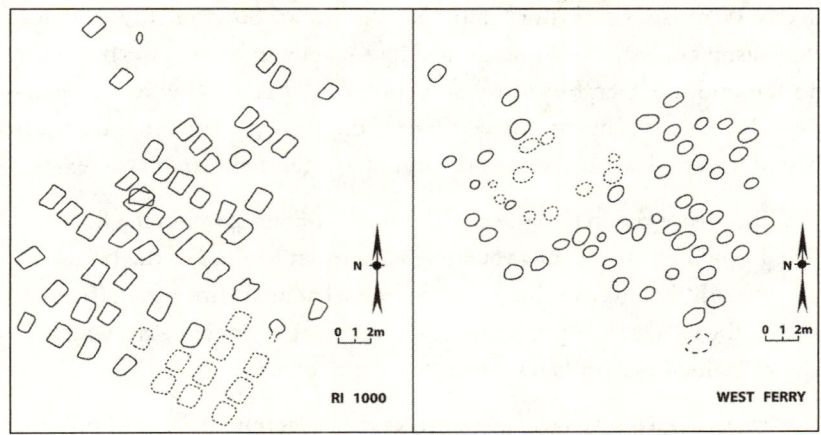

FIGURE 8.3. The West Ferry site. (Redrawn from Simmons 1970; published with permission from the artist, Oliver Mueller-Heubach.)

or after the body was interred. Europeans who began arriving in the late fifteenth century became the source of new goods that were incorporated into local economies and/or exchange networks in ways that did not replicate European customs of trade or reciprocity (Thomas 1991; Strathern 1988).

Intensified fur trade activities in the early seventeenth century and the adoption of shell beads as currency (wampum) between 1620 and 1650 likely accelerated economic trends toward capital accumulation among elites. This was accompanied by new symbolic ways of marking differences between groups, as well as increased hostility among them and, perhaps, increased ritual activity (Starna 1992; Axtell 1985; Rubertone 2001; Robinson et al. 1985; Simmons 1970), some of which may also have been reflected at these cemeteries. The richness of their grave furniture suggests that, as a result of this increased capital, some lineages gained power and influence at the expense of others. Among the most important trade goods often found in graves were objects of metal, particularly brass and iron kettles, which, while frequently buried whole, were sometimes broken up into pieces that were reshaped into points, knives, and, particularly, ornaments (Martin 1975).

Special symbolic efficacy seems to have been associated with these kettles, as well as metal and items of metal manufacture. For example, the Burr's Hill cemetery, in Warren, Rhode Island—located within what was likely Wampanoag territory and near the site of Sowams, the capital of Massasoit's domains—was excavated by amateur archaeologists beginning in the mid-nineteenth century and contains burials dating to the seventeenth century (Gibson 1980). One of the most prominent excavators, Charles Carr, described one of the multiple interments found there:

> They were laid in two rows, with the feet of one row and the heads of the other practically touching each other.... One of the bodies was a little lower in the line and somewhat apart from the others. At the head of this particular body was a large copper kettle, which contained two broken skulls.... (Gibson 1980, 13)

These cemeteries have been seen as the reflection of stepped-up ritual activity in the face of introduced epidemic disease (Starna 1992), a rapid growth of the signaling of wealth among elite families as coastal societies evolved toward centralized chiefdomships (Nassaney 1989), and a protective response to European interference with native grave sites (Axtell 1985). It is also likely, as Stephen Gudeman (1986) suggests, that relations with the supernatural were modeled on everyday social relations, and thus gift giving and the gifts of grave furniture were forms of exchange in which supernatural beings and ancestors were placed in a relationship of obligation to the living in the same way that those to whom gifts were given were expected to reciprocate. This view of grave goods also emphasizes the multigenerational nature of all mortuary exchanges. Recent reanalysis of the Titicut burial ground near modern Taunton, Massachusetts, for example, suggests that grouped interments at this place of power (Zymroz 1997; Simmons 1990) strengthened ties to supernatural forces for the good of the living community. Edward Winslow describes the goods so deployed:

> A great spacious house, wherein only some few (that are, as we may term them, priests) come. Thither, at certain known times, resort all their people, and offer almost all the riches they have to their gods, as kettles, skins, hatchets, beads, knives, etc., all which are cast by the priests into a great fire that they make in the midst of the house, and there consumed to ashes. (Winslow 1910, 345)

Although the excavations of contact-period cemeteries and individual graves seem to confirm the descriptions of contemporary observers that objects of wealth and symbolic importance were disposed of or given at death, much less is known about other exchanges that may have taken place among the living prior to, during, or following the obsequies. It is known, however, that mourning rituals took place over several weeks following death, particularly for high-status individuals and *sachems* (e.g., Williams 1988, 160). As gift giving and feasting were common features of all ritual activity among the native people of southern New England in the early seventeenth century, it is likely that further exchanges took place among native families after the death of a community member (Bragdon 1996, 229–230). It is the case that even after the adoption of Christianity among native people was widespread, graves of those who were clearly Christian Indians were still in many cases accompanied by grave goods (e.g., MHC 1980, 1991), suggesting that these ideas had long currency in the region. This suggests that although literacy and the adoption of Christianity had an impact on native people's ontology, long-standing mortuary practices survived. The writing of wills for and by native people in the eighteenth century also supports this argument.

The Native Wills

After the establishment of seasonally occupied European trading posts in the early seventeenth century and the first permanent settlements at Plymouth, Boston, and Hartford between 1620 and 1640, native communities were increasingly circumscribed, and also diminished by introduced epidemic diseases. Missionaries working among the survivors—especially among the Massachusett and Wampanoag of eastern Massachusetts, Cape Cod, and the islands of Martha's Vineyard and Nantucket—introduced Christianity, adding new dimensions to native personhood, while literacy and employment within the European economy made other ways of being Indian possible. Native communities on Martha's Vineyard had only limited autonomy at the beginning of the eighteenth century, and some surviving writings in their native language reflect their increasing incorporation into the English governance of the island, which required the production of certain official documents, such as census and marriage records, deeds or land transfers, and wills.

Native deeds and other documents suggest that principles of precontact kinship were retained well into the eighteenth century in many parts of native southern New England (Bragdon 2009a) and that *sachems* continued to allot land orally in front of witnesses well after the adoption of

Document no. 7. Clements Library, University of Michigan.

FIGURE 8.4. Will of Naomi Ommaush, 1749. (Published with permission from the Clements Library, University of Michigan.)

vernacular literacy allowed these transactions to be set down in writing (Little 1980; Goddard and Bragdon 1988; Bragdon 2009a). Documents in the native language, which began to appear on Martha's Vineyard and Nantucket in the mid- to late seventeenth century, seem at first to have taken the form of "recorded oral land transfers" in which the words of the *sachems*, their beneficiaries or heirs, and witnesses were recorded as direct quotes. A significant feature of these transfers is reference to "use rights," which were often carefully specified (Bragdon 2009b). Later documents confirming the transfer of land rights took a similar form, while including additional passages that appear to mimic English legal phraseology. However, the models for these documents, English deeds and wills, were never followed exactly. In fact, the few native wills that survive provide a unique window into the ways that native people defined themselves after the adoption of Christianity and literacy.

Thinking of Gay Head on Martha's Vineyard in the eighteenth century as a linguistic community allows us to make sense of the complexity of this Christian native place. In this case, the communicative economy of Gay Head was influenced by the newly introduced English legal terminology and practices, as well as Christian conversion and its associated texts. The new medium, a written text, is also evidence of the transformation of this communicative economy. In addition, the development of "legal consciousness" and the acquisition of a new communicative repertoire allowed native people to function adequately in two worlds. Natives drew on the literate tradition in English and their own indigenous practices to create a polyphonic discourse.

Among the surviving vernacular writings by speakers of the native languages of southern New England, only two wills are known. A half dozen other wills, written in English on behalf of island natives, also survive. The most interesting will was written in the Massachusett or Wampanoag language for Naomi Ommaush, wife of a native preacher, by Zachary Hossueit, the Gay Head justice of the peace, Congregationalist minister, and descendant of a *sachem* line (Figure 8.4).

At first glance this will appears to indicate both a profoundly Christian view of the afterlife and an emerging "legal consciousness" reflecting an effort on the part of native people who adopted both the style and concept of record keeping to protect land and moveable property from loss to the encroaching English by virtue of their command of literacy and English rules of inheritance. The writing of wills, moreover, appears to reflect a growing sense of individuality: the "autonomous person" of Western understanding. In particular, the first passage, quoting from the Bible, appears to be modeled after English wills of the same period. A more thorough reading, however, tells a slightly different story, one that makes these new native written forms consistent with earlier beliefs and practices—those that resemble more closely the "communal" concept of the person reflected in other aspects of native ontology.

This will is atypical in many respects. First, although her husband, Nehemiah Ommaush, was still alive at the time this will was written, he is not mentioned (Segal and Pierce 2003). Instead, Naomi leaves her principal belongings to two categories of people: the minister Hossueit and his wife, and several other relatives, none of whom appear to have been siblings (Bragdon 1998, 2009a).

Second, the most important of the bequeathed objects are an object made of pewter or other metal and seventeen pewter spoons. The spoons appear to have been heirlooms, perhaps given to a member of Naomi's family by the Society for the Propagation of the Gospel as an award or payment for service as a minister or teacher (Bragdon 2009a). Aside from the status they represent and conferred, these objects may have been significant because they were metal and thus durable. As described in the native language, these spoons, although of English origin, are given animate gender endings, just as their indigenous counterparts, made of bone or wood, would have been. Anthropologist Irving Hallowell (1960) argues that this potential for animacy produces a profoundly different understanding of the character of objects and their potential social roles.[4] Naomi's bequests of durable, animate, possibly heirloom metal objects may be compared to the distribution of metal grave goods found in contact-period cemeteries. In both cases, the gifts were multigenerational and "reproductive" in the sense that Weiner's (1992) work implies.

The will written for Naomi Ommaush can also be compared to one written in English on behalf of the native woman Juday Chipnock in March 1709–1710:

The last will and testament of Juday an Indian woman dafter of Chipnock one of the Indian Sachims of the north shore near a p_ called Manamsha on Martha's Vineyard the wife of an Indian called Caperonend. First, I do give unto my dafter Sarah one Iron Kittle that my mother left me, nextly, I do give unto her my sd dafter a piece of land that was given me by my father, at a place called the old pond field; nextly I do order one iron pot unto such person as shall provide a coffin for me to be buried in; and lastly I do give all my sachem right unto sd dafter and my husband Caperonend equally to be divided between them & also I do appoint my husband to be executor to this my last will and testament & in witness thereof I have hereunto subscribe with my hand and put to my seal this twenty-and sixth day of November 1707. Witnessed by Ephriam (Nico)demus and Japhet Hannit, Thomas Mayhew Justice of the Peace, proved 1709/10. (Goddard and Bragdon 1988, doc. 48 [D1, 30])

This will, which shares features with earlier "recorded oral land transfers," is, along with Naomi Ommaush's, what might be termed "traditional" in intent. Among other features, it mentions the bequest of a metal kettle. In addition, it marks the intergenerational relationship between Juday Chipnock, her mother, and her daughter, Sarah.

Another native will, written in Wampanoag for the Gay Head preacher Peter Ohquanhut in 1735, is different.

Ohquanhut left his house, evidently divided into three chambers, to his wife and daughter, along with cattle, sheep, and other livestock. Household items are not enumerated but are to be "used as I have used them." The need to bequeath a fixed-in-place English-style house, which unlike a wigwam represented a new kind of residential permanency, may account for the will's content. Here Ohquanhut employs what appears to be a traditional concept of "use ownership" reflected in earlier recorded oral land transfers described above (see also Little 1980). On the other hand, this will may also reflect a deeply transforming Christianity, which eschewed material links between generations expressed through grave goods. Some other native Christian communities of the period had also adopted this perspective; the Waldo Farm native historic cemetery near Taunton, for example, located near an English Quaker community, contained multiple burials with no grave goods at all.

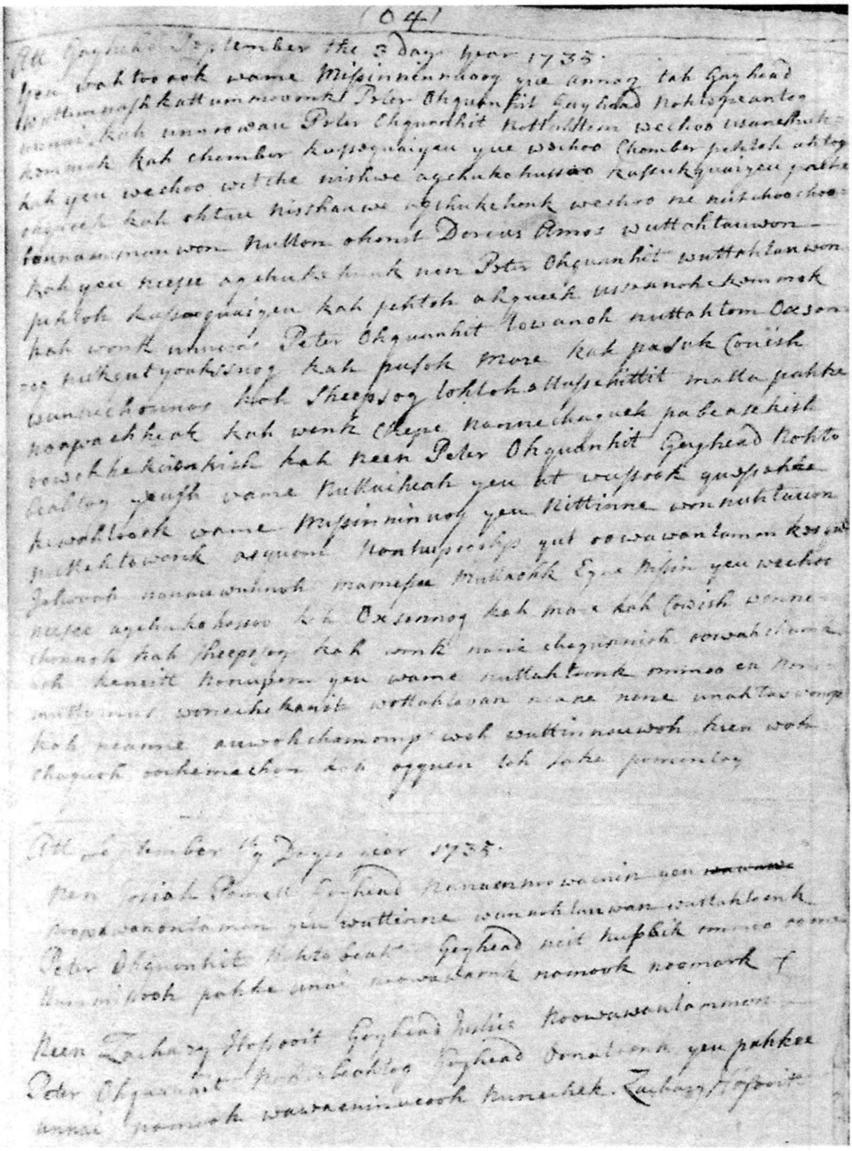

FIG. 8.5 Will of Peter Ohquanhut, 1735. (Published with permission from the Dukes County, Massachusetts, Registry of Deeds.)

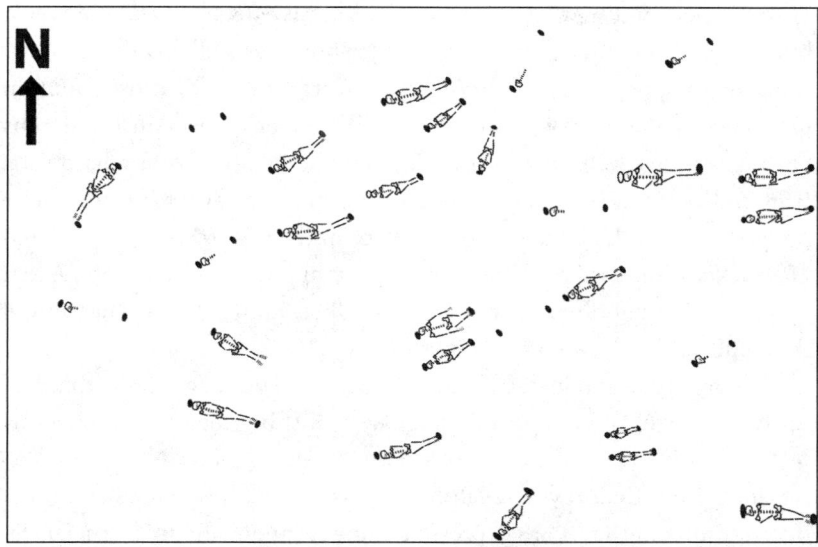

FIGURE 8.6. The Waldo Farm site. (Redrawn from Hodge 2005; published with permission from the artist, Oliver Mueller-Heubach.)

Conclusions: Mortuary Rites in Cross-Cultural Perspective

In recently described chiefly societies such as those that persist in Melanesia, individuals are defined in part by their ancestral links, social ties, and community membership. This understanding of personhood makes the processes of mortuary rituals significantly more important as a context for understanding both individuals and the groups they belong to. For example, central to Strathern's (1988) and Weiner's (1992) analyses is the detailed treatment of mortuary exchanges in chiefly level societies, which frequently foreground female roles and activities.

Significant wealth objects, originally given in exchange, may be reclaimed years or generations later, and in this way the replacement process gives an exchange system a dimension of reproductive potential. From this perspective, death, rather than marriage, operates as a regulatory force, allowing for the replacement of wealth and the long-term regeneration of social relations.

Another central feature of funerary prestations is the frequently durable nature of these gifts (Weiner 1992) and the fact that such objects were also often seen as animate (that is, having the potential for animate action). Significant attention has been paid to shell objects and ornaments at Burr's

Hill, RI 1000, and Crescent Beach (e.g., Robinson et al.; McBride 1990), but less has been said about metal objects; however, Dillaplane (1980, 79) notes that copper, iron, and brass kettles were among the most common grave offerings at Burr's Hill, along with other metal objects such as spoons (Beaudry 1980), bells, medallions, firearm parts, and furniture hardware. Iron and brass objects also appear in the probate inventories of native people living in the Natick praying towns and on Martha's Vineyard and Nantucket (Goddard and Bragdon 1988). It appears likely, therefore, that bequests of metal objects were symbolically significant as a reflection of durability of family or community ties.

It is argued here that data from archaeological investigations, ethnohistorical research, and indigenous languages must be viewed over a lengthy period to understand the nature of these transformations. Native people's writings about their own eschatological beliefs and their views about the distribution of property as expressed in the form of wills are a crucial element of this examination. Among the new social elements of personhood revealed in these wills are the importance of rank in Christian communities, the role of heirlooms in symbolizing social ties through time, and the importance of literacy in evolving native societies. Each of these, in turn, is relevant to an understanding of personhood in colonized native societies in southern New England.

In sum, these wills, all modeled after English wills and written by and for members of the Christian Indian community at Gay Head, are testimony to the changing nature of both eschatology and social order there. Ministers and preachers had replaced those of hereditary rank as prominent leaders. Additionally, people secured their descendants' futures not through oral transfers made in front of witnesses, but through a written and curated document. But both feature heirloom objects, including durable metal goods to be "passed" down to respected members of the community and to relatives, and all link past and future generations together through objects. Thus a variety of practices and beliefs could be accommodated in the new order. Some wills continued to reflect the "communal" nature of native personhood, still connected to and defined by communities. These bequests also define the legatees in the same way. Native wills, although comparatively few in number, testify to the complexity of Christian Indian communities, but not to their demise.

Will of Naomi Ommaush
(in the hand of Zachary Hossueit)

Transcription

(Goddard and Bragdon 1988, 52–55
[Clements Library, University of Michigan])
Eyeu waeht8ok wame peantamwae ummissininumoh God nen
[[wam]] naomai ommaush Gayhead Eyeu noowahtom passummesuh
numonchem en wame umayut ohke ne matta pish wonk waj woh
quske & yeuyeu nuttaonnous tohneit woh nunuppun yeu kattumm8
woh nuttohtom ohquontamunat nummatcheusseonkash nashpe
8shquehonk nussonchumom Lord Jesus Christ & wonk n8wahtom
togkonnogque nohhog nuppuk & mache pussohquat pish wonk
ommohke maiish ne kasukoh [[.]] & wonk nukketeahogon[[oh]] pish
wonk pettuttauonnuk ne massag ommohkeyae mohtompan nonche
[[..]] nogkushkauonat Lord ut mamahchekesukqut. & neit pish
numicheme wetomomun Lord & nen naomai omaush yeu nissin ut
anuhquabit God yeu noowekontamwe [[a.]] annishkottummauwonnau
nuttohtoonk nuttauwamaog nishnoh pasuk pish wunneemmunnumun
mache nuppon ne asque auwohteau Zachary hossueit nohtompeontog
nuttanniskottumau pasuk ohquoh samp8nnakuss8 mussiken [[&w]] &
wonk punnueter wunnokash nukquttuh tashshunash & wonk punnueter
kunnommaog piogqussueog wonnoh Enattuh [[& Eyeu]] &-- wonk
ummuttummussoh butthiah hossueit nuttannuskottumau pasuk
nuttogk8 uttauyeu wamunnog nagum pish uppepenamun neit mache
nuppon & nissum yeu ohquombai matta pish howan wamequttamm8
upputch8wunnonat wutche nish anniskottummauwake wunah nam8k
wawaeinueooh [[nu..rk n …l]] n8mark . & . wonk nooseal naomai
omaush her X mark . seal S
wawaeninueog
Jude hossueit his mark X
buthiah accomus her mark X att July the .8 year. 1749
      att . July . 8 year.1749 . ne noquat wonk nissim nuttanniskottummau
[[nema]] nuttauwatueonk Calab Elisha pasuk punnakit
      att . July the 8 year. 1749 ne noquat nissim nuttanniskottumau
nuttauwatueonk Jeanohumun pasuk ohquohkoome kaskepessue & wonk
pasuk nuttogkoo

att July . the 8 year. 1749 ne noquat nuttaniskottumau nuttauwam
Henry amos—neit woh ahtau ne numonag ne masquag pish 8tohtauwun
pasuk penchens neeanoo wamussit

att July .the. 8 year. 1749 ne noquat nuttaniskottumau nuttauwaeh
Ezther henry pasuk nuttogkoo oneyeu Conneko nuttattaamonah
oohkassuk & pish wuttohtauwun

att July . the .8 year. 1749 nekasukoh nuttanniskottumau nuttauwam
marcy noah pasuk patukkoot

& nish ongatoganash kooche ahtau monmachaiyeuash nish
pish nuttauwonkonnash toh sohke pomontam . & neit matta wame
auwhoteaon [[.]] & nish pish kutchachabunnumaatinash neit mache
nuppon Yeu wame unnai nuttanniskottumauwaonkan8 nuttauwamoog
n8wekontamweussen yeu nohquah ut anuhquabit nu[m.]nt8m Lord
Jesus Christ
[na] mook noomark &wonk nooseal naomai omaush her X mark
and seal S
[--w]aeninueog
[--]hossueit his mark X
[---i.h] accomus her mark X

Translation

Know ye all Christian people of God. I Naomai Ommaush of Gayhead
know that very soon I go the way of all the earth, whence I shall not be able
to return again. And now I hope, if I should die this year, I would have my
sins forgiven by the blood of my Lord, the Lord Jesus Christ. And again
I know that although my body dies and has rotted (?) it shall rise again
on the last day, and also my soul shall also enter where he is, on the great
day of resurrection, to go to meet the Lord in heaven. And then we shall
dwell with the lord forever. And I Naomai Ommaush say this before God:
I willingly bequeath this property of mine to my kin. Each shall take, after
I die, what I have not yet used. To Zachary Hossueit, the minister, I bequeath one [ohquoh?]—it is straight looking and large—and also six pewter dishes, and also seventeen pewter spoons. And also to his wife Butthiah
Hossueit I bequeath one of my dresses—whichever one she pleases she
shall choose when I have died. And I say at this time, no one shall have
the authority to defraud them of these things I bequeath to them. And,
witnesses, see my mark and also my seal.

July 8, 1749, on that date I also say I bequeath to my kinsman Calab Elisha one blanket.

On July 8, 1749, on that date I say that I bequeath to my kinswoman Jeanohumun one [ohquohkoome kaskepessue] and also one of my dresses.

On July 8, 1749 on that date also I bequeath to my kinsman Henry Amos some of that cloth of mine that I may then have; of the red he shall have one penchens because of how kind he has been to me.

On July 8, 1749 on that date I bequeath to my kinswoman Ezther Henry one dress of mine of blue (?) calico; I bought it of her late mother, and she shall have it.

On July 8, 1749, on that day I bequeath to my kinswoman March Noah one petticoat.

And those other things more that I have of household goods, those I shall use as long as I live. Then if I do not use them all, you shall divide them when I have died. My bequeathing of all this to my kin was done; I willingly do it on this date before my God the Lord Jesus Christ.... (Goddard and Bragdon 1988, 55)

Notes

1. Anthropologists have traditionally categorized societies according to a hierarchical scheme of social organization. Chiefly societies are characterized by centralized rulership, often hereditary, with distinctions of rank and privilege. These societies are thought to be transitional between band and state societies.
2. Strathern (1988, 13) uses the phrase "dividuate person," in contrast to the Western notion of "individual."
3. One of the few exceptions, an examination of early-seventeenth-century English wills by Dan Beaver (1992), suggests that even in early modern English contexts, the wider community was always recognized in the form of gifts to "charity," frequently dispersed at death.
4. Animacy was certainly a feature of Algonquian cosmology, as described both in ethnohistoric literature and inscribed in Algonquian grammatical structure as a category of gender. Grammatical gender is assigned to a variety of beings and features of the natural world; humans and animals were animate, along with items of personal use such as pipes, some trees and plants, and often stone. Speakers of Algonquian languages thus express a "culturally constituted cognitive set," recognizing "potentialities for animation in certain classes of objects under certain circumstances." Writing about the Ojibwa, Irving Hallowell (1938) recalled, "Since stones are grammatically animate, I once asked an old man: Are *all* the stones we see about us here alive? He reflected a long while and then replied, No! But *some* are."

References

Axtell, James. 1985. *The Invasion Within: The Contest of Cultures in Colonial North America*. New York: Oxford University Press.

Beaudry, Mary C. 1980. "Spoons from the Burr's Hill Collection." In *Burr's Hill: A 17th Century Wampanoag Burial Ground in Warren, Rhode Island*, edited by Susan Gibson, 72–78. Providence, R.I.: Haffenreffer Museum of Anthropology, Brown University.

Beaver, Dan. 1992. "Sown in Dishonour, Raised in Glory: Death, Ritual and Social Organization in Northern Gloucestershire, 1590–1690." *Social History* 17.

Bragdon, Kathleen J. 1991. "Native Christianity in Eighteenth-Century Massachusetts: Ritual as Cultural Reaffirmation." In *New Dimensions in Ethnohistory: Papers of the Second Laurier Conference on Ethnohistory and Ethnology*, edited by Barry Gough and Laird Christie, 118–126. Canadian Ethnology Service Mercury Series Paper 120. Quebec: Canadian Museum of Civilization.

———. 1993. "The Material Culture of the Christian Indians of New England, 1650–1775." In *Documentary Archaeology in the New World*, edited by Mary C. Beaudry, 126–131. New York: Cambridge University Press.

———. 1996. *Native People of Southern New England, 1500–1650*. Norman: University of Oklahoma Press.

———. 1999. "Ethnohistory, Historical Archaeology, and the Rise of Social Complexity: Case Studies in Native New England." In *Old and New Worlds*, edited by Geoff Egan and Ronald L. Michael, 84–96. Oxford, U.K.: Oxbow Books.

———. 2009a. *Native People of Southern New England, 1650–1775*. Norman: University of Oklahoma Press.

———. 2009b. "The Pragmatics of Language Learning: Graphic Pluralism on Martha's Vineyard, 1660–1720." *Ethnohistory* 57(1): 35–50.

Brenner, Elise. 1986. "Archaeological Investigations at a Massachusetts Praying Town." *Bulletin of the Massachusetts Archaeological Society* 47(2): 69–78.

———. 1988. "Sociopolitical Implications of Mortuary Ritual Remains in Seventeenth-Century Native Southern New England." In *The Recovery of Meaning*, edited by Mark P. Leone and Parker B. Potter, Jr., 147–181. Washington, D.C.: Smithsonian Institution Press.

Brück, Joanna. 2006. "Death, Exchange, and Reproduction in the British Bronze Age Europe." *European Journal of Archaeology* 9(1): 73–101.

Comaroff, John L., and Jean Comaroff. 2010. "On Personhood: An Anthropological Perspective from Africa." In *Contemporary Archaeology in Theory: The New Pragmatism*, edited by Robert Preucel and Stephen A. Mrozowski, 244–255. 2nd ed. Oxford, U.K.: Wiley-Blackwell.

Dillaplane, Timothy L. 1980. "European Trade Kettles." In *Burr's Hill: A 17th Century Wampanoag Burial Ground in Warren, Rhode Island*, edited by Susan Gibson, 79–84. Providence, R.I.: Haffenreffer Museum of Anthropology, Brown University.

Fowler, Chris. 2005. "Identity Politics: Personhood, Kinship, Gender and Power in Neolithic and Early Bronze Age Britain." In *The Archaeology of Plural and Changing Identities: Beyond Identification*, edited by Elinor Casella and Chris Fowler, 2:109–134. New York: Kluwer Academic/Plenum.

Gibson, Susan. 1980. *Burr's Hill: A 17th Century Wampanoag Burial Ground in Warren, Rhode Island*. Providence, R.I.: Haffenreffer Museum of Anthropology, Brown University.

Goddard, Ives, and Kathleen Bragdon. 1988. *Native Writings in Massachusett*. Memoir Series no. 185. 2 vols. Philadelphia: American Philosophical Society.

Gudeman, Stephen. 1986. *Economics as Culture: Models and Metaphors of Livelihood*. London: Routledge.

Hallowell, Irving. 1960. "Ojibwa Ontology, Behavior and World View." Reprinted in *Teachings from the American Earth*, edited by Dennis Tedlock and Barbara Tedlock, 141–179. New York: Liveright.

Hess, Sabine. 2006. "Strathern's Melanesian 'Dividual' and the Christian 'Individual': A Perspective from Vanua Lava, Vanuatu." *Oceania* 76(3): 285–296.

Hodge, Christina J. 2005. "Faith and Practice at an Early-Eighteenth Century Wampanoag Burial Ground: The Waldo Farm Site in Dartmouth, Massachusetts." *Historical Archaeology* 39(4): 73–94.

LaFantasie, Glenn. 1988. *The Correspondence of Roger Williams*, vol. 1, *1629–1653*, vol. 2, *1654–1682*. Hanover, N.H.: University Press of New England.

Little, Elizabeth. 1980. "Three Kinds of Indian Land Deeds at Nantucket, Massachusetts." In *Papers of the Eleventh Algonquian Conference*, edited by William Cowan, 61–70. Ottawa: Carleton University Press.

Martin, Calvin. 1975. "Four Lives of a Micmac Copper Pot." *Ethnohistory* 22(2): 111–133.

Massachusetts Historical Commission (MHC). 1980. "Miacomet Indian Village and Burial Ground, Nantucket." Manuscript, NAN-HA-2, MHC, Boston.

———. 1988. "Santuit Pond Road Cemetery, Mashpee." Manuscript, MAS-HA-4, MHC, Boston.

———. 1995a. "Paskamanset River Burial, Dartmouth." Manuscript, MAS-DA-04, MHC, Boston.

———. 1995b. "Waldo Farm Cemetery, Dartmouth." Manuscript, MAS-DA-05, MHC, Boston.

———. 1999. "Mizzenmast Road Mashpee Indian Cemetery." Manuscript, MAS-HA-20, MHC, Boston.

McBride, Kevin. 1990. "The Historical Archaeology of the Mashantucket Pequots, 1637–1975. In *The Pequots in Southern New England: The Fall and Rise of an Ancient American Nation*, edited by L. M. Hauptman and J. D. Wherry, pp. 96–116. University of Oklahoma Press.

———. 1994. "The Source and Mother of the Fur Trade: Native-Dutch Relations in Eastern New Netherland." In *Enduring Traditions: Native Peoples of New England*, edited by Laurie Weinstein, 31–51. Westport and London: Bergin and Garvey.

Mosco, P. 1992. "Motherless Sons: 'Divine Kings' and 'Partible Persons' in Mela-
    nesia and Polynesia." *Man* (n.s.) 27: 697–717.
Nassaney, Michael S. 1989. "An Epistemological Enquiry into Some Archaeologi-
    cal and Historical Interpretations of Seventeenth Century Native American-
    European Relations." In *Archaeological Approaches to Cultural Identity*, edited
    by Stephen J. Shennan, 76–93. Boston: Unwin Hyman.
Porter Poole, Fitz John. 2010. "Symbols of Substance: Bimin-Kuskusmin Models
    of Procreation, Death, and Personhood." *Mankind* (online) 14(3): 191–216.
Robinson, Paul, Marc Kelley, and Patricia E. Rubertone. 1985. "Preliminary
    Biocultural Interpretations from a Seventeenth Century Narragansett Indian
    Cemetery in Rhode Island." In *Cultures in Contact: The European Impact on
    Native Cultural Institutions in Eastern North America, A.D. 1000–1800*, edited
    by William Fitzhugh, 107–130. Washington, D.C.: Anthropology Society of
    Washington and Smithsonian Institution Press.
Rubertone, Patricia E. 2001. *Grave Undertakings: An Archaeology of Roger Williams
    and the Narragansett Indians*. Washington, D.C.: Smithsonian Institution Press.
Salisbury, Neal. 1982. *Manitou and Providence: Indians, Europeans, and the Making
    of New England, 1500–1643*. New York: Oxford University Press.
Salwen, Bert. 1978. "Indians of Southern New England and Long Island: Early
    Period." In *Handbook of North American Indians*, vol. 15, *Northeast*, edited by
    Bruce G. Trigger, 160–176. Washington, D.C.: Smithsonian Institution.
Segel, Jerome, and R. Andrew Pierce. 2003. *The Wampanoag Genealogical History
    of Martha's Vineyard, Massachusetts*, vol. 1, *Island History, People, and Places
    from Sustained Contact through the Early Federal Era*. Baltimore: Genealogical
    Publishing Company.
Silliman, Stephen. 2001. "Agency, Practical Politics, and the Archaeology of Cul-
    ture Contact." *Journal of Social Archaeology* 1(2): 190–209.
———. 2009. "Change and Continuity, Practice and Memory: Native American
    Persistence in Colonial New England." *American Antiquity* 74(2): 211–230.
Silverman, David. 2005. *Faith and Boundaries: Colonists, Christianity, and Commu-
    nity among the Wampanoag Indians of Martha's Vineyard, 1600–1871*. Cam-
    bridge: Cambridge University Press.
Simmons, William S. 1970. *Cautantowwit's House: An Indian Burial Ground on the
    Island of Conanicut in Narragansett Bay*. Providence, R.I.: Brown University
    Press.
———. 1986. *Spirit of the New England Tribes: Indian History and Folklore,
    1620–1984*. Lebanon, N.H.: University Press of New England.
———. 1990. "Of Large Things Remembered: Southern New England Indian
    Legends of Colonial Encounters." In *The Art and Mystery of Historical Ar-
    chaeology: Essays in Honor of James Fanto Deetz*, edited by Mary Beaudry and
    Anne Yentsch, 317–329. Boca Raton, Fla.: CRC Press.
St. George, Robert Blair. 2000. Introduction to *Possible Pasts: Becoming Colonial
    in Early America*, edited by Robert Blair St. George, 1–29. Ithaca, N.Y.: Cornell
    University Press.

Starna, William A. 1992. "The Biological Encounter: Disease and the Ideological Domain." *American Indian Quarterly* 16(4): 511–519.

Strathern, Marilyn. 1988. *The Gender of the Gift: Problems with Women and Problems with Society in Melanesia.* Berkeley: University of California Press.

Thomas, Nicholas. 1991. *Entangled Objects: Exchange, Material Culture, and Colonialism in the Pacific.* Cambridge, Mass.: Harvard University Press.

Trigg, Heather B. 2003. "The Ties That Bind: Economic and Social Interactions in Early-Colonial New Mexico, A.D. 1598–1680." *Historical Archaeology* 37(2): 65–84.

Trigger, Bruce G. 1985. *Natives and Newcomers: Canada's "Heroic Age" Reconsidered.* Montreal: McGill-Queen's University Press.

Tuma, Stuart John, Jr. 1985. "Contact Period (1500–1675) Burials in Southeastern New England." Master's thesis, Department of History and Historical Archaeology, University of Massachusetts at Amherst.

Turnbaugh, William A. 1984. *The Material Culture of RI 1000, a Mid-17th Century Burial Site in North Kingstown.* Kingstown: University of Rhode Island.

———. 1993. "Assessing the Significance of European Goods in a Seventeenth-Century Narragansett Society." *In Ethnohistory and Archaeology: Approaches to Postcontact Change in the Americas,* edited by J. D. Rogers and S. M. Wilson, 133–160. New York: Plenum.

Weiner, Annette. 1992. *Inalienable Possessions: The Paradox of Keeping While Giving.* Berkeley: University of California Press.

Williams, Roger. 1936. *A Key into the Language of America.* Providence: Rhode Island Tercentennial Committee.

Willoughby, Charles C. 1935. *Antiquities of the New England Indians.* Cambridge, Mass.: Peabody Museum of Anthropology, Harvard University.

Winslow, Edward. 1910. "Relation." Reprinted in *Chronicles of the Pilgrim Fathers,* edited by Ernest Rhys, 267–356. London: J. M. Dent and Sons.

Wyss, Hilary. 2000. *Writing Indians: Literacy, Christianity, and Native Community in Early America.* Amherst: University of Massachusetts Press.

Zymroz, Desiree. 1997. "The Titicut Site Burials: An Alternative Perspective on Native Actions and Experiences During the Contact Period." Master's thesis, Department of Anthropology and Archaeology, University of Massachusetts, Boston.

CHAPTER 9

The Testament of
Gerónimo Flores, 1660

A Nahuatl-Language Writing
from a Mixe Community in Colonial Mexico

LISA SOUSA

In 1669, fifteen Mixe men and women from Santa María Asunción Toton-tepec appeared before Spanish officials to file a civil suit against the people of Amatepec over land. Although the community of Amatepec possessed a royal decree granting them the contested land, the people of Totontepec had an impressive arsenal of native-language documents of their own to support their claims. Significantly, their records were written in Nahuatl. Among the records was the lengthy will of Gerónimo Flores, which was made in the presence of community officials as he lay on his deathbed in 1660 (AJVA, Civil 1:7, 1630–1675).[1]

The testament of Gerónimo Flores is one of approximately eighty Nahuatl-language documents from Villa Alta that are now preserved in the collection of colonial civil and criminal records at the judicial archive in Oaxaca City. The Villa Alta jurisdiction included Zapotec, Mixe, and Chinantec communities, as well as the Nahua settlement of Analco, a barrio of Villa Alta proper.[2] The documents date from 1572 to 1774, and the majority of the extant records were produced in the seventeenth century. The 1572 testament of Domingo Atocmatz is the earliest dated writing (AJVA, Civil 1:11, 1672).[3] The three latest Nahuatl documents are translations of royal decrees dated 1753, 1761, and 1774.[4] While locally produced Nahuatl writings seem to have declined by the 1750s, the translation of royal decrees into

TABLE 9.1. Provenance of Mixe Nahuatl-language documents

Amatepec	Temascalapa	Totontepec
Ayutla	Tiltepec	Xareta
Metepec	Tlahuilotepec	Xayacastepec
Ocotepec		

Nahuatl for Mixe audiences suggests the continued importance of Nahuatl as a lingua franca in the region in the second half of the eighteenth century.

The provenance of these documents makes them especially intriguing. Nearly all of the Nahuatl-language records in the judicial archive come from ten Mixe-speaking towns of the Villa Alta (see Table 9.1). Only a handful of the Nahuatl-language writings in the collection come from a Zapotec-speaking place, and none originate from the Nahua barrio of Analco in Villa Alta.[5] The absence of Mixe-language notarial documents and the continuation of Nahuatl-language writing for a century and a half suggests that the Mixe never wrote their own language. Consequently, Nahuatl was not a transitional written language as it was among other indigenous groups, such as the Mixtecs, who went on to develop alphabetic writing in their own language (Terraciano 2001, 45–48); for the Mixes, Nahuatl was their written language. In fact, Nahuatl-language writing seems to have precluded the development of Mixe-language alphabetic writing. The extant records from the Mixe communities of Villa Alta make up one of the largest collections of Nahuatl written as a second language.

The Mixe Nahuatl corpus from Villa Alta contains several genres of writing, including testaments, land documents, bills of sale, inventories, town council records, and translations of royal decrees. As in the Nahua, Maya, and Mixtec spheres, the testament is the most common type of civil document.[6] Testaments appear earliest and survive through the latest stages of native-language writing from the region. Nahuatl-language criminal records from Villa Alta, mainly notifications of crimes that had been committed, also survive in the judicial archive. Maps and genealogies with Nahuatl-language glosses provide examples of the combination of pictorial and alphabetic writing in the colonial archival record.

Several important studies have examined politics, spirituality, and the economy of the Villa Alta jurisdiction under Spanish rule.[7] However, these studies focus mainly on the region's Zapotec population, and little has been

written on colonial Mixe communities. No previous study of the region
has used Mixe Nahuatl-language archival documents. These records provide evidence of regional variation in the evolution of Nahuatl in contact
with Spanish, advancing our understanding of the history of the language
and of multiethnic interaction during the colonial period. This chapter
provides a transcription and translation of Flores's testament and offers
a preliminary study of landholding and social relations as reflected in this
and other Mixe Nahuatl-language documents. A comparative analysis of
terms and concepts in the Nahuatl-language documents from Villa Alta
and central Mexico illuminates similarities and differences in the Mixes'
practices and ideology.

Lands and Landholding

At the time of the conquest, Mixes lived in dispersed communities in the
steep, mountainous terrain of the Sierra Alta. They were at war with Zapotecs of the region when the Spaniards arrived, and they had intermittently
fought with Chinantecs as well. In his study of the Spanish conquest and
the imposition of colonial rule in the sixteenth-century, Alonso Barros
van Hovell tot Westerflier (2007) shows how Spaniards exploited these
preexisting ethnic rivalries—much to the detriment of the Mixes, who
lost control over vital resources because they failed to form alliances with
colonial authorities. During much of the colonial period, Mixe communities fell under two jurisdictions: Villa Alta and Nejapa.[8] In his study of
colonial Villa Alta, John Chance notes that Spanish friars and crown officials undertook various campaigns in the sixteenth and early seventeenth
centuries to congregate and relocate Mixe settlements, often with limited
success (Chance 1989, 82–85).[9] At this time, little is known about Mixe
sociopolitical organization or economic relations in the late Postclassic
and early colonial periods. However, colonial wills provide a window onto
Mixe landholding concepts and practices.

The final statements of Mixe testators reveal both similarities and differences between Mixe and Nahua land tenure systems. As was common
throughout Mesoamerica, Mixes held multiple plots of scattered lands,
which allowed them to take advantage of the region's environmental diversity and to deal with problems of soil depletion and erosion.[10] Dispersed
landholdings recorded in seventeenth-century wills may also reflect dis-
ruptions caused by congregation efforts, as Mixes attempted to hold tra-

ditional lands and also claim lands in newly settled regions. In his last will and testament, Gerónimo Flores claimed forty-five fields, suggesting that the plots were small. Like the Nahuas, Mixe men and women acquired land through purchase, inheritance, or grant, and they freely alienated property through sale or bequest. Flores had inherited fields from his grandfather, grandmother, father, and sisters, and he purchased a few plots as well. Mixes used a complex land classification system with numerous categories, including *amilli* (irrigated field), *ichcamilli* (cotton field), *tonalmilli* (sunny or warm field? Or a field assigned to someone?), and *quauhmilli* (field enriched with decayed tree matter?). Flores mentioned these four different types of land as he bequeathed his property and belongings to his heirs.

Like documents from other regions in Oaxaca and central Mexico, the Mixe testaments list proper names to identify specific fields, most likely referring to *parajes* (larger tracts) where the lands were located.[11] Thus, as Flores identified five of his irrigated lands, he noted: "the fourth [field] is named Cohonhoucp; the fifth [field], also there, is Cohonhoucp." The fact that two plots shared the same name and that Flores specified that the fifth land was "also there" at Cohonhoucp suggests that he was referring to a larger place where the fields were located. Later in the testament, Flores mentions yet another irrigated plot named Cohonhoucp that his sisters had left to him. Similarly, he refers to two *tonalmilli* called Xitzp, which were his grandfather's lands. The wording here further supports the interpretation that such names referred to general locations rather than specific plots.

One striking difference between central Mexican and Mixe Nahuatl testaments is the virtual absence of indigenous or Spanish land measurement terminology in the Villa Alta corpus.[12] In this regard, Mixe wills are like those of the Mixtecs and Zapotecs of Oaxaca, which sometimes refer to neighbors and locate the lands in a certain tract but rarely use measurements to describe the fields. As discussed below, Mixe testators also frequently mentioned the people from whom they had inherited or purchased specific fields as though to situate lands in the community's social memory.

Testaments demonstrate that the Mixe had complex arrangements in which several individuals formed partnerships and took turns working lands that they held jointly. The documents use terms such as *tlayahualoa* (to go around, as in a procession; to rotate) and *patla* (to trade or exchange) that emphasize rotation of privileges and responsibilities. In his 1660 testament, Flores described such an arrangement concerning an irrigated field whereby he worked the land for two years, and another man cultivated it the following year. Flores also described another arrangement in which he alternated the rights to work an irrigated field with another man. Although more research is needed to clearly understand these types of arrangements, it appears that he had invested more and therefore had a claim to work it for longer periods of time than his partner, who had invested less. These complex types of landholding arrangements described in the Villa Alta Nahuatl documents appear to be unusual in the Nahua world.

The Nahuatl-language corpus from Villa Alta reveals Mixe concepts and principles of organization. The evidence provided on landholding shows that rotation was a fundamental organizational concept, just as it was among the Nahuas and other Mesoamerican groups. Like Nahuas of central Mexico, Mixe testators often expressed expectations of reciprocity and cooperation when they left property to designated heirs, doing the deceased the favor of helping their souls.[13] This sense of cooperation and long-term obligation also shaped concepts of land sale and tenure. For example, in the testament of María Caco, which was among the documents submitted by the people of Totontepec in their suit against Amatepec, she explained that don Joseph González had purchased land from her for five pesos, and she instructed her heirs to return the money to him if he should decide that he no longer wanted it. This practice, also seen in other Mixe testaments, suggests a fluid understanding of exchange and land ownership.

Mixe testators retained a clear memory of the origins of the lands that they held, and they rarely claimed fields as theirs alone. Flores described only two purchased fields as "my lands," and even then he identified the person who had sold them to him. Other properties listed in the testament were "lands of my grandfather," "the property of my grandmother," or "the land of my father." When he left his house to his grandchild, he was careful to acknowledge that he did not have a claim to the lot itself: "this lot is the property of his grandmother. It is not my property." His statement conveys more of a sense of stewardship over land than outright ownership, and his emphatic statement made this complex arrangement clear. Furthermore, his initial arrangement with his mother, who owned the lot, represents another type of partnership that Mixes formed to manage lands and resources.[14]

The Mixe Nahuatl-language corpus also reveals some Spanish influence on concepts of landholding. The Spanish term for the primary household land, *solar*, is ubiquitous in the Villa Alta documents, just as it is in central Mexican records. As Caterina Pizzigoni (2012, 30) points out, Spaniards strictly understood the term *solar* to mean house lot. Based on his research with Nahuatl-language documents, James Lockhart (1992, 68–69) notes that while Nahuas borrowed the Spanish term, they conceived of a *solar* differently than Spaniards did; for Nahuas, a *solar* referred to a house lot with some agricultural lands attached to it. This may very well have been the case among the Mixe; however, further research is necessary to determine the precise meaning of the term in these documents. More unusual in the Mixe corpus is the use of the Spanish loanword *pedazo* (piece, parcel), which may relate to concepts of joint landholding and cultivation.

In addition to lands, Mixe testaments often described houses and occasionally other household items that the testator bequeathed to his or her heirs. Spanish household furnishings, tools, and personal effects listed in the testament of Flores and other Mixe testators include *santos* (saints), *sillas* (chairs), *mesas* (tables), *vigas* (beams), *hachas* (axes), *sierras* (saws), *escoplos* (chisels), and Spanish-style clothing such as *jubones* (jackets), *cuellos* (collars), and *sombreros* (hats). Flores concluded his testament by making special mention of an image of Saint Joseph that he had purchased for fifty pesos, which he ordered to be placed in the church "for eternity." The high price that he paid for the icon suggests that this must have been a very large and well-crafted image. The references to Spanish goods and concepts reflect considerable Spanish influence on Mixe society and culture, and the presence of European goods in the market, even in the rather remote reaches of the Sierra Alta.[15]

Social Relations

Bequests of land and other property shed light on Mixe social organization and family relations. Mixe testators often left fields to a group, some of four or more people, including both men and women, who were admonished to always cultivate the land together. In contrast, Nahuas tended to bequeath scattered plots to individuals. Mixes who had joint ownership of land could bequeath their portions of the partnership to heirs, and these complex arrangements survived through several generations. Flores made the partnership he had concerning his irrigated field even more complex by ordering that his two grandchildren, his daughter, and his two uncles inherit the property and jointly work it. The fact that he left all of his lands to the same group suggests that they lived together and made up a multi-generational household unit of extended kin.

Flores used the occasion of ordering his testament to reinforce the ties among family members, living and deceased. By acknowledging the previous holders of the lands that he was passing on to his own heirs, he honored the memory of his ancestors. With his family assembled around him and the local officials present, Flores made a final plea to his heirs to follow his wishes. He warned, "If someone turns out to be a scoundrel, if my grandchildren, my child, or my uncles argue with each other someday, I say now that I place it in the hands of the officers of the law, who will instruct them." His statement opened the door for community officials to intervene in family conflicts over the inheritance, thereby blurring the boundaries between public and private realms. His final words allowed him to admonish family members to stay in line and to avoid conflict with one another. His parting concerns were for the welfare and harmony of the family.

Testament of Gerónimo Flores, 1660

Transcription

1660 aºs   +   testamento

<u>v</u> yca ytocatzin dios tetatzin yuā dios tepiltzin dios despiritu sto ma y mochihua amen jesus axcan cempohuali ome tona metztli de março yuā ypan xihuitl de i y 660 aºs nehual nicocoxqui ninotoca gerᵐᵒ flores ca huel nimococohua axcan ypampa nechmotlaocoliz ttº dios axcan ca ypampa axcan nicnotza mochintin aldes regidores ypampa nicchihua notestamento yxpan yni Sʳᵉˢ alles regidores axcan ac nimochicahua acmo niyelemiqui acmo ni[tla]yecoltia acmo nicpia tomines ca ya nihuehuentzi acmo nicpia tomines

<u>v</u> ys catqui nictenehua achtopa ypalehuilo noanina matlactli ome Pºs momacas ⁿᵒmisa teopixqui yuā yey peso ᵇⁱᵍⁱˡˡᵃ yua nahui tonin ychquich momacas teopixqui yuā nahui tomin momacas cantores

<u>v</u> ys catqui nictlali ce peso limosna momacas totlaçonantzi Sᵗᵃ
Mᵃ ylhuicaccihuali Sᵗᵃ cofradia ypampa yehual quipalehui noanima
quitlatlauhtis ttº dios

<u>v</u> ys catqui nictenehua nomili yc ce ytoca nocoocm onicohuili ce
pedaço yuā oc ce pedaço onicohuili gaspar tooyphopop yuā occe pedaço
onicpatla ynahuac simon gonzales ca mochintin nicmaca noyxhui
gerᵐᵒ yuā Juᵃ yuā nopiltzi felicita yuā ome notiyo pº garᵃ yuā Juº capⁿ
mochintin calaquisque quiyelemiquisque motlayahualosque cece xihuitl

<u>v</u> ys catqui ytlali nocoltzi macuili yc ce ytoca pacexp yc ome yto
quetzcuep yc yey ytoca coytocpanam yc nahui ytoca maxontzexm yc
macuili ytoca noyhaotm yc chicuace ytoca tzotzoquetzm yc chicome
ytoca aoctzonhuayyom yc chichuey ytoca tzocomoh yc chicnahui ytoca
aoctzonhuinm yc matlactli ytoca pahoncaum yc matlactli ce ytoca
+copohayom yc matlactli ome ytoca xacecacem ysquich ytlali nocoltzi ca
çano yuqui mochintin nicmaca noyxhui ome yuā nopiltzi yuā ome notiyo
motlayahualosque cecexihuitl

<u>v</u> ys catqui tlali amili yaxca noxitzi macuili yc ce ytoca hayhaun yc
ome ytoca mocxop yc ye ytoca copoom yc nahui ytoca cohonhoucp yc
macuili çano ompa cohonhoucp yuā oc ce quauhmili ytoca hayhaotm
ysquich ytlali noxitzi ca çano yuqui mochintin yelemiquisque ome
noyxhui yuā ce nopiltzi yua ome notiyo cecexihuitl quimotlayahualosque

<u>v</u> yuā oc ce notlali amili yaxca no~~tzitzi~~coltzi ytoca nouxp çano yuqui
mochintin nicma noyshui yuā nopiltzi yuā notiyo ome

[f 1v]

<u>v</u> ys catqui nictenehua ytlali notatzi yc ce ytoca tzintocm oquicohuili
Juº Rey to mayor yc ome ytoca nicopnoap otli yehual yahui amatepec yc
yey ytoca [---------------] yaxca nocoltzi yc nahui ytoca tlali picoctzam yc
macuili ˢᵃ ⁿᵒ ʸᵘʰqᵘⁱ ytoca poli ytoca mnaxhuinm çano yaxca nocoltzi yc
chiccuace ytoca cahaxtocm yaxca notatzi yc chicome ~~ytoca huinxocxom~~
yaxca nocoltzi yno tlali yni tlali ca amo yaxca neli

<u>v</u> ys catqui ome tonalmili ytoca xitzp çano yaxca nocoltzi
nimocuauhxochnamiqui ynahuac a°l guttz yua çano yuqui mochintin
nicmaca quiyelemiquisque ome noyshui yuā ce nopiltzi yuā ome notiyo
quimotlayahualosque cece xihuitl

<u>v</u> ys catqui nictehua notlali yaxca noxitzi nehual nicpia yc ce ytoca
noxctzam amili ynahuac ocotepec tlacal tlaco noaxca yuā tlaco yyaxca
yc ome tlali amili ytoca pixam çano ynahuac ocotepec tlacatl ytoca ben°
ome xihuitl niyelemiqui yuā ce xihuitl yehuatl yc yey ytoca tlali tzaycam
amili ycuac niquiças pixam nicalaqui tzaycam çano yuqui ome xihuitl
niyelemiqui onca no yc nahui tlali ytoca notzocom amili ce xihuitl noaxca
yuā ce xihuitl onicohua ça nocel ypampa yno niyelemiqui mochipa
cece xihuitl çano yuqui quipiasque quiyelemiquisque noyxhui ome yuā
nopiltzi yuā ome notiyo

<u>v</u> ys catqui nictenehua noychacamili ytoca pohotahom
nimocuauhxochnamiqui ynahuac tlacatl metlaltepec çano yuqui nicmaca
mochintin ⁿoyshui yuā nopiltzi yuā notiyo ome amohaqui quiquixtisque

<u>v</u> ys catqui oc nahui noychcamili ce ytoca xaxam yuā yc ome
ytoca naptahom yc yey yto mohoyocm yuā occe ytoca ma°tzom yni
tlali ca yaxca nocoltzi çano yuqui ymac noyxhui ger^{mo} yuā Ju^a yuā
nopiltzi felicita yuā ome notiyo Ju° Cap^n yuā p° gar^a ca yni quipiasque
quiyelemiquisque

<u>v</u> ys catqui oc nahui notlali ca yaxca noher^{nas} ce yto barbula yuā oc
ce ytoca felicita ome catca ya noher^{nas} yni tlali nahui ca yca testamento
onechmaca amo çan nicpiya amo çan niyelemiqui ce ytoca mehopaom
yc ome ytoca mehop yc yey caltempa çolar campa motlaliliyayaya Ju°
gonzales cauh yc nahui tlali ytoca cohonhoucp amili ysquich yni tlali
onechmaca noher^{nas} yuā çano yuqui mochintin noyshui yuā nopiltzi yuā
ome notiyo quipiasque quiyelemiquisque

[f 2]

<u>v</u> ys catqui nictenehua axcan yni nocali ca ycel yni noyxhui ger^{mo}
quipias yuā yni çolar yaxca yxitzi amo noaxca amo quitenehuas nopiltzi

felicita yuā çano yuqui ycel quipias felicita campa motlalia axca yno çolar
ycuac momiquilis quemania tlamis ynemiltlistli nica tlalticpac cenca yni
quimati haquin quima^ca ome yni tlali ça ysquich yuā mochi quesquich
o[---]a ^tlali ytech yni notestamento ycuac momiquilis haqui aço onca
ypiltzi haqui mocahua oc ce ytech mocahuas yni tlali mochi huelis oc
cecni tlacatl quimacas

v ys catqui nictehua axcan ce S^to onicohua S^n Joseph y ompohuali ma
tlactli p^os yuā yca noyolocacopa axcan nictlali teopa ompa ye cemicac
ca çan ysquich niquitoa nicchihua notestameto yxpan S^res alles omentin
Ju^o gar^a yuā ben^o her^des yuā yeyntin Regidores p^o de gusman yuā luis
melchor yuā Ju^o bernal ca ynin quineltisque mochihuas quemania
yuā aço haqui tlahueliloc quiça aço noyxhui aço nopiltzi aço notiyo
mochalaniya quemaniya ymac Justi^a nictoa nictlalia axcan yehual
quimachtis ca çan ysquich mitoa yuā micuiloa cempoali tona metztli de
março ytencopa cocoxqui

Ju^o lopez de escobar
otlacuilo
Ju^o gar^a aldes   ben^o her^des
                                    Alde

Luis melchor regidor   p^o de gusman regidor

              Ju^o ber^l regidor

Resebi las missas y vijilia conte[---]
des en este testamento por el anim[a]
de geronimo flores y por verdad [-----]
[-----]

Fr Andres [---]

[f. 4]
yuā oc ome tlali ytoca huinxocxox yuā paocm

ca yaxca Ju° de la cruz ya omoxelo yni tlali
amo ystlacaltis quemania yni ger^mo flores ca ya oquixe-
lohua hehantzitzi

Translation

1660 years   +   testament

In the name of God the Father, God the Son, and God the Holy Spirit, may it be done. Amen. Jesus. Today, the twenty-second day of the month of March in the year of 1660, I, the sick person named Gerónimo Flores, am very ill. Our Lord God will soon have mercy on me, I summoned all the *alcaldes* and *regidores* today so that I can make my testament in the presence of these *señores alcaldes* and *regidores*—for no longer am I strong, no longer do I cultivate, no longer do I provide for myself, no longer do I have money, for I am an old man, no longer do I have money.

Item, I mention first the help of my soul. Twelve pesos will be given to the friar[16] for my masses, and three pesos and four reales for the vigil, it will all be given to the friar. Four reales will be given to the singers.

Item, I order that one peso offering will be given to the holy Confraternity of Our Precious Mother Santa María, the Heavenly Lady, so that she will help my soul and pray to our God.

Item, I declare my fields: the first named Nocoocm, I bought one piece and another piece from Gaspar Tooyphopop and another piece I exchanged with Simon González. I give it to all of them, my grandchildren, Gerónimo and Juana, and my child, Felicidad, and my two uncles, Pedro García and Juan Capitán. All of them will enter and work it. They will rotate each year.

Item, there are five lands of my grandfather: the first is named Pacexp; the second is named Quetzcuep; the third is named Coytocpanam; the fourth is named Maxontexm; the fifth is named Noyhaotm; the sixth is named Tzotzoquetzm; the seventh is named Aoctzonhayyom; the eighth is named Tzoconeh; the ninth is named Aoctzonhuinm; the tenth is named Pahoncaum; the eleventh is named Copohayom; the twelfth is named Xacecaum.[17] That is all of the land of my grandfather. Likewise, I give it to all of them, my grandchildren, my child, and my two uncles. They will rotate each year.

Item, there are five lands, irrigated fields, that are the property of my grandmother: the first is named Hayhaun; the second is named Mocxop; the third is named Copoom; the fourth is named Cohonhoup; the fifth, also there, is Cohonhoup, and another field with decayed tree matter[18] called Hayhaotm. That is all of the land of my grandmother. Likewise, all of them, my grandchildren, my child, and my two uncles are to cultivate it. They will rotate each year.

And another of my lands, an irrigated field, called Nouxp, was the property of my ~~grandmother~~ grandfather. Likewise, I give it to all of them, my grandchildren, my child, and my two uncles.

Item, I declare the land of my father: the first is named Tzintocm, which he bought from Juan *regidor mayor*; the second is named Nicopnoap and is on the road that goes to Amatepec, and the third [marked out] is the property of my grandfather; the fourth land is named Picoctzam; the fifth is named Poli; and the one named Mnaxhuinm is also the property of my grandfather; the sixth is named Haxtocm and is the property of my father; the seventh is this land that is not his property, truly it is the property of my grandfather.[19]

Item, two *tonalmilli* [warm, sunny?][20] fields called Xitzp that border with [the land of] Alonso Gutiérrez also are the property of my grandfather. Likewise, I give it to all of them, my two grandchildren, my child, and my two uncles, and they will work it and rotate each year.

Item, I declare my lands that are the property of my grandmother: the first, named Noxctzam, is an irrigated field along with a person from Ocotepec; half is my property and half is his property. The second land is an irrigated field named Pixam also jointly with a person of Ocotepec called Benito. Two years I work it and one year he does. The third land, named Tzaycaym, is an irrigated field. When I leave Pixam, I enter Tzaycaym. Likewise, I work it for two years. There is also a fourth land named Notzocom that is an irrigated field. It has been my property for a year; a year ago I bought it all by myself so that I always work it each year. My two grandchildren, my child, and my two uncles will keep it and work it in the same way.

Item, I declare my cotton field called Pohotahom that borders with [the land of] a person from Metlaltepec, likewise, I give it to all of them, my grandchildren, my child, and my two uncles. No one is to take it from them.

Item, four more cotton fields, one named Xaxam and the second named Naptahom, the third named Mohoyocm, and the fourth named Mactzom, these lands are the property of my grandfather. Likewise, it is in the hands of my grandchildren, Gerónimo and Juana, my child Felicidad, and my two uncles, Juan Capitán and Pedro Gaspar, who will keep and work it.

Item, four more of my lands are the property of my sisters, the first named Bárbola and the second named Felicidad; both of them were my sisters. They gave me these four lands in their testaments; I'm not just keeping it and working it [without their approval]. One is named Meho-paom; the second is named Mahop; the third is at the edge of the house on the lot where Juan González used to reside; the fourth land, named Cohonhoucp, is an irrigated field. My sisters gave me all of this land, and likewise, all of them, my grandchildren, my child, and my two uncles will keep and work it.

Item, I declare now that my grandchild Gerónimo will have this, my house by himself, and as for this lot which is the property of his grand-mother, it is not my property, my child Felicidad is not to mention [claim] it, and likewise Felicidad will keep the lot by herself where she has already settled. When she dies someday and her life here on earth ends, she will decide to whom she will give these two lands. That is all. And as for what-ever land is in this my testament, when [he?] dies, perhaps there will be some child of [his?] left with whom the land will remain. (If there is no child, he can give it to a person from elsewhere.)

Item, I declare that I bought one saint, Saint Joseph, for fifty pesos. With all of my heart, I now place it in the church where it will be for eter-nity. That is all that I say. I am making my testament in the presence of the two *señores alcaldes*, Juan García and Benito Hernández, and three *regi-dores*, Pedro de Guzmán, Luis Melchor, and Juan Bernal. They will carry this out and it will be done someday. If someone turns out to be a scoun-drel, if my grandchildren, my child, or my uncles argue with each other someday, I say that now I place it in the hands of the officers of the law, who will instruct them. That is all that is said and written the twentieth day of the month of March. By order of the sick person.

[Signatures]

[on the back of the document]
And two more lands, named Huinxocxocx and Paocm, that are the prop-erty of Juan de la Cruz, were divided. Gerónimo Flores is not to tell lies someday, for they already divided it.

Notes

I would like to thank James Lockhart for encouraging me to pursue a Mixe Nahuatl project and for his comments on my preliminary translation of this document. All errors are my own.

1. The reader should note that since I conducted this research, the archive has been reorganized and the numbering of the *expedientes* has been changed.
2. See Gerhard 1993, 367–373.
3. The date of the *expediente* is 1672, but it contains several earlier documents.
4. These royal decrees are contained in AJVA, Civil 4:217 and 5:260, and Civil Anexo 1:25, respectively. Fifty-nine of the eighty documents are dated.
5. Whether there are Nahuatl documents in other collections from the Zapotec communities of Villa Alta or Analco remains to be seen.
6. See Lockhart 1992, 353, 367–73 on Nahuatl; Terraciano 2001, 45-48 on Mixtec; Restall 1997, 237; and Restall, Sousa, and Terraciano 2005, 15.
7. Hamnett 1971; Chance 1989; Romero Frizzi 1996; Baskes 2000; Oudijk 2000; Yannakakis 2008; Tavárez 2011.
8. It is not clear to me at this time whether Mixe communities in Nejapa also wrote in Nahuatl.
9. See Chance 1989 for an introduction to the background of the region.
10. On scattered landholdings in Mesoamerica, see, for example, Lockhart 1992; Restall 1997; Terraciano 2001.
11. This might also suggest that the fields were named. Terraciano (2001, 210) observed the practice of naming lands based on his analysis of Mixtec-language records from the Mixteca Alta. He suggests that naming may have compensated for lack of standardized measurements.
12. Terraciano (2001, 210) also observes this in the Mixtec region.
13. Lockhart 1992, 172–174, 255; Pizzigoni 2012, 188.
14. James Lockhart confirms that although Nahuas sometimes mentioned the person they had inherited land from, they did not actually call it the forebear's property, as the Mixes did in their testaments (personal communication, 2013).
15. Much of the introduction of Spanish goods in Villa Alta was the result of the practice of *repartimiento de efectos*. For various interpretations of the impact of this institution see Hamnett 1971; Chance 1989; Baskes 2000; and Yannakakis 2008.
16. Perhaps by this time *teopixqui* refers more generally to a priest, which was the case in central Mexico (James Lockhart, personal communication, 2013). This will require additional research in the corpus, to be sure.
17. It is puzzling that Gerónimo Flores states that there are five lands but then lists twelve. Also, note that the names are locative (referring to the places where the lands are located).
18. The translation of *quauhmilli* is tentative. *Quauhtlalli* or *quauhmilli* could also refer to lands given to deserving or high-ranking people (James Lockhart, personal communication, 2013).

19. Note that he seems to identify two fields as the fifth of his properties.
20. *Tonalmilli* could also refer to a land that is assigned to someone.

References

Barros van Hovell tot Westerflier, Alonso. 2007. "Cien años de guerras mixes: Territoralidades prehispánicas, expansion burocrática, y zapotequización en el Istmo de Tehuantepec durante el siglo XVI." *Historia Mexicana* 57(2): 325–403.

Baskes, Jeremy. 2000. *Indians, Merchants, and Markets: A Reinterpretation of the* Repartimiento *and Spanish-Indian Economic Relations in Colonial Oaxaca, 1750–1821.* Stanford, Calif.: Stanford University Press.

Chance, John. 1989. *Conquest of the Sierra: Spaniards and Indians in Colonial Oaxaca.* Norman: University of Oklahoma Press.

Hamnett, Brian R. 1971. *Politics and Trade in Southern Mexico, 1750–1821.* Cambridge: Cambridge University Press.

Lockhart, James. 1992. *The Nahuas After the Conquest: A Social and Cultural History of the Indians of Central Mexico, Sixteenth Through Eighteenth Centuries.* Stanford, Calif.: Stanford University Press.

Oudijk, Michel. 2000. *Historiography of the Bénizáa: The Postclassic and Early Colonial Periods (1000–1600 AD).* Leiden: Research School of Asian, African, and Amerindian Studies, Leiden University.

Pizzigoni, Caterina. 2012. *The Life Within: Local Indigenous Society in Mexico's Toluca Valley, 1650–1800.* Stanford, Calif.: Stanford University Press.

Restall, Matthew. 1997. *The Maya World: Yucatec Culture and Society, 1550–1850.* Stanford, Calif.: Stanford University Press.

Restall, Matthew, Lisa Sousa, and Kevin Terraciano, trans. and eds. 2005. *Mesoamerican Voices: Native-Language Writings from Colonial Mexico, Oaxaca, Yucatan, and Guatemala.* Cambridge: Cambridge University Press.

Romero Frizzi, María de los Angeles. 1996. *El sol y la cruz: Los pueblos de indios de Oaxaca colonial.* Mexico City: CIESAS.

Tavárez, David. 2011. *The Invisible War: Indigenous Devotions, Discipline, and Dissent in Colonial Mexico.* Stanford, Calif.: Stanford University Press.

Terraciano, Kevin. 2001. *The Mixtecs of Colonial Oaxaca: Ñudzahui History, Sixteenth through Eighteenth Centuries.* Stanford, Calif.: Stanford University Press.

Yannakakis, Yanna. 2008. *The Art of Being In-Between: Native Intermediaries, Indian Identity, and Local Rule in Colonial Oaxaca.* Durham, N.C.: Duke University Press.

CHAPTER 10

Disposing of the Body
and Aiding the Soul

Death, Dying, and Testaments
in Colonial Huexotzinco

ERIKA R. HOSSELKUS

In May of 1613, Ana Xiuhpetlacal, an indigenous resident of the town of Huexotzinco in Puebla, Mexico, dictated her testament in her native tongue, Nahuatl, to a notary. She asked to be wrapped in a cloak and buried, perhaps near a chapel, statue, or painting of Santa María de la Asunción. She requested one mass to speed her soul's release from purgatory and set aside four pesos for the *cofradía* (lay religious fellowship) of San Diego so that the steward would provide and deliver candles to the church for the mass (BNAH, Archivo Histórico, 3rd series, leg. 28, doc. 14/23).

For Ana Xiuhpetlacal and her contemporaries, execution of a testament represented one step toward an ideal Catholic death that would facilitate the soul's swift entry into heaven.[1] The burial instructions and mass requests outlined in the testament served to shepherd one's earthly remains to consecrated ground, and the transcendent soul into the afterlife. Despite their sometimes formulaic nature, the spiritual clauses of the testaments of New Spain's indigenous inhabitants demonstrate personal, local, and indigenous understandings of Catholic death-related practices. This chapter explores the spiritual directives of Huexotzinco's indigenous testators and the ways in which they illuminate that region's vibrant and unique Catholicism as exercised at the time of death.

By 1613, the year of Ana Xiuhpetlacal's death, Huexotzinco was a provincial colonial town inhabited by Nahuas, Spaniards, Africans, and mixed-heritage individuals. Residents provided labor and supplies to the regional capital, Puebla de los Ángeles. When the Spaniards first entered this region, the powerful ethnic state of Huexotzinco allied with Hernando Cortés, contributing warriors and goods to the 1521 conquest of the Aztec Empire. However, despite loyal service and an impassioned 1560 letter directed to King Philip II of Spain, in which they argued that their dedication to Spain and to Christianity surpassed that of neighboring Tlaxcala, Huexotzinco never attained the rewards, protection, or enduring recognition granted to the latter polity by the Spanish crown (AHNE, Diversos Colecciones 24, n. 42, p. 2).[2] Tracts of land passed from indigenous to Spanish hands, and by the seventeenth century, Tlaxcala had eclipsed Huexotzinco as New Spain's "most loyal" indigenous city (Prem 1988).[3]

Nonetheless, the community of Huexotzinco remained home to indigenous nobles and commoners who produced a notable corpus of Nahuatl-language documents during the seventeenth century, including approximately fifty testaments, dozens of bills of sale, and other assorted items, very few of which have been examined by scholars. This chapter examines the testament of Ana Xiuhpetlacal and twenty-three other testaments from the region.[4] All were produced by Huexotzinco's most prolific indigenous notary, Esteban de Coto.[5] They date from 1612 to 1634, with clusters occurring in certain years, as indicated in Table 10.1.[6]

In some ways, Huexotzinco's testaments and the spiritual directives of its indigenous invalids resemble those seen in other parts of New Spain or the wider Spanish Empire. In other ways, however, Huexotzinco is quite idiosyncratic, drawing attention to the eminently local nature of indigenous Catholicism in New Spain.

Disposing of the Body

Among the spiritual concerns addressed by early modern testators, burial instructions came first. In those instructions, and in their requests for masses, Huexotzinco's invalids invoked their relationships with local friars and priests, part of the larger social network uniting indigenous society. They relied on those individuals to carry out or oversee the execution of their spiritual desires. Ana Xiuhpetlacal, like most testators in this sample, ordered that her body be interred at "our church" (BNAH, doc. 14/23). All testators in the sample died prior to secularization of parishes, enacted under Bishop Juan de Palafox y Mendoza in 1640–1642. Thus, "our

TABLE 10.1. Huexotzinco testaments produced by notary Esteban de Coto, 1612–1634

Source and Document No.	Name of Testator	Testament Date
BNAH 25	Juana Caxtillanxochitl	12/29/1612
BNAH 20	Juana Caxtillanxochitl	1/6/1613
BNAH 22	Sebastián Pérez	2/21/1613
BNAH 14, 23	Ana Xiuhpetlacal	5/21/1613
BNAH 27	Francisco de la Peña	9/3/1613
BNAH 21	Isabel Cacaloxochitl	10/24/1617
BNAH 49	Gaspar Méndez	8/30/1618
BNAH 47	Ana Nenca	9/4/1618
BNAH 51	Agata Nenca	12/28/1618
BNAH 45	Francisco Pérez	8/12/1622
BNAH 44	Juan García	12/23/1626
BNAH 40	Tomás Tlilli	1/24/1630
AGN, fol. 281, Testament 1	Andrés Muñoz	8/18/1630
BNAH 41	Ana María	5/6/1631
BNAH 29	Ana Teocuitlaxochitl	6/3/1631
BNAH 42	Pedro Gante	8/16/1631
BNAH 50	Baltasar García	2/21/1632
AGN, fol. 322, Testament 6	María Cacaloxochitl	3/21/1632
BNAH 33	Lucas Pérez	3/26/1632
BNAH 28	Ana Neçahualxochitl	5/22/1632
BNAH 43	Juan Miguel	5/23/1632
BNAH 31	Melchior de la Cruz	9/15/1633
BNAH 19	Francisco Pérez	5/19/1634
BNAH 48	Mariana	7/20/1634

Note: BNAH = Biblioteca Nacional de Antropología e Historia, Archivo Histórico, 3rd series, legajo 28; AGN = Archivo General de la Nación, Tierras, vol. 3712.

church" meant the Franciscan church of the friary of San Miguel, located in the town's principal neighborhood of San Juan Tecpan. Culhuacan's sixteenth-century Nahuas likewise preferred to be buried at their town's main church, San Juan Evangelista, and the eighteenth-century indigenous residents of Toluca requested burial at the major Franciscan friary church in their region—all of which suggests that church burials were standard in New Spain, as elsewhere in the early modern Catholic world (Cline 1986, 24; Pizzigoni 2007, 16).

More specifically, Ana Xiuhpetlacal requested burial near Santa María de la Asunción, referring perhaps to a chapel, statue, or painting within the church.[7] In fact, all but one of the twenty-four Huexotzinco testators identified a precise burial location. They asked to be interred inside or outside

TABLE 10.2. Huexotzinco testators' burial locations, 1612–1634

	Location, Fixture, or Feature	Number of Testators Requesting Burial
Location	Within the church (*tecalco*)	2
	In the patio or courtyard (*ithualco*)	2
	In the thatched structure (*tzacalco*)	1
Fixture(s)	At the foot of the altar stairs (*apetlac*)	2
	At the foot of the altar stairs (*apetlac*) and near the holy water font (*yn tlateochihuallatitlan*)	2
Feature	San Juan	5
	Before (the grave of) our redeemer/savior (*totemaquixticatzin seporero*)	3
	Santa María de la Asunción	1
	San Pablo	1
Fixture and Feature	At the foot of the altar stairs (*apetlac*) near San Miguel	1
Location and Feature	Within the church (*callitec*) near San Francisco	2
	Within the church (*tecalco*) near San Diego	1
	No specifics	1

Note: Features are statues or sculptural elements located within the friary church.

of the friary church or near certain church fixtures or features, including the altar, saints' images, an entombed Christ sculpture, and the holy water font, as outlined in Table 10.2.[8]

The individuals represented in Table 10.2 clearly attributed significance to specific locations within the sacred space of the friary complex. Are the burial preferences of Huexotzinco's Nahuas unique, or do they resemble those of the larger Spanish Empire and other parts of indigenous New Spain? What do such choices reveal about Catholicism and its relationship to death and dying in the region?

In early modern Spain, "the closer one could be to the eucharist, the better," with the ideal burial location being closest to the altar (Eire 1995, 99). Wealthy, influential individuals and families tended to secure prime spots, often through generous donations to the church. Those of more modest means commonly asked for interment near specific saints' images, the holy water font, or other church features that attracted devotees and prayers from which the deceased might vicariously benefit. Family members frequently asked to be buried near one another. Only the wealthiest families could afford to establish and maintain private chapels with salaried chaplains responsible for masses for the souls of deceased family members

(Eire 1995, 100–101; Nalle 1992, 184–185). Similar practices obtained in colonial Mexico City, where noble families established familial sepulchers
in prized locations, sometimes near the altar (Zárate Toscano 2000, 260).
In colonial Lima and Cuzco, indigenous caciques likewise expressed interest in being interred near relatives and close to specific church fixtures
and features, including the altar (Ramos 2010, 189, 197–198). Similarly, in
eighteenth-century Toluca some Nahua testators sought interment near
family members, while many asked to be buried near specific saints' images
(Pizzigoni 2007, 16–17).[9]

In contrast to the pattern that seemed to prevail in much of the Spanish
Empire, no testator in Huexotzinco requested burial near a family member.[10] There is some evidence that Huexotzinco's Nahuas considered the
altar a sacred and desirable interment site; however, other features within
the San Miguel friary church attracted as much or more attention. Only
five of the twenty-three Huexotzinco testators who addressed burial location mentioned the altar directly, asking to be interred at the foot of the
altar stairs (*apetlac*) (BNAH, docs. 20, 28, 45, 48; AGN, Ramo Tierras,
vol. 3712, p. 322). Two of those five testators further asked to be buried
near the holy water font (*tlateochihuallatitlan*) situated nearby (BNAH,
doc. 20; AGN, Ramo Tierras, vol. 3712, p. 322). Many more testators—a
total of eleven—requested burial near a specific saint's statue or image
(BNAH, docs. 14/23, 19, 21, 22, 25, 40, 42, 43, 45, 49, 51). In Huexotzinco,
however, electing burial near a saint did not preclude interment near the
altar. San Miguel had only one nave, and most of its statuary adorned the
area near the altar. This particular architecture and interior adornment
meant that those who requested burial near a saint also, by default, asked
to be buried close to the altar (Hosselkus 2011).[11] For example, six of the
eleven Huexotzinco testators who specified a saint chose San Juan or San
Miguel (BNAH, docs. 21, 22, 42, 43, 45, 49). Sixteenth-century artist Simón
Pereyns designed the altarpiece of San Miguel's single nave to include fifteen sculpted saints, each approaching six feet in height, among them a
statue of San Juan Bautista and one of San Miguel that measured a few
inches taller than the others (Berlin et al. 1958, 72). It is quite likely that the
six testators referred to these very altar sculptures.[12]

Two of the eleven testators chose interment near San Francisco
(BNAH, docs. 25, 40). Huexotzinco's Nahuas instructed Pereyns to incorporate into the altarpiece a painted representation of "the history of Señor

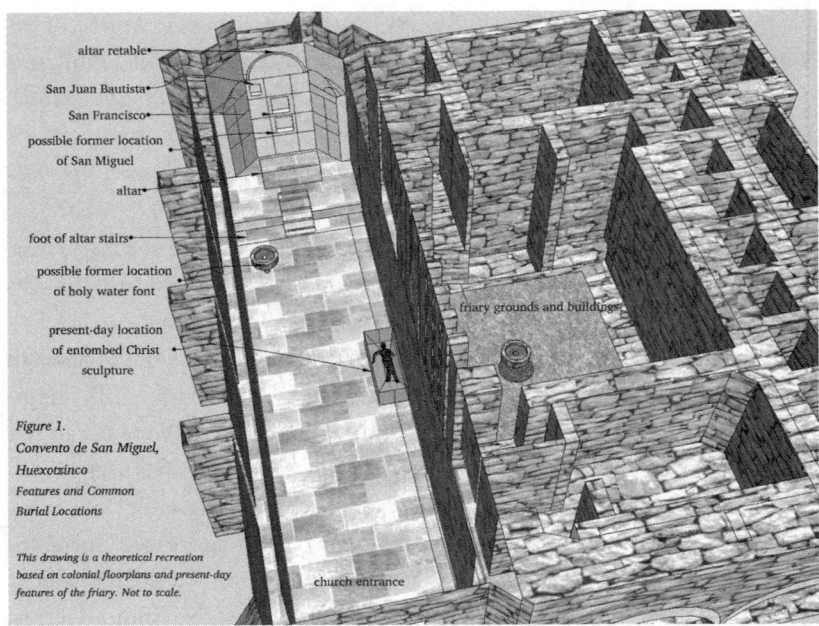

altar retable
San Juan Bautista
San Francisco
possible former location
of San Miguel
altar
foot of altar stairs
possible former location
of holy water font
present-day location
of entombed Christ
sculpture

Figure 1.
Convento de San Miguel,
Huexotzinco
Features and Common
Burial Locations

This drawing is a theoretical recreation
based on colonial floorplans and present-day
features of the friary. Not to scale.

friary grounds and buildings

church entrance

FIGURE 10.1. Convento de San Miguel, Huexotzinco.

San Francisco, in greater than one-half relief, of how he received the stigmata, with his companion and the angel" (Berlin et al. 1958, 72). This painting is quite possibly the San Francisco to whom two testators, Tomás Tlilli and Juana Caxtillanxochitl, referred, placing their earthly remains close to the altar as well. The remaining three testators identified saints' images not included in the altarpiece but likely positioned near the altar, meaning that a total of fifteen testators asked—directly or indirectly—for interment near San Miguel's altar (BNAH, docs. 14/23, 19, 51).[13] It seems, then, that Huexotzinco's seventeenth-century Nahuas, like their counterparts elsewhere in the empire, considered the altar—the place from which the friar offered salvation, by offering the true body and blood of Christ—a sacred and desirable location for their earthly remains.

The altar was important, but the language of many testaments prioritizes proximity to certain saints over nearness to the altar. Although sixteenth-century Spaniards often sought burial near saints' images, Nahuatl testaments from sixteenth-century Culhuacan and sixteenth-century Ocotelulco, Tlaxcala, in New Spain rarely mention specific saints (Cline and León Portilla 1984; Rojas Rabiela et al. 1999).[14] In fact, Nahua devotion to the cult of saints is not uniformly evident in a corpus of testaments until the eighteenth century, when the Nahua invalids of Toluca often specified burial sites oriented to a saint's image or chapel (Pizzigoni 2007, 16). When compared with these published studies of Nahuatl testaments, the Huexotzinco corpus, dating to the first three decades of the seventeenth century, constitutes a relatively early example in New Spain of indigenous devotion to the saints.[15] Of the eleven individuals electing burial near a saint, six chose the saint associated with their own neighborhoods (BNAH, docs. 21, 25, 40, 42, 43, 51). Others, including two testators from the neighborhood of Santa María Almoyahuacan (both named Francisco Pérez), identified regionally popular saints such as San Miguel and San Diego (BNAH, docs. 19, 45). Archangel San Miguel enjoyed prominence as the patron saint of Huexotzinco's Franciscan convent and also drew considerable followings in Tlaxcala and as an early patron saint of the city of Puebla.[16] Local devotion to San Diego dates to the late sixteenth century, when a young boy miraculously survived a fall into a well after his mother prayed to the saint (Vetancurt 1982, 58).

A final group of three testators wished to be buried "facing the tomb of our redeemer" (BNAH, docs. 29, 41, 44). Even today a life-sized sculpture of the deceased Christ adorns the San Miguel church, housed in a glass coffin or sepulcher situated under part of a penitential mural. During the sixteenth century, Huexotzinco's indigenous *cofradía* members carried a piece like this in the yearly Holy Week reenactments of the Descent from the Cross (Webster 1997, 29). These testators' wish to be buried near the statue attests to the legacy of Franciscan evangelization in the region. It also reflects the Christ-centered religiosity evident in the impressive Passion iconography of the San Miguel friary.

The burial preferences of Huexotzinco's indigenous testators—interment near the altar, near the holy water font, in front of specific saints, or near the entombed Christ—resemble preferences expressed in wills from other parts of the early modern Spanish Empire. They are not entirely unique or novel; they do, however, reflect personal, regional, and indigenous influences. Individual testators honored their personal devotions by choosing from a variety of burial locations, often near saints of regional importance, such as San Miguel, San Francisco, San Juan, or San Diego. Some, such as Francisco Pérez, who asked to be buried before San Miguel and at the foot of the altar stairs, identified with multiple fixtures or

features within the sacred space of the friary church. Its single-nave construction, something particular though not unique to San Miguel, enabled
Huexotzinco's invalids to do this.

Testators in Huexotzinco never asked to be buried near family members, a regional idiosyncrasy not readily evident elsewhere in the empire.
Nor does their wealth appear to correlate to burial location; for example,
testators of diverse means requested interment near the altar. This is also
particular though not necessarily unique to the region, due perhaps to
Huexotzinco's provincial status and small population relative to Mexico
City and other seventeenth-century urban centers. While there is nothing
evidently indigenous about the testators' burial choices, the testaments
from Huexotzinco do demonstrate devotion to the cult of saints in a Mexican indigenous community in the first decades of the seventeenth century—something not apparent in earlier Nahuatl testaments. All of these
findings point to the variable and flexible nature of Catholic practice in
indigenous New Spain. All early modern Catholic testators made spiritual
directives as they approached death, but the nature of those directives reflects personal, regional, and ethnic preferences.

Aiding the Soul

Testators also disposed of their earthly remains through their burial instructions, aiding their transcendent souls on the journey to heaven with
masses, a major component of testaments in the early modern Spanish Empire. Souls that received no masses or prayers risked languishing
eternally in purgatory. In Spain the number of masses requested by testators increased over the course of the sixteenth century and into the seventeenth century in some areas (Eire 1995, 176; Nalle 1992, 187). Nahuatl
testaments from New Spain usually contain at least one mass request and a
corresponding offering (Cline and León Portilla 1984; Pizzigoni 2007, 14).
For example, Ana Xiuhpetlacal of Huexotzinco left two pesos for one mass
for her soul (BNAH, doc. 14/23). In fact, all twenty-four testators in this
sample requested at least one mass near the beginning of the testament,
almost as if the notary, Esteban de Coto, included the provision without
exception. They left between two and five pesos for each mass, with two to
three pesos being standard, and did not specify mass type.

Five Huexotzinco testators requested one additional mass later in the
body of the testament (BNAH, docs. 19, 21, 29, 31; AGN, Ramo Tierras,

vol. 3712, p. 322). One requested two additional masses (AGN, Ramo Tierras, vol. 3712, p. 281). Another individual requested six extra masses (BNAH, doc. 20). Those requesting more masses were not uniformly wealthier in land or personal property. All testators in this sample interacted with the same notary. In turn, we might speculate that spiritual concerns or priorities compelled some individuals, though a minority, to spend modest amounts of money on extra masses rather than bequeath it all to heirs. Ana Xiuhpetlacal was the only testator to provide for masses for the souls of deceased family members. She ordered the sale of part of a plot of land to pay for a mass for her sister, Elena de Santa María, and one for her nephew, Matías de Santa María. Ana also possessed her deceased sister's skirt, *huipil*, and head covering. She ordered that the *huipil* be sold to fund an additional mass for Matías de Santa María (BNAH, doc. 14/23). Overall, the mass provisions outlined by Huexotzinco's seventeenth-century indigenous testators remained quite modest, deviating from the standard request of a single mass in relatively few instances; however, those few instances show personal preference at work. Individual spiritual concerns and priorities drove some to request additional masses for themselves or family members and helped to define the nature of death-related practices in indigenous New Spain, as elsewhere in the early modern Catholic world.

Five of this sample's twenty-four Huexotzinco testators also turned to *cofradías*, another part of the social network binding society, when death approached and spiritual concerns arose (BNAH, docs. 14/23, 21, 41, 47, 49). These lay religious organizations—associated with a particular church, chapel, or devotion—frequently participated in death rites in New Spain and elsewhere in the empire. They accompanied funeral processions in which the deceased's body traveled from the home to the church for mass and burial. They helped the poor with burial expenses, prayed for the souls of the dead, and funded masses for the souls of deceased members. Testators in sixteenth-century Spain frequently requested the presence of multiple *cofradías* at their funerals to offer prayers and spiritual support as the soul transitioned to the afterlife, even if they were not members (Eire 1995, 134–141; Nalle 1992, 196). In contrast, testaments from sixteenth-century indigenous Culhuacan and Ocotelulco, Tlaxcala, show no evidence of functioning *cofradías*. Nor did they seem to play a significant role in the funerals of indigenous residents of eighteenth-century Toluca (Pizzigoni 2007, 18).

For Huexotzinco, evidence indicates that *cofradías* were more integral to indigenous death rites than suggested by the five testamentary references. For example, Vetancurt (1982, 58) found eleven indigenous *cofradías* functioning in the town in the second half of the seventeenth century. Extant records prove that at least four of those predated secularization (Archivo Parroquial de San Miguel, Sección Disciplinar, Cofradías, caja 123, libros 1, 2, 3, 5). In addition, Webster (1997) has convincingly shown that the Cofradía de San Diego y la Santa Veracruz, introduced by the Franciscans, served as a vehicle for indigenous religiosity in the sixteenth century. It also regularly funded two high masses per month at the San Miguel friary church dedicated to "all the *cofrades*, living and deceased" (Archivo Parroquial de San Miguel, Sección Disciplinar, Cofradías, caja 123, libro 5, n.p.). Furthermore, the town's Cofradía de las Ánimas Benditas de Purgatorio de los Naturales performed a variety of death-related duties. The entity's constitution directs officials to use donations to buy the wax necessary for all the masses and burials requested by *cofrades*. It also orders them to fund a sung requiem mass each month for the souls in purgatory, and the entity's accounts record regular payments for such masses. Whenever a *cofrade* died, the organization was to arrange and pay for the funeral mass. Finally, officials were to set up an annual anniversary mass in which the living *cofrades* would participate in memory of the deceased (Archivo Parroquial de San Miguel, Sección Disciplinar, Cofradías, caja 123, libro 6, n.p.).

When Huexotzinco testators invoked *cofradías*, their requests generally echoed that of Ana Xiuhpetlacal, who ordered that "an offering of four reales, from which candles will come, is to be delivered to [the *cofradía* of] San Diego" (BNAH, doc. 14/23). Four of the five testators, including Ana, requested candles for the funeral mass from the area's oldest *cofradía*, dedicated to San Diego y la Santa Veracruz (BNAH, docs. 14/23, 21, 47, 49).[17] Ana María, the fifth testator, made her offering to the Cofradía de las Ánimas Benditas de Purgatorio de los Naturales (BNAH, doc. 41). Above all, the language used in these testaments indicates that Huexotzinco's *cofradías* provided candles for funeral masses in return for a donation. All masses required a specific minimum number of candles, which were also an integral aspect of religious processions. *Cofradías* could purchase wax in bulk, store it, and pay for it to be worked into candles of various types and sizes that could be distributed to *cofrades* when appropriate or given as charity to those who could not afford to purchase them.

In Huexotzinco the standard offering made to a *cofradía* in return for funeral mass candles was four reales (equivalent to half a peso). Interestingly, three of the nineteen testators who did not invoke a *cofradía* left mass offerings of two pesos and four reales (BNAH, docs. 20, 29, 48). It is possible that they envisioned the extra reales being exchanged for candles. One of those three testators also ordered that one peso be distributed "so that candles will come from it," surely referring to those provided by a *cofradía* (BNAH, doc. 20). Such evidence suggests that obtaining mass candles from a *cofradía* was a relatively common practice, not always requiring full explication. Although not entirely visible in the spiritual directives of testators, combined evidence indicates that *cofradías* played a significant role in the death practices of Huexotzinco's Nahuas. In this way the region differs from sixteenth-century indigenous Mexican communities. It also differs from eighteenth-century Toluca. Nor does the marked association with mass candles emerge from testaments from early modern Spain. Huexotzinco appears quite unique in this regard. This may reflect the legacy of Franciscan evangelization. It clearly demonstrates the regional nature of indigenous Catholicism as exercised at death in New Spain.

Only one testator in this sample made charitable bequests unrelated to funeral masses. Juana Caxtillanxochitl, the individual who requested a total of seven masses, left a castrated pig to the community for the feast day of the Trinity and three chickens to "San Diego," perhaps the chapel or the *cofradía* (BNAH, doc. 20). A skilled weaver, Juana possessed many lengths of cloth in various patterns and colors, half-finished shirts and skirts still on the loom, yarn, considerable land (some with magueys), and livestock. Her testament provides a final example of the personal nature of spiritual directives made at death. Her relative wealth enabled her to request many masses and leave charitable donations, yet many equally well heeled Nahuas disposed of their wealth by passing it all on to heirs. The precise reasons for Juana's decision elude us, but her Christian generosity is evident. Her case also reminds us of the many variations within Catholic death practices in indigenous New Spain and elsewhere in the Spanish Empire. Some individuals specified burial location, while others did not. Some requested and funded multiple masses; others were content with one standard mass. Some belonged to *cofradías* and sought their participation in funeral processions and masses; others perhaps belonged to but did not invoke the entities in their testaments.

The findings of sixteenth-century ecumenical and provincial councils defined and refined the Church's vision of a proper, or ideal, Catholic death, especially with regard to the role of extreme unction and good works in salvation.[18] The testamentary model organized and standardized the spiritual directives of the dying across the early modern era; however, personal, regional, and ethnic concerns emanate through the testaments. Although Huexotzinco's testators did not explain why they wished to be buried near San Miguel rather than San Juan, or San Francisco rather than San Pablo, their choices highlight the individual's contribution to the testamentary genre. Their devotion to the cult of saints, in contrast to their counterparts elsewhere in central New Spain, illustrates the eminently regional nature of religious practice in the early modern era. Recognizing and examining these types of idiosyncrasies is a critical part of understanding the nature of Catholicism and its relationship to death in the minds and lives of the indigenous residents of New Spain.

Last Will and Testament of Ana Xiuhpetlacal, Huexotzinco, 1613

Transcription

(BNAH, Archivo Histórico, 3rd series, leg. 28, doc. 14/23, fols. 19–23v)
[fol. 19]

y̱ yn ica . ytocatzin tetatzin . yhuā tepiltzin [yhuā] Espu Sancto . nicpehualtia . yn notestamēto . ma qui[ma]ticā . yn ixquichtin . quitazq̄ . ynī amatl ca yn nehuatl notoca . aña . xiuhpetlacal . nicā nochā Ciudad huexo^co . ytech nipohui . yn perochia . yn itoca . S . pa^o . ocotepec nicchiua . yn notestamēto . macihui . yn mococohua . yn nonacayo . yece yn noyollo . yn noçialliz . yn notlanequilliz – yn notlacaquia . anquē ca . çā pactica . auh nicchixtica yn miquiztli . yn aac huel yxpāpa yehua . yn aac huel quitlalcahuia . yc nicā nictlallia . yn notestamēto yn ça tlatzōco . yn ça tlatzaccā . yn notlanequilliz . ynic mochipa mopiaz . ynic ayac quitlacoz . ca yehuatli . yz catqui yc nicpehualtia .

y̱ huellachto yehuatl . yn nanimatzin ymactzinc[o] nocōtlallia . yn tote^o dios . ca oquimochiuilli . yhuā nicnotlatlauhtillia . ynic nechmotlaocolilliz . nechmopopolhuilliz . yn notlatlacol ynic nechmohuiq̄lliz . yn ichātzinco . yn ilhuicatl yhtec yn ihquac contlalcahui . yn nanima . yn nonacayo . auh yn nonacayo ytech nicpohua . yn tlalli .

ca ytech oquiz . ca tlalli — ca çoquitl yhuā nicnequi . ça ce tilmahtli . yc
moq̄milloz . ynic motocaz . yhuā nicneq́ onpa motocaz . yn toteopā . Sta
ma.ª asump.º · onpa nechmomachiotilli[z] yn teopixq́ yn nosepultora
yn notecoch yn n[otla]tatac . yhuā nicneq́ . yn ipāpa . yn nanima [ipale]
huilloca . ynic am̄o onpa . huecahuaz yn porga[to]rio cētetl missa . nopā
mihtoz . auh ytlacamo hue[li]tiz . ma ya qui y moztlatica . mochiuaz .
mocahuaz huētzintli . teopa ome pesus . auh . ynic quiçaz cātella . S. diego
. mocahuaz . huētzintli nahui rs

v̲ ynic cētlamātli . nitlanahuatitiuh . nicpia . nosular cētetl
matlamatl . yni hueyac cēpohualli . yn tlanipa . jular . yn ihuicpa . norde
. nictepanohua . diego gotierez . yn acopa . nictepanohua . ytoca .
gaspa. maldonado . yn amilpā[fol. 19v]pa nictepanohua . ytoca . simō .
tollipanecatl . yhuā ypā mani nocalhua . sacaltin ontetl auh . yn nosular
[nojular] yhuā nocalhuā . nicmacatiuh . ytoca . Juā de s. tiago . yehuatl
tlapiaz .

v̲ ynic ōtlamātli nitlanahuatitiuh . yn teuhcyotl ytech niccauhtiuh . yn
itoca . Juā de s. tiago . yehuatl teuhctlalliloz . yn ipā . ylhuitzin . S . Simō .
nimā teochiualloz . yehuatl tlacateuhctli tocayotilloz . yhuā yn ipā ylhuitl
quichiuaz . yn quexquich monequiz . – amo ytla . quitlacoz .

v̲ ynic yetlamātli . nitlanahuatitiuh . nicpia . sular [jular] hu[sic ; prob.
huel] yehuatl . yn tecalli . ypā mania . ynic hueyac cenpohualli onmatlactli
. ynic patlahuac ynic hueyac cenpohualli . yn tlanipa . nictepanohua .
hellias . monoz yn ihuicpa . norde jular . yn acopa jular . yn amilpāpa .
nictepanohua . gaspar . maldonado . ynin . nicma[ca]tiuh . yn itoca . Juā
de . s. ti²go . oncā teuhctiz . ayac quellehuilliz . yhuā yn tepātli . yhçiuhca
. quichihuaz . oncatq̄ . yn calquauitl . mopia . hepo[hual]li onmatlactli .
ynic mochiuaz . calli . ça nimā yhçiuhca . quichiua . yn Juā de s.tiago .

v̲ ynic nauhtlamātli . nitlanahuatitiuh . nicpia . notlal ytocayocā
quauhquiyahuac . ynic hueyac . onpa onaci . yn itepāco . fran^{co} . hernādez
. beroz . ynic patlauac cēpohualli oncastolli . oncā onpehua . yn itepāco
. gabriel cehuanotl yn amilpāpa . notepanecapo Esteua p̲z catca . yn
ihuicpa . norde notepanecapo . Juā de . s .tiago ynic tlani temohua . ytech
onaci - tlaxcaltecayotli . auh yepohualli . monamacaz yn tlalli . oncā quiçaz
ontetl missa . cētetl ymissa . hellena . de . sta ma.ª yhuā cētetl ymissa . yn
nopillotzin ytoca . mathias . de s. ta ma.ª yn ihquac monamacaz - yn tlalli
. yhquac mochiuaz . yn missa yn quexquich mocahuaz . yn tlalli . ytech
nicpouhtiuh . Juā de . s . tiago ayac quellehuilliz . –

<u>y</u> ynic maCuillamātli . nitlanahuatitiuh . quipia tomi.ˢ ytoca . Barnabe chalchiuhtepehua . nahui tomi.ˢ yhciuhca . tlaxtlahuaz . quimacaz . yn itoca . Juã de . s .tiᵃgo [fol. 23] <u>y</u> ynic chiquacētlamātli . nitlanahuatitiuh . ytoca Jua de cardo quipia . tomi.ˢ chiquacē tomiˢ . quimacatehuac nopitzin catca . ytoca . hellena de s . ta ma.ᵃ auh . yhciuhca . tlaxtlahuaz . macoz . yn noaruaceashuā

<u>y</u> ynic chicōtlamātli . nitlanahuatitiuh . yn yehuatl nopillotzin sebastiana . quihuicaz . yn icuetzin yhuā ytlapachiuhca auh . yn huipilli monamacaz . oncā quiçaz . cētetl . missa . ypā mochiuaz yn nopillotzin mathias de . s . ta ma.ᵃ catca . m[...]c[...]uaz huētzintli [...] pesus . yn ihquac omonamacac huipilli . –

<u>y</u> auh yz catqui y niquimixquetztiuh . yn niqũɪteneuhtiuh . yn quimoCuitlauizq̃ . yn notlatlalil . yn notestamēto . ynic ce ytoca . pasqual metina . ynic ome . diego <u>pz</u> tlacochcalcatl ynic mochi . neltiz . mochiuaz ma ypaltzinco . yn tot"º dios . quimochiuillizque q́ motequipanilhuizq̃ . yn yehuatli . yn notestamēto . hanoço nocōdicillo . hanoço notzōquizcatlanequilliz . yn iuh ca . nahuatilli . yn mellahuac tlahtolli . ynic yhçiuhca . mochiuaz . neltiz yn izquitl[a]mātli . yn itech nictlallitiuh . yn notestamēto au[h] occepa niquinotlatlauhtillitiuh. Pasqual metina. yhuā diego . <u>pz</u> . tlacochcalcatl ynic nopā motlatoltizque ynic yhçiuhca mochiuaz . auh yntla yhciuhca . mochiuaz . yc nicnotlatlauhtillia . yn yehuatzin yn tote"º dios . ynic qũɪmotlaocoliliz . ynic no yuhqui . ypā mochiuaz . yn ihquac momiquillizque yntla oc cētetl notestamēto . yn canapa neciz mochi nicpollohua . ātle ypā pohuiz . yuhqui yna[...] hanoço aca ytla niquilhui . notlahtol n[...]nehuilli . mochi nicpollohua . çā ye yyo . ne[...] yn axcā nicchiua . omochiuh . ypā martes . yc 21 . ylhuitl ỹ mes de mayo . 1613 . aºs auh yn cocoxqui quitlalli . ce cruz . auh . yn imixpa testigo . omochiuh . mathias . de gande alguacil Pasqual de . s . fran.ᶜº Esteuā de coto . escriº

+ + āna xiuhpetlacal

[fol. 23v] [right margin: + ytestamēto aña xiuhpetlacal . ocotepec]

+ mathias . de gāde Pasqual de . S . francº

Esteuā de coto

<u>y</u> çatepā oniquilnamic mopia . amatl ypatiuh . nahui pesus . cōfesio . naria . auh monamacac . mo[...]ci ome pesus yhua chiquace tominˢ

Translation

[fol. 19]

ẙ In the name of the father, the child, and the Holy Spirit, I begin my testament. Know all who see this document that I, named Ana Xiuhpetlacal, whose home is here in the city of Huexotzinco and who belongs to the parish called San Pablo Ocotepec, make my testament. Although my body is ill, nevertheless nothing is wrong with my spirit, will, and understanding; rather, they are sound. I am awaiting death, from which no one can flee, which no one can avoid. Therefore, I here issue my testament, my last and final will, so that it will always be kept and that no one will go against it. This is it, here it is, with this I begin:

ẙ First of all, I place my soul in the hands of our lord God who made it, and I beseech him to favor me by pardoning me my sins, and taking me to his home in heaven when my soul has abandoned my body. I assign my body to the earth, for it came from it and is earth and clay. I want my body to be wrapped just in a cloak for burial, and I want it interred at our church, Santa María de la Asunción. The priest will designate my grave for me there. I wish, on account of the help of my soul, so that it will not be long in purgatory, a mass to be said for me, and if it cannot be done, let it be later, the next day. A two-peso offering is to be delivered to the church. An offering of four reales, from which candles will come, is to be delivered to [the cofradía of] San Diego.

ẙ First, I am ordering that I have a *solar* that is 10 *matl* [wide] and 20 long. Below the *solar*, toward the north, I share a border with Diego Gutiérrez and above I border on one named Gaspar Maldonado; toward the irrigated fields [south] [fol. 19v] I border on Simón Tolipanecatl, and my houses, two thatch structures, are there on it [the lot]. I am giving my *solar* and my houses to the one named Juan de Santiago; he is to be in charge.

ẙ Second, I am ordering that I am leaving the lordship to the one named Juan de Santiago, and he is to be installed as lord on the day of San Simón and thereupon he is to be consecrated. He will be given the name of Tlacateuctli, and on the saint's day he will do all that is necessary so that he will do nothing wrong.

ẙ Third, I am ordering that I have a *solar* on which the palace [lordly house] used to be, 30 wide and 20 long. Below, I share a border with Elías Muñoz; toward the north is a lot; above is a lot; and toward the irrigated

fields I border on Gaspar Maldonado. I am giving this to the one named
Juan de Santiago and there he will hold forth as lord and no one else is
to desire it from him. And he is to build the walls soon, and there are 70
house timbers with which to make the house; Juan de Santiago is to do it
very quickly.

y Fourth, I am ordering that I have land in a place named Quauhquiyahuac and on the long side it reaches the border of Francisco Hernández
Beroz[?]. In width it is 35 and it starts from the border of Gabriel Cehuanotl; toward the irrigated fields my neighbor is Esteban Pérez, deceased,
and toward the north my neighbor is Juan de Santiago. Below it descends
and reaches Tlaxcalan territory. Sixty [matl] of the land are to be sold, and
out of the proceeds will come two masses, one mass for Elena de Santa
María and one mass for my nephew named Matías de Santa María. When
the land is sold and the masses are performed, I assign however much of
the land is left to Juan de Santiago; no one is to covet it of him.

y Fifth, I am ordering that Bernabé Chalchiuhtepehua owes four reales
and he is to pay soon and give it to the one named Juan de Santiago.

[fol. 23] y Sixth, I am ordering that Juan de Galdós has [owes] money,
six reales, that my deceased older sister, Elena de Santa María, gave to him
before she died. He is to pay soon and it is to be given to my executors.

v Seventh, I am ordering that my niece Sebastiana is to have her [Elena
de Santa María's] skirt and her veil/ head covering. The huipil is to be sold
and [the cost of] a mass is to come out it; it is to be performed for my deceased nephew, Matías de Santa María. An offering is to be delivered when
the huipil has been sold.

y Here are those who I am appointing and naming to take care of my
orders and my testament, first Pasqual Medina and second Diego Pérez
Tlacochcalcatl. By means of our lord God they are to execute and carry
out this my testament, or codicil, or last will according to the law, a proper
statement, so that each of the things I am issuing in my testament will be
done and carried out quickly. Again, I implore Pasqual Medina and Diego
Pérez Tlacochcalcatl to see to it on my behalf that it be done quickly. And
if it is done quickly, I pray our lord God to grant them that it will be done
that way with them when they die. And if another testament of mine
should appear, I cancel it; it is to count for nothing. Or if I made a statement of promise to someone, I cancel it all. Only the one I make today is
authentic. It was done on Tuesday the 21st day of the month of May of the

year 1613. The sick person put a cross [instead of signing her name]. It was done before the witnesses Matías de Gante, *alguacil*, and Pasqual de San Francisco. Esteban de Coto, notary.

++ Ana Xiuhpetlacal.

[fol. 23v] [right margin: The testament of Ana Xiuhpetlacal of Ocotepec.]

+ Matías de Gante. Pascual de San Francisco.

Esteban de Coto.

<u>v</u> Afterward I remembered that a book is preserved that cost four pesos, a confessional book. It was sold and came to two pesos, six reales.

Notes

My thanks to Jim Lockhart for his invaluable translation assistance.

1. In addition to preparing a testament, the Catholic faithful were directed to anticipate and contemplate the moral and existential struggles associated with leaving the terrestrial world for the hereafter. They could prepare for that final agony by utilizing an *arte de bien morir* (good death manual) during life. As the name suggests, works of this genre were designed to inform the faithful about the nature of the deathbed experience and thereby enable them to ward off demons, remain faithful, and repent deeply during their last hours (see Bastante 2006). The Church also required that invalids issue a final confession and receive absolution, last communion, and the sacrament of extreme unction, though of course not everyone was able to do so.

2. In the years following the conquest, the Huexotzinca faithfully delivered cloth, corn, and other supplies to Mexico City on the orders of the first *audiencia* (high court). They also sent warriors, slaves, arrows, loincloths, and more to accompany the conquest expedition into western New Spain, led by Nuño de Guzmán (see *Codice de Huexotzinco* 1995).

3. A particularly impressive study of the development of Tlaxcala's unique indigenous identity during the colonial era is developed in Cuadriello 2011.

4. With the guidance of Jim Lockhart, I have translated forty-one of approximately fifty extant testaments. I have also translated some of the assorted materials, including a contract between a painter and a *cofradía* for the repair of a statue, two reports of concubinage, a warning issued to a musician, and records of deaths and births. These documents—a corpus of Nahuatl testaments, bills of sale, and other miscellaneous documents from the polity of San Andrés Cholula—and abundant Spanish-language documents are treated in my doctoral dissertation (Hosselkus 2011) and constitute part of my ongoing work on indigenous life and death in colonial Puebla.

5. The testaments produced by Coto are stylistically similar, close in date, and constitute a more cohesive and logical sample than the entire corpus of

forty-one translated testaments. They are largely representative of the total corpus. Citations for each document appear in Table 10.1. Coto shared his name with a Spaniard, Esteban de Coto, notary of the king (*escribano del rey*), who acquired a land grant in the Huexotzinco region in 1591 and recorded the details of a miraculous event associated with the holy host that occurred at the Franciscan friary of San Miguel in the same year (Mendieta 1997, 454).

6. Thirteen of the Huexotzinco testators in this sample (54 percent) were male, and the remaining eleven (46 percent) were female. Nine testators were married, including eight men and one woman. Fourteen testaments, five corresponding to male testators and nine to female testators, do not mention a spouse. One testator was a widow. Seventeen testators (71 percent) mentioned children in their testaments. They resided in eight different neighborhoods of Huexotzinco. The testators' wealth and social status varied greatly; some were lords, possessing significant real and personal property, while others owned no land.

7. Although the pertinent section of Ana Xiuhpetlacal's testament might be translated as "I want it interred at our church of Santa María de la Asunción," there was no such church in Huexotzinco in the first half of the seventeenth century. One of San Miguel's *posa* chapels was dedicated to Santa María de la Asunción, and fragments of a fresco dedicated to the Virgin can still be detected there. It is possible that Ana wished to be buried near that chapel, but burial near a statue or painting is more likely.

8. The practice of specifying burial location within the friary complex was not common in sixteenth-century Culhuacan. In contrast, it was quite common in eighteenth-century Toluca, suggesting that this tendency may be related, in some way, to the development of notarial tradition over time or to developments in Catholic practice over time (Pizzigoni 2007, 16).

9. I utilize selected studies and collections of testaments for comparison throughout this chapter. Other scholars have worked with testaments from the early modern Spanish Empire, but the studies addressed here are most directly relevant.

10. Perhaps testators expected friars to know where their relatives were buried in this relatively small community, or perhaps the notary, Esteban de Coto, did not prompt testators regarding locations of relatives' bodies. Ultimately, we are left to speculate.

11. See Hosselkus 2011, chap. 4, for more on this. The saints do not appear to correspond to Huexotzinco's *posa* chapels despite Vetancurt's (1982, 58) findings for the sixteenth century.

12. The testator who cited San Miguel requested burial before his image at the foot of the altar stairs, providing evidence of saint imagery at the altar.

13. Testator Ana Xiuhpetlacal is a possible exception. She requested burial near Santa María de la Asunción. One of Huexotzinco's *posa* chapels was dedicated to Santa María de la Asunción; however, it seems unlikely that

Xiuhpetlacal wished to be buried outside of the church walls when most of her contemporaries preferred burial inside the structure.

14. This corresponds with Lockhart's (1992, 243) finding that no Nahuatl testament dated prior to the 1580s makes explicit reference to the cult of saints.

15. As scholars uncover and analyze testaments from the seventeenth century, we are likely to better understand the development of devotion to the cult of saints in indigenous New Spain. For example, Jonathan Truitt's chapter (this volume) suggests that the cult of saints was part of Nahua religious practice in Mexico-Tenochtitlan in the seventeenth century, as in Huexotzinco.

16. On San Miguel in the region's art history, see Báez Macías 1979.

17. For more on the *cofradía* of San Diego y la Santa Veracruz see Webster 1997.

18. The Council of Trent and the First and Second Mexican Provincial Councils addressed the importance of extreme unction, with the councils addressing the sacrament's administration in indigenous communities (*Concilios provinciales* 1796).

References

Báez Macías, Eduardo. 1979. *El Arcangel San Miguel*. Instituto de Investigaciones Estéticas, Monografías de Arte. Mexico City: Universidad Nacional Autónoma de México.

Bastante, Pamela. 2006. *The Arte de Bien Morir: Changes in the Church's Official Discourses from Fifteenth-Century Spain to Eighteenth-Century Mexico*. Vancouver: University of British Columbia.

Berlin, Heinrich, Pedro de Carvajal, and Cristóbal Gutiérrez. 1958. "The High Altar of Huejotzingo." *The Americas* 15(1): 63–73.

Cline, S. L. 1986. *Colonial Culhuacan, 1580–1600: A Social History of an Aztec Town*. Albuquerque: University of New Mexico Press.

Cline, S. L., and Miguel León-Portilla. 1984. *The Testaments of Culhuacan*. Los Angeles: UCLA Latin American Center Publications.

Codice de Huexotzinco. 1995. Library of Congress, Coca-Cola Export Corporation. Mexico City: Ediciones Multiarte.

Concilios provinciales primero y segundo, celebrados en la muy noble y muy leal ciudad de México. 1796. Mexico City: Imprenta de el Superior Gobierno.

Cuadriello, Jaime. 2011. *The Glories of The Republic of Tlaxcala: Art and Life in Viceregal Mexico*. Translated by C. J. Follett. Austin: University of Texas Press.

Eire, Carlos M. N. 1995. *From Madrid to Purgatory: The Art and Craft of Dying in Sixteenth-Century Spain*. New York: Cambridge University Press.

Hosselkus, Erika R. 2011. Living with Death Between the Volcanoes: Nahua Approaches to Mortality in Colonial Puebla's Upper Atoyac Basin. Ph.D. dissertation, Department of History, Tulane University.

Lockhart, James. 1992. *The Nahuas After the Conquest: A Social and Cultural History of the Indians of Central Mexico, Sixteenth Through Eighteenth Centuries*. Stanford, Calif.: Stanford University Press.

Mendieta, fray Gerónimo de. 1997. *Historia eclesiástica indiana*. Vol. 1. Mexico City: Consejo Nacional para la Cultura y las Artes.

Nalle, Sara Tilghman. 1992. *God in La Mancha: Religious Reform and the People of Cuenca, 1500–1650*. Baltimore: Johns Hopkins University Press.

Pizzigoni, Caterina, trans. and ed. 2007. *Testaments of Toluca*. Nahuatl Studies Series No. 8, edited by James Lockhart. Stanford, Calif.: Stanford University Press.

Prem, Hanns J. 1988. *Milpa y hacienda: Tenencia de la tierra indígena y española en la cuenca del Alto Atoyac, Puebla, México (1520–1650)*. Mexico City and Puebla: CIESAS, Estado de Puebla, Fondo de Cultura Económica.

Ramos, Gabriela. 2010. *Death and Conversion in the Andes: Lima and Cuzco, 1532–1670*. Notre Dame, Ind.: University of Notre Dame Press.

Rojas Rabiela, Teresa, Elsa Leticia Rea López, and Constantino Medina Lima. 1999. *Vidas y bienes olvidados: Testamentos indígenas novohispanos*. Vol. 1. Mexico City: CIESAS, Consejo Nacional de Ciencia y Tecnología.

Vetancurt, fray Agustín de. 1982. *Crónica de la provincia del Santo Evangelio de México*. Biblioteca Porrúa 45. Mexico City: Editorial Porrúa.

Webster, Susan Verdi. 1997. "Art, Ritual, and Confraternities in Sixteenth-Century New Spain: Penitential Imagery at the Monastery of San Miguel, Huejotzingo." *Anales del Instituto de Investigaciones Estéticas* 70: 5–43.

Zárate Toscano, Verónica. 2000. *Los nobles ante la muerte en México: Actitudes, ceremonias y memoria, 1750–1850*. Mexico City: Instituto de Investigaciones Dr. José María Luis Mora.

CHAPTER 11

"Networks of Trust"

Debtors and Creditors in the Wills of Indian Nobles and
Commoners in the Lima Valley, 1596–1607

PAUL J. CHARNEY

In recent years scholars have made greater use of the wills of non-Europeans as a source for the social history of colonial Latin America. Wills have served as barometers of piety and spirituality, of confraternal devotion and cultural transformation among blacks, Indians, and other nonwhites. Of course, many did not make wills because of impoverishment, geographical isolation, or unwillingness. Members of the Indian nobility were more likely to testate, owing to the desire to protect their status and wealth, as well as to authenticate their own political legitimacy, as Conway's chapter in this volume makes clear. Some Indian commoners nonetheless testated, and their wills—along with those of the Indian nobility—provide insights into the indigenous past and the extent of changes wrought by the Spanish intrusion.[1]

This study is based on thirteen wills chosen for their geographical and chronological proximity. They were all testated in the Valley of Lima between 1596 and 1607, six by the Indian nobility, and seven by Indian commoners who all did so in 1596, two of whom drew up codicils and one who died intestate. The titles *don* and *doña* and/or their political and economic status distinguished nobility from commoners; the former included two caciques (chiefs), one male *principal* (subordinate chief) and his wife, one female *principal*, and a cacique's wife. The nobles claimed their birthplace in the valley's Spanish-created Indian communities (Figure 11.1 and Table 11.1). Of the seven commoners, six lived in Surco and one in Surquillo (Table 11.2). Each community consisted of *ayllus* (a sociopolitical

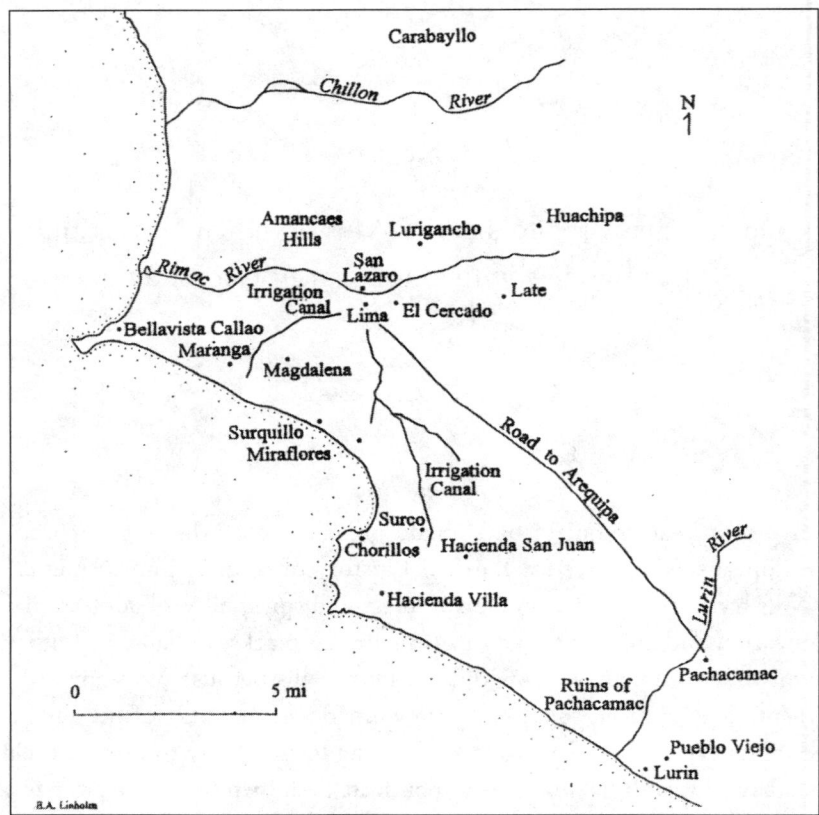

FIGURE 11.1. Spanish-created Indian communities in the Valley of Lima during the colonial period. (Redrawn from Keith 1971, 68; and Gunther Doering 1983, Map 18.)

unit headed by a cacique whose members are linked to a common lineage or ancestor-deity) that were relocated in the 1560s from their original areas to more compact communities because of depopulation and the desire of royal officials and priests for more effective tribute collection and evangelization. As epidemic diseases reduced the size of the coastal Indian population, the number of Spaniards, Africans, and people of mixed ancestry increased, and Indians from different parts of the Peruvian viceroyalty migrated to Lima (Charney 2001, chap. 1). The native-born of the valley who survived nonetheless managed to adapt to the market economy on their own terms.

One part of a standard will reveals much about small-scale commerce: the relationship between debtors and creditors. In her study of the Nahua

TABLE 11.1. Noble testators

Testator	Year	Notary[a]	Office[b]	Town	Year	Population	
1 Don Juan Casapacsi	1607	*	C	Magdalena	1602	321	
2 Francisca Chani	1596	**		Surco	1602	684	
3 Francisco Chumbimaycha	1596	**	P	Guadca	1602	250	R1[c]
4 Doña Isabel Caxaquilla	1598	***	P	Lurigancho	1591	128	R2[d]
5 Doña Maria Guacha	1601	****		Chuquitanta	1591	89	R2
6 Don Fernando Nacara	1600	****	C	Collique	1784	26	R2

Sources:

1. "Título de una chacra y tierras que Pedro de Garate poseia en el valle de la Magdalena....
(1641)," Archivo General de la Nación de Perú (AGNP), Títulos de Propiedad, cuaderno 241, fols.
14v–16r.

2. "Testamentos de indios," AGNP, one legajo, unnumbered folios.

3. Ibid.

4. Rodrigo Alonso Castillejo (1597–1598), AGNP, Protocolos Notariales (PN) 21, fols. 1471v–477r
(copy of original).

5. Castillejo (1599–1602), AGNP, PN 22, fols. 899r–902v.

6. Ibid., fols. 672v–675r.

7. Paul Charney, *Indian Society in the Valley of Lima, Peru, 1532–1824* (2001), app. 5.

[a] Notaries: * Don Felipe Chatan of Magdalena; ** Don Lorenzo Yanchichumbi of Surco; ***Juan de
Herrera (Spanish); **** Rodrigo Alonso Castillejo (Spanish)

[b] Office: C = *cacique*, P = *principal*.

[c] R1: *ayllu* reduced to Magdalena

[d] R2: *ayllu* reduced to Carabayllo.

in Coyoacan, Rebecca Horn (1998, 77) sees such commerce as an important vehicle of cultural change. But what kind of change? Aside from the
debate on the existence of marketplaces in the Andean world, it is clear that
many Andean men and women came to view money and trade as not entirely alien. In fact, the ethnohistorian Waldemar Espinoso Soriano found
in his linguistic and lexical research that trade was not unheard of before
the Spanish arrival, while according to the late Thierry Saignes (1999, 94),
"today a debt is called *wanu* in Quechua ('manure') because it fertilizes
interpersonal relationships."[2] Therefore, this debt of alien origin was "given
symbolic meaning" (Restall 1998, 143) and did not necessarily indicate
total cultural loss.

The testators' listings of their creditors, in addition to what was owed
to them, reveal a "network of trust" (Graubart 2007, 77). Such a network—
rural and intimate, and possibly built upon the *wanu*—also included Spaniards who had financial and fictive kin ties to men and women of the Indian
nobility. Early modern Europeans also attached a similar symbolic meaning to debt, referring to it as "an obligation, a relational debt, which was not

TABLE 11.2. Debts and credits of commoners, 1596

Name/Ayllu	Date	Debt	Credits
Antonio Haique / Callca	10/1		2 p (work); 2 p (rent); 2 pt; 1 pt; 1 pt (chicha); 2 bo of chicha; 15 p for use of chestnut mare
Simon Saoni / community of Surquillo	10/24	2 pt (rent)	5 pt (trousers); [7 pt loose-fitting trousers, shirt, hat]
Miguel Cocssi / Cintaulli	10/26		8 r, 8 r, 8 r, 2 p, 6 r
Maria Capan / Ydcar	?		new taffeta shirt; 8 r; 12 r; 4 r (chicken); ½ fa sora (maize); 8 r (ca of chicha); 8 r (ca of chicha); 13 pt (3 ca of chicha)
Elvira Coyti (intestate) / Cuncham	2/2	4 pt, 1 pt	8 r (chicken)
Juan China / Ydcar	4/17	2 p (firewood), 10 p (firewood), 5 p	2 p (for cutting firewood); 10 p (lost fishing net)
Codicile	4/17		forgive debt of fishing net
Constanza Ticlla / Tauli	4/17		6 r
Codicile	4/20	8 r (ca of chicha)	

Source: "Testamentos de indios," AGN, one legajo.
Notes:
Currency: p = peso (8 reales); r = real; pt = patacones (cheaper silver coinage worth 8 reales);
pc = peso corriente (9 reales in sixteenth century; 8 reales in seventeenth century).
Measurements: bu. = bushel; ca = cántaro (15 liters); bo = botija (8 liters); fa = fanega
(1.5 bushels in dry measure; 1 hectare in area).

quantified in financial terms but could be repaid within a complex, flexible network of reciprocity" (Guzzi-Heeb 2004, 106). This might have found relevance in the Andean world, where most kin and non-kin relationships were defined by acts of reciprocity, with the introduction of currency becoming just another ingredient of the social glue.

The *wanu*, however, did not often leave a paper trail. Jane Mangan's (2003) study of Andeans in colonial Potosí shows that their small-scale transactions often went unnotarized; instead, those outside the traditional sources of credit (e.g., church, patron, merchant guilds, *caja de censos* [general Indian fund]) used "cues like place of residence, ethnic identity, and gender" to identify debtors or creditors (Mangan 2003, 109, 115–116; and 2005, 118–119, 124–127; see also Graubart 2007, 76–80).[3] Although they were not city Indians, the testators of the Valley of Lima used similar cues, and others had cultural connotations. One stemmed from the

Spanish custom of addressing the "wife of...," implying the secondary place of the maiden name. Don Juan Casapacsi's creditors included "wife of Juan Vinco," "wife of Alonso Toribio," "Juan Fernández, husband of Petrona," "the son-in-law of María Bilbao," and "the mother of don Esteban" (AGN, Lima, Títulos de Propiedad [hereafter TP]), "Título de una chacra...(1641)," 241, fols. 15r–15v). Francisca Chani also used Spanish forms in identifying some of her debtors, but two of the three revealed an Andean preference for retaining their maiden names: "the wife of Pedro Cancho Haiqui" (the son of Antonio Haiqui [Surco]), one of the common testators); "Juana Yca, wife of Felipe Mosta"; and "Leonor Mitan, the wife of Martín Hayhim," also identified as an "yndia de la Magdalena" (AGN, Lima, "Testamentos de indios," one *legajo*). Commoners did the same: Constanza Ticlla identified Ana Quilltin, "wife of Julio Larac," as her creditor, and Juan Caotay, "son of Pedro Pachoy," owed Miguel Cocssi for a small loan (ibid.).[4] This acknowledgment of the debtor's or creditor's partner reflects the social intimacy of a rural community whose members knew one another and thereby constituted a supporting network. In contrast, most of the urban Indians studied by Mangan lived in multiethnic, interconnected neighborhoods that compelled them to rely more on ethnic markers and the precise locations of residences in order to identify debtors or creditors.

The social and physical proximity naturally necessitated a certain level of trust to facilitate an array of transactions. For the valley's testators, big and small loans, goods pawned for cash, and what was owed for labor services, rent, clothing, or animals loaned out perhaps depended on an existing "network of trust" that straddled pre- and postconquest times. Unfortunately, the testator's relationship with the debtor or creditor and his or her race were not always made clear. When clarity prevailed, those transactions, more so for the nobility than commoners, occurred in and outside the community, among Indians and non-Indians, men and women, and real and fictive kin. Not surprisingly, the amount of debt and income differentiated commoners from nobles (compare Tables 11.2 and 11.3). Large sums usually involved Spaniards and were often notarized, though some Indians and other nonwhites had cash to spare that must have impressed or inspired envy from their fellow villagers (Restall 1998, 143).

Don Juan Casapacsi claimed notarizing the largest debts to three Spaniards, and another to his Spanish *padrino* (godfather), Miguel Galas; he

TABLE 11.3. Debts and credits of nobles

Testator (c = creditors; d = debtors)	Debts	Credits
1. D. Juan Casapacsi 17 c; 1d	950 p*; 553 pt*; 3 fa wheat; golden ring; 30 pt (pawn: altarpiece) [10 pt (rent), 3 pt]	400 p censo
2. Francisco Chani 1 c; 7 d	4 r	1 fa wheat (rent); ca chicha = 8 r; 6 r broken ca = 8 r; 2 lost ca = 16 r; 62 pc = 5 fa wheat
3. Francisco Chumbimaycha 4 c; 7 d	16 r; 6 pt (pawn: choker of pearls, 28 p)	7 pc = wheat; 20 r; 8 r = half fa maize;12 r maize (holds two old black plumes); 9 p (of 30 p yearly rent); 80 pc (2 year rent); 9 pt (rent)
4. D. Isabel Caxaquilla 1 c; 1 d	350 p	400 p censo
5. D. Maria Guacha 7 c; 5 d	50 pc; 5 pt; 20 pt (pawn: silverware, 2 silver vessels, 30 pieces of silver) 5 pt (of goods); 16 pt (pawn: silver rider); 16 pt; 9 pt (pawn: silverware)	100 p (rent); 2 pts (2 bo of chicha) 2 pts and 6 r (chicha); 2 pts (chicha); 8r 8r (chicha)
6. D. Fernando Nacara 9 c; 4 d	500 pc; 26 pt; 40 p; 20 pt [20 p, 10 pt]; [10 pt, 3 pt]; 1 fa maize [100 pt, 20 pt, 6 pt]; roan horse	171 p (censo); mare; 14 p (rent); [72 pt (rent), 1,200 pt (8 years back rent)]

Sources:

1."Título de una chacra y tierras que Pedro de Garate poseia en el valle de la Magdalena.... (1641)", Archivo General de la Nación de Perú (AGNP), Títulos de Propiedad, cuaderno 241, fols. 14v–16r.

2. "Testamentos de indios," AGNP, one legajo, unnumbered folios.

3. Ibid.

4. Rodrigo Alonso Castillejo (1597–1598), AGNP, Protocolos Notariales (PN) 21, fols. 1471v–1477r (copy of original).

5. Castillejo (1599–1602), AGNP, PN 22, fols. 899r–902v.

6. Ibid., fols. 672v–675r.

7. Paul Charney, Indian Society in the Valley of Lima, Peru, 1532–1824 (2001), app. 5.

Notes:

Currency: p = peso (8 reales); r = real; pt = patacones (cheaper silver coinage worth 8 reales); pc = peso corriente (9 reales in sixteenth century; 8 reales in seventeenth century).

Measurements: bu. = bushel; ca = cántaro (15 liters); bo = botija (8 liters); fa = fanega (1.5 bushels in dry measure; 1 hectare in area).

* Total debts

[ ] = one individual

also owed money to seventeen people, including four women (see Table 11.3) (AGN, TP, "Título de una chacra … (1641)," 241, fols. 15r–15v). Galas resided in Magdalena, and a number of the cacique's Spanish creditors were related to him. Although the creditors' residences and races remain uncertain, the smaller debts suggest that Casapacsi owed for labor services: nine ranged from one to eleven *patacones*, and two amounted to three *fanegas* of wheat (1 *fanega* = 1.5 bushels). Substantial debts could easily be balanced on the credit side. Doña Isabel Caxaquilla's single debt to her *compadre* (godparent) Juan Delgado was wiped clean by what was owed her by another Spaniard, Gonzalo Ramírez (see Table 11.2). Both held farmland in the Lurigancho area, but by way of the *compadrazgo* (godparenthood) relationship, Delgado knew Ana Chumbi, Caxaquilla's relative through marriage, and consequently Chumbi appointed him executor. Delgado also rented land from Caxaquilla's brother-in-law, don Bartolomé Ayculi, the *alcalde* (mayor) of Lurigancho.[5] Thus, fictive kinship ties in both cases connected men and women who otherwise might not have done business together, or, alternatively, the transactions themselves facilitated such ties.

Don Fernando Nacara's nine creditors represented a cross-section of society. He owed the *mulata* María Lizara—"the neighbor of Juan de Ysla" (possibly resident in Lima) and wife of the *mulato* Alonso de Talabera— forty of a seventy peso loan; the *encomendero* (who collected tribute from his assigned Indian communities); Lima's *alguacil mayor* (constable), Francisco Severino de Torres; and three farmers. He also owed the Spanish farmer Francisco Sánchez the enormous sum of 500 pesos, Sanchez's son-in-law Juan Baptista de Uribe twenty pesos, and his *compadre* Diego Chumbi of Carabayllo a roan horse. Familiarity and kinship worked the other way for Nacara's debtors. Gabriel Flores, the brother-in-law of Diego Peréz, a mestizo barber, owed Nacara for the use of a mare he had borrowed to carry wood. The same Peréz, a resident of Carabayllo, rented land from Nacara and paid three *fanegas* of wheat as part of the rent, both formalizing an agreement before a notary public. Being related through marriage might have enabled Flores and Peréz to do business with Nacara. Debts could also accumulate as a consequence of unfulfilled agreements. Don Diego Sacayachumbi, cacique of Huancayo, owed Nacara eight years of back rent totaling 1,200 *patacones*, the deal apparently having been made before a Mercedarian priest.[6] Knowing individuals and their relatives in high places or having fictive kin and the ability to reach across racial and gender lines no doubt facilitated money lending, promoted economic enterprise, and reinforced diverse social networks.

The financial dealings of other nobles were equally diverse. Doña María Guacha of the *ayllu* Chuquitanta tapped into a sizable network that transcended racial, gender, class, and *ayllu* boundaries. Moreover, despite her request to be buried in Lima, her residence, she did not sever ties to the community. María Mulatta (whose surname probably indicates her ethnicity) had loaned doña María Guacha twenty *patacones* for pawning two silver-inlaid gourds, an item of more value but perhaps necessary for future loans. Doña María also owed her *parienta* (kinswoman) Madalena Mansa, a single Indian woman who resided in Carabayllo, and Ana Aya, owner of a *pulpería* (general store), for goods she bought on credit, and the five *patacones* that her deceased aunt, Madalena Casache, gave her to say masses, which she ordered to be fulfilled. Her debtors included a servant and members of two *ayllus* of Carabayllo, the testator don Fernando Nacara of Collique and Francisco Huanica of Huancayo. After her executor collected the debts from the "Indians of Carabayllo," the proceeds were to be converted into alms for that community's *cofradía* (lay confraternity) Nuestra Señora de Rosario, to which she belonged.[7] But she did have an important connection in Lima: she owed nearly fifty pesos to Domingo Indio, an embroiderer and the *mayordomo* of the Indian *cofradía* San Miguel of Lima's Augustinian convent. At the same time, her deceased husband's nephew, don Juan Anaquivi, owed her 100 pesos for land rental, and the widow of Francisco Sanchez, resident of Carabayllo, ten *fanegas* of maize and six of wheat.[8] Such transactions marked doña María Guacha as an independent women of means with an extensive network to rely upon, who had not forgotten where she came from. (The women testators in part 1 of this volume demonstrated equal economic force.)

Francisca Chani's debt of four reales to Surco's Spanish *tambero* (Q [Quechua] for "owner of a *tambo*," an inn that also sold supplies to travelers), Jinéz de Córdoba, was "for my children," and as owner of a *tambo* he was probably an important, though not the only, source of loans. A steady source of rental income would better provide for her children after she passed away. In fact, the Indians of Cuncham, one of the *ayllus* in Surco, owed her two *fanegas* of wheat as *terrasgo* (rent) for sowing on her land. Her husband, Francisco Chumbimaycha, owed money to five Indians:

two from Surco, where he resided; two from his birthplace, Magdalena; and his brother Juan Chaocha, who was working possibly for wages on a farm owned by the Dominican order. The tailor, Francisco de Sansolis, held a choker of pearls worth twenty-eight pesos for a two *patacón* loan; the difference might be explained by the difficulty in procuring cash, or perhaps because Chumbimaycha was planning to borrow more from the tailor. Other creditors included Diego de Carvajal, the *principal* of Surco; two Indians of unknown origin; and a Spanish rentier (AGN, Lima, "Testamentos de indios," one *legajo*). Both husband and wife (and women, in general) illustrate well how a married couple had a variety of debts and debtors independent of one another. And Chumbimaycha still had ties to his home community.

This flow of cash was perhaps the "manure" fertilizing interpersonal relationships as well as financing traditional economic activities, such as the production of *chicha* (an Andean alcoholic drink, traditionally made from maize), in which both nobles and commoners (men and women) participated. Chani produced *chicha*, and her husband, Chumbimaycha, probably supplied her with maize from his own land. Domingo Chicnesumo witnessed for Chani and owed her eight reales on behalf of a fisherman from Trujillo for a *cántaro* (jug of fifteen liters) of *chicha*; another owed her for a "broken *cántaro*." Some of her possessions included four new ollas (cooking pots) for heating the corn (AGN, Lima, "Testamentos de indios"). A *cántaro* was likely used for distribution to individual customers; an olla must have been larger and more suited for fermenting or storage purposes (Figure 11.2). Doña María Guacha's three debtors owed her for *chicha* she had sold them, and her eleven ollas that the *corregidor* (Indian affairs agent), perhaps her business partner, deposited in the tavern of Carabayllo strongly suggests that she produced *chicha* on an even larger scale than Chani (Castillejo 1599–1602, AGNP, PN 22, fols. 899v–901v). No doubt, profits from *chicha* sales helped pay her debts. Of course, this commercialization, which is also seen in commoners' wills, does not mean that it ceased to be distributed for ritual or ceremonial occasions. In fact, Leo Garofalo's (2005, 108) study finds an extensive market for *chicha* even in the city of Lima, where authorities suspected it was being used for prehispanic ceremonies (Garofalo 2005, 108). Thus, despite their largest debts to Spaniards, the evidence suggests a variety of sources for small loans effectuated within a "network of trust" that included men and women crossing racial, community, and class lines.

FIGURE 11.2. Drinking *chicha* at a tomb. (From Poma de Ayala [1615] 1992, 262.)

Commoners had debts and were owed money, too, though in smaller amounts and generally with other Indians and a few noble persons.[9] Besides *chicha*, labor, animals, and clothing also had negotiable monetary value. Three of the testators—Haqui, Cocssi, and Capan—produced and sold *chicha*, probably out of their homes, and tended to handle the most cash (see Table 11.3). Significantly, three nobles owed Antonio Haiqui: the cacique-*principal* of Surco, Francisco Tantachumbi, for cutting wood and renting the *chacara* of Haqui's son; don Miguel, *principal* and public notary of Magdalena, two *patacones* for *chicha*; and don Juan Casapacsi, one of the testators, one *patacón*. Two other debtors were Bartolomé Lloma, for two *botijas* (eight liters) of *chicha*, and Miguel Malca, fifteen reales for use of a chestnut mare. Of course, only caciques were allowed to ride a horse, but nothing was said about ownership. Miguel Cocssi claimed being debt free, but five individuals owed him money; two were Indians, and the other three had Indian-sounding surnames: Hoqui, Malas, and Cala. Cocssi paid Juan Coro, "indio de este pueblo," two pesos for renting his lands, and the two *cántaros* of *chicha* prepared for Coro were not deducted as intended from the rent, so Coro still owed this amount, in addition to six reales that Juan Caotay, an Indian, had loaned him. Simon Saoni owed *terrasgo* to Lucía Caman on land that he cultivated in beans. He instructed Martín Chumpa to keep the trousers (probably a "rental"), but he still owed five *patacones*, and Diego Valca, "yndio," owed him seven *patacones* for "renting" a pair of trousers, a shirt, and a hat used in dancing. Similarly, María Capan loaned to another resident of Surco, Diego Mita Paca, a new taffeta shirt "for dancing...[and]...if it is damaged or there are some *cascavélas* (bells) missing, he pays whatever the value determined by justice." The Spanish chronicler Bernabé Cobo ([1609] 1990, 244) wrote that in Inca times one of the adornments for their dances were "little round bells...on the instep of the foot." Whether such European clothing with sewn-in bells was adapted to prehispanic rituals is unclear, though when *chicha* was referenced, Capan used the Quechua term for it, *sora* (Arriaga [1621] 1920, 211), to describe the debt owed her by Diego Guaman, "indio de este pueblo." Four others, probably Indians, owed for small loans or for *chicha* purchased on credit.

Chicha thus generated an income that could, in turn, be used for money lending, and it must have sustained pottery making as well. The "renting"

of traditional or manufactured clothing, one's labor or land, and even animals was another way of raising cash and indicated their value. These petty
transactions harbored as much significance as the larger ones since most
were intracommunity, thereby contributing to the *wanu* of long-lasting,
trusting relationships—so long as everyone paid their debts.

While material wealth and status separated them, commoners and
nobles came together on *chicha*. In prehispanic times, on the coast it was
mainly men who made *chicha*, exchanging it for maize, wool, and other
items; in the highlands, however, women prepared it for their families.
Much of this trade was bartering between specific kin-related groups.
Indian leaders also provided *chicha* to cement political alliances and to display their hospitality and generosity, and it became central to ritual and
ceremonial occasions (Rostworowski de Diez Canseco 1974, 180; Bruins
1994, 278–280).[10] After the conquest, both men and women in the Valley of
Lima became involved in producing *chicha* for their own families and communities—and possibly for the market in Lima, where it had widespread
multiethnic participation (Garofalo 2005, 108). Nobles (Chani, Guacha,
and Chumbimaycha) and commoners (Haiqui, Cocssi, and Capan) considered *chicha* a marketable commodity and used it as such. Along with
Casapacsi and Chumbimaycha, five of the commoners had maize fields
that likely generated cash that could be available to loan out to their neighbors, up or down the social hierarchy. Doña María Guacha's will indicates
that the Spanish *corregidor* was involved as well; that would not be unusual,
for during his tenure (1577–1580), the *corregidor* Hernán Vásquez exploited
Indian labor from Carabayllo and Surco to work his maize fields and make
chicha at the behest of their caciques in order to market it in Lima. He also
used Surco's oxen and mares for plowing his fields. None of this Vásquez
paid for, but he owed a number of caciques and Indian officials for loans
(BNP, A537, fols. 8r–11r, 56r–56v, 205r, 216v, 230r–236v). Thus, a market
for maize and *chicha* took shape despite complaints that the Indians were
drinking to excess. In fact, Viceroy Francisco de Toledo attempted to regulate it by ordering that in any Indian community it should be sold from
one specific, secure *casa*, and no more than one *azumbre* (two liters) for
each Indian daily or a *cántaro* for eight. However, perhaps owing to their
status and larger household, the caciques were allowed to drink two *cántaros* daily (Rivera Serna 1975/1976, 175–176). Of course, as has been shown,
the Indians ignored Toledo's regulations.

As did maize and *chicha*, clothing became commodified as well (see Terraciano, this volume). Cotton fields could be found up and down the Pacific coast and in the hot highland valleys. According to the chronicler Guaman Poma ([1615] 1992, 47), Andean men and women had learned to make clothes in the third age, after the flood, and under Spanish rule it was still highly valued because of the time required to make clothes by hand (Figure 11.3). Arnold Bauer (2001, 26, 105–106) extrapolates that the weaving done with the tools used in colonial and prehispanic times was (and is) a time-consuming task that involved male and female members of the household in cleaning, combing, beating, and spinning cotton (see also Cieza de León [1553] 1984, 294). The testators, and no doubt the larger society, thereby assessed the value of loaned-out clothing and used it or unworked cloth to pay debts or as pawn in order to obtain cash. Francisco Chumbimaycha held an item from prehispanic material culture, "two old black plumes" that Benito Caravajal, an Indian resident of Magdalena, gave him in exchange for maize worth twelve reales (AGN, Lima, "Testamentos de indios"). These plumes might once have been sewn into the high collar (*tanta*) or headgear that nobles and priests wore in prehispanic times, adding to the symbolic value of the clothing as well as marking the wearer's status. In fact, the Quechua words *tanta* and *chumbi* (garment) referred to the clothing donned by anyone of high status and made up part of the surnames of coastal caciques (Rostworowski de Diez Canseco 1974, 45–46).[11] Unfortunately, Chumbimaycha saw their value decline because they were "already decayed" and instead ordered that the twelve reales be collected and the plumes returned so he could continue to cherish them.

Like the growing of cotton and the weaving of cloth, fishing continued into the colonial era, as illustrated in debtor-creditor ties. Juan China used a codicil on the same day he testated his will to forgive the debt owed by Bartolomé Santillán (Indian of Surco), a large fishing net that Santillán claimed losing:

> …since the said Bartolomé Santillán has repaired it at his cost, it is his (China's) will that he keep it, though it is not only his but that the net pertains to four people—Julio Chahancassa, Antonio Chaca, Gonzalo Maylla, Diego Tamassa—for the said four supplied the pieces of netting from their own to repair it. (AGN, Lima, "Testamentos de indios")[12]

QVARTA CALLE
OVCOC·CVMO

TERZERAEDADDEIÑS
PVRVMRVNA

QVINTA CALLE
CIPAS·COÑA

PRIMERA CALLE
AVACOCVARMI

FIGURE 11.3. Learning to weave. (From Poma de Ayala [1615] 1992, 47.)

He indicated using the fishing net to catch *corvina* (like redfish or channel bass) and *chita* (white ocean fish), perhaps in partnership with those four individuals. Such a partnership possibly alluded to prehispanic norms such as resource sharing and collective work in which an *ayllu* shared its resources with another, usually under cacique supervision. China further stated that *they* hauled fish from the *mar de cuncham* (Cuncham's sea), a reference to that *ayllu's* prehispanic access. Although a member of another *ayllu*, Ydcar, China apparently had no problem passing through Cuncham's former right-of-way so long as he "paid" something, like part of the day's catch (AGN, Lima, "Testamentos de indios"). This payment did not acknowledge Western-style ownership. To be sure, Cuncham collectively "possessed" the beaches but did not have permanent or exclusive rights, and outsiders could probably harvest the *ayllu's* reed patches in order to construct their boats (Rostworowski de Diez Canseco 1977, 216, 245, and 1978, 59; Ramírez, 1996, 18–19, 47).

Of course, such non-ownership of land became less viable when a monetary value was imposed and cacical authority appeared to be absent. Although China's interest apparently faded, other Indians continued to fish and even organized under the Spanish *gremio* (guild) system, remaining so until the end of the colonial period. Its importance should not be underestimated, as Indian fisherman also established their own villages, including Chorrillos and San Pedro de Quilcay, where a number of Surco's residents went to live (Charney 2001, 25–25). Precontact collective activities could thus be incorporated into colonial institutions, the old juxtaposed with the new.

Conclusion

Identifying debtors and creditors revealed a broad set of relationships—kin and quasi- or fictive kin, economic and social, Indian and non-Indian, men and women, commoners and nobles—that the testators had relied upon, in varying degrees, for large or small loans, whether in cash or in kind. Wills became one of the means through which such relationships were publicly acknowledged and remembered. At the same time, the many *different* people named, including some identified by their race and status, who were the testators' lenders or borrowers, composed an extensive network of trust that upheld societal obligations and order. Understandably, nobles obtained the large loans from Spaniards and tended to have a greater number of contacts outside the communities than did commoners. After all, they were ultimately responsible for any shortfalls in the community tribute (*tasa*) and therefore needed to have access to ready cash. Of course, their material possessions echoed their proximity to the Spanish world.

The cultural hybridity evident in wills from the Valley of Lima was not mutually exclusive but often interdependent and accommodating, for traditional goods and economic activities had become grafted onto the new market economy whose participants, men and women, came from different classes and races. Moreover, while kin-based collective tasks and the sharing of resources—whether at the household or village level—did not disappear, the transition to new relationships based on creditor-debtor ties increasingly took hold, undergirding networks of trust in the Valley of Lima. Such networks provided some stability to those battered by Spanish colonialism, as well as maintaining links to the indigenous past.

The Will of Don Juan Casapacsi

Transcription

[*"Título de una chacra y tierras que Pedro de Garate poseia en el valle de la Magdalena… (1641)," Archivo General de la Nación, Lima, Títulos de Propiedad, cuaderno 241, fols. 14–16, 1641*]

[fol. 14r] En el nombre de la Santísima Trinidad Padre Hijo y Espíritu Santo tres personas y una esencia divina sepan quantos esta carta de testamento vieren como yo don Juan Casapacsi cacique principal desta dicho pueblo de la Magdalena estando enfermo del cuerpo y sano de la voluntad y en mi buen juicio y entendimiento natural qual Dios nuestro Señor fue servido de me dar teniendo de la muerta que es cosa natural y deseando poner mi anima en la carrera de salvacion creyendo come creo fiel y catolicamente en el misterio de la Santissima Trinidad y en todo aquella que tiene y crei y confiesa la Santa Madre yglesia de Roma como Catolica cristiano que soy tomando como tomo por mi abogada y yntersesora a la serenissima virgen Santa Maria y con todo los santos y santas de la corte celestial a quien suplico yntersedan por mi anima ante su divino hijo otorgo y conosco que hago y ordeno este dicho mi testamento y postrimera voluntad en la manera siguiente.…

Primeramente encomiendo me anima a Dios nuestro señor que la crio y rredimio por su preciosa sangre y el cuerpo mando a la tierra de

que fue formado y que me cuerpo sea supultado en esta Santa yglesia
deste dicho pueblo de la Magdalena a donde soy natural y de padre cura
y vicario me acompane el cuerpo con cruz alta y los hermanos veynte
cuatros de la Madre de Dios de la Limpia Conçepcion con todas las çeras
de la dicha cofradía porque yo soy uno dellos y si fuere ora me digan
una missa de mi cuerpo presente o si no otro dia siguiente y se pague las
limosna de mis bienes porque es mi voluntad....

Yten mando que me entierren con el habito de nuestro Padre Sant
Francisco....

Yten mando que me digan doze misas cantadas y cuatro rezados y se
pague la limosna de mis bienes....

Tierras/Deudas

Yten mas declaro que yo tengo por mis bienes quatro fanegadas de
tierras de sembradura de maiz que lindan con el pueblo de la Magdalena
y por otra parte con tierras de Nuestra Señora y con tierras de Martín
Canij y con tierras de Lorenzo Villa y estas dichas tierras los tengo
arrendados a Miguel Galas mi padrino y sobre ello me presto el dicho
Miguel Galas quatro çientos y treynte

[fol. 14v] patacones en rreales de contado digo embeçes como consta
de çedulas que tiene fechas y firmados de su nombre y asi confieso
deberlos quiero y es mi voluntad que se vayan desquitado en las tierras
que le tengo arrendados y que mis herederos no las puedan quitar hasta
desquitar la cantidad sino fuera pagando la dicha deuda cumplida esta
dicha deuda mando que lo aya y herede doña Magdalena Sala mi hija y
esto es mi voluntad digo que estos quatro çientos y treynte patacones es
fuera de las cartas de pago que estan en la escritura....

Yten mas declaro por mis bienes en la chacara que llaman vallai
nueve fanegadas de tierras. La una fanegada en la cabeçera de las tierras
dejo para la cofradía de la Madre de Dios de la Limpia conçepcion y con
condicion de que me han de decir una misa cantada cada un ano que
cayere dia de los santos y el restante destas dichas tierras quiero que lo
aya y herede don Juan Casapacsi y Pedro Calpa mis nietos y esto es mi
voluntad....

Yten declaro que tengo una cuja en que yo duermo mando a mi hija
doña Magdalena....

Yten mas declaro que tengo una casa de mi morada con su huerta y un
cuarto en la entrada con un pedazo de huerta mando a mi mujer legitima

doña María Choque mientras que ella viviere en ella no le puedan quitar y que pueda sembrar lo que quisiera en la dicha huerta para su menester esto es mi voluntad....

Yten mas declaro que dejo a mis nietos un solar hacia a la esquina en que puedan vivir y que si doña María mi mujer se fuere a su tierra dejando la dicha casa y huerta mando que mis nietos puedan heredar del dicho pedaso de casa y huerta por que es mi voluntad....

Yten mas declaro una caja labrada mando a la dicha mi mujer llamada doña María Choque....

Yten mas declaro que tengo otra caja grande de cedro y un bufete grande y cuatro sillas de sentar la una quebrada y las tres sanos/ una silla de caballo nuevo con todo su adereso y su caparason....

Yten mas declaro que tengo otra silla de caballo ya vieja con sus estribos....

Yten un banco grande de sentar y otro banquillo....

Yten mas tengo un rretablo de lienso de Santo Crucifijo....

[fol. 15r] Yten mas tengo otro rretablo de lienso guarnesido de chromo

Yten mas tengo otro rretablo pequeno de Nuestra Señora de Rosario /los quales mis bienes se venda en la almoneada o fuera de ella como mis albaceas les paresiere....

Yten mas tengo sembrado una fanega de trigo y de lo prosedido se haga bien por mi anima y esto es mi voluntad....

Yten mas declaro que yo debo las personas siguiente....

- a Santiago Cayma çincuenta y dos patacones (52pt)
- a Catalina Delgada treynta patacones (30pt)
- a Francisco Merlo español no me acuerdo quanto mas conforme mi çedula se pague
- a Juan de Alba de Herao labrador dos çientos y çincuentas pesos por una escritura que le tengo hecho (250p)
- a Juan Fernandes Vitarte dies patacones (10pt)

Yten mas debo a Juan de Parra dos çientos pesos las quales parecera por una escritura (200p)

- a Juan Fernandes marido de Petrona dos fanegas de trigo
- a Hernando Cayma dos patacones (2pt)
- a la madre de don Esteban un anillo de oro que le empene casas en Lima

Yten mas declaro que tengo un solar y casas en Lima la qual estas

dichas casas las tiene Miguel Pablo español por los seisçientos pesos
que les debia yo y por nuestro concierto fue que los dichos seisçientos
pesos fuese desquitando en el dicho solar y asi se cumpla conforme
nuestro concierto y cumplido esta dicha cantidad los aya y herede doña
Magdalena Salla mi hija....

Deudas

Yten mas debo al yerno de María Bilbao treynta patacones y sobre
ello me tiene un rretablo empagando los dichos treynta patacones se
vuelva y se de a mis herederos....

- a Juan Tanta sacristaño no me acuerdo lo que debo que el dijere se
  pague
- a María Martín tres patacones (3pt)
- a Lorenzo Moscoso dies patacones (10pt)
- a Miguel Cayma tres patacones (3pt)
- a la mujer de Alonso Toribio dose rreales (12rr)
- a don Esteban Vacay once patacones del alguilar de sus tierras (11pt)
- a don Francisco Chayque una fanega de trigo....
- a la mujer de Juan Vinco dos patacones (2pt)

[fol. 15v] Yten mas declaro que tengo sembrado una fanega de maiz
quita por beneficiar es mi voluntad que de lo procedido della se le de a mi
mujer doña María y a mi hija doña Magdalena....

Yten mas declaro que tengo unas tierras llamadas vachicolli las
quales tierras tiene Francisca de Salas viuda en que se conciertó
conmigo la susodicha en seisçientos y veynte pesos de a nueve reales los
quatroçientos pesos de la nueve reales a censo/ dosçientos y veynte pesos
restantes se me habia de pagar luego y del censo de los quatroçientos
pesos me ha de pagar en cada un año treynta pesos de la nueve reales
por la transación y conçierto de la deuda y del pleito que traya con
la susodicha como consta en la escritura que paso ante Diego Ñieto
Maldonado escribano real mando que mis albaceas hagan cuenta con la
dicha Francisca de Salas viuda conforme la escritura que en veynte nueve
dias del mes de marzo y milliseisçientos y siete anos y hecha la cuenta
paguen mis deudas conforme este mi testamento es mi voluntad que
cumplido de pagar mis deudas los aya y herede mis herederos....

albaceas pagan sus deudas

Para cumplir y pagar este mi testamento dejo y nombre por mis
albaceas y testamentarios a Miguel Galas español y mi padrino residente

en este pueblo de la magdalena y a don Esteban Vacay y a los quales y a
cada uno dellos doy mi poder cumplido para que entren en mis bienes
y vendan en la almoneda o fuera de ella como les pareciere y de lo
procedido della cumplan y paguen las limosnas de las misas que dijieren
por bien de mi anima y cobrar de los personas que asi me deben y pagar
a los personas a quien yo debo conforme va declarado en differentes
clausulas y rrevoco y doy por ninguno qualquier testamento o codicilios
que yo haya hecho antes desta quiero que no valga ni hagan fe dello
salvo esta que el presente hago quiero que valga y hagan fe dello por
mi testamento y ultima voluntad y con la forma que mas haya lugar de
derechos siendo testigos Diego Cayma alcalde y don Francisco Chatan
y Alonso Vallahunan y don Diego Vaza y don Franisco Chazque y
Juan Tacuri y por ser verdad firmaron los quien supieron firmar en la
Magdalena este dia catorce del mes de octubre y de mill seiesçientos
y ocho anos y asimismo declaro por mis herederos legitimos a doña
Magdalena Salla mi hija y a don Juan Casapacsi y a Pedro Calpa mis
nietos....

[fol. 16r] Yo el presente escribano de cabildo deste dicho pueblo doy
fe que paso este testamento ante me and conosco al otorgante y no firme
por que dijo que no podia y rogo a uno de los testigos que firmase por el

Ante mi don Felipe Chatnan
Escribano de cabildo

Translation

[fol. 14r] In the name of the Holy Trinity—Father, Son, and Holy Spirit—
three persons in one divine being, oversee this will and testament, and
witness that I, don Juan Casapacsi, cacique-*principal* of said town, Magdalena, being ill of body and healthy of will and of sound mind, with the
understanding that God our Lord saw fit to give me, that death is a natural
thing, and wishing to place my soul on the path to salvation, believing myself faithful to the Holy Mother Church of Rome and the mystery of the
Blessed Trinity, as I am a Christian of Roman Catholic faith, having chosen
as my advocate and intercessor the Blessed Virgin Mary and all the saints
of the Heavenly Court whom I request intercede for my soul before their
divine Son, I promise and I am aware that I make and order the following
will and testament.

First, I entrust my soul to God our Lord, who has raised and redeemed it for His precious body and blood that was sent to the Earth from which it was formed, and that my body be buried in this Holy church in said town, Magdalena, which is my birth town, and that the Priest and Vicar accompany my body in a procession with high cross, and with the twenty-four brothers (high officers) from the Confraternity of Saints and the Mother of God of the Immaculate Conception, with all candles lit, representing said Confraternity, because I am one of them, and at my time of death, I wish my requiem mass be said with my body present, or if not, the following day, and that the alms be paid with my assets because it is my will.

Item: I order that I be interred with the shroud of our Father Saint Francis.

Item: I order that twelve high masses and four low masses be said for me, and that the alms be paid from my assets.

Land/Debts

Item: I also declare that I have for my property four *fanegadas* [1 *fanegada* = 2.9 hectares] of corn fields, which border the town of Magdalena on one side, and with the land of Our Lady on the other, and with the lands of Martín Canij and Lorenzo Villa, and said lands I have rented to Miguel Galas, my godfather, and for which he loaned me four hundred and thirty *patacones* in reales, [fol. 14v] which I pay him at specified times, and as noted in official documents, signed and dated. In this way, I confess to owing them, I desire and it is my will that the debts be paid on the lands that I have rented him, and that my heirs cannot take them away until the debts be paid, except for when the debt be paid I will that doña Magdalena Sala, my daughter, inherit that debt. This is my will that these four hundred and thirty *patacones* be removed from the promissory notes in which they are recorded.

Item: I also declare as my property in the farm they call Vallai, nine *fanegadas* of land. The one *fanegada* at the head of the lands I leave for the Confraternity of the Mother of God of the Immaculate Conception, under the condition that they say a high mass each year on All Saint's Day, and the rest of the said lands shall be inherited by don Juan Casapacsi and Pedro Calpa, my grandsons, and this is my will.

Item: I order the one bedstead on which I sleep be given to my daughter, doña Magdalena.

Item: I also order my house of residence, with its garden and one room at the entrance with a smaller garden, be given to my legitimate spouse, doña María Choque, and that, while she still lives, no one can take it away from her, and that she may grow what she wishes in said garden for her well-being. This is my will....

Item: I also declare that I leave my grandsons the corner lot, in which they may reside, and that if my wife, doña María Choque, were to pass on, leave them said houses and garden. I will that my grandsons inherit said piece of garden and home.

Item: I also declare an elegant box that I order be given to my wife, doña María Choque.

Item: I also declare another cedar box and a large desk with four chairs, one broken and three intact, and one new saddle with all its adornments and nosebag.

Item: I also claim to own another saddle, which is now older and used with its stirrups.

Item: One large bench and a stool.

Item: I also own a canvas altarpiece of the Blessed Crucifixion.

[fol. 15r] Item: I also have another canvas altarpiece trimmed in color

Item: I also have another small altarpiece of Our Lady of the Rosary/ goods that may be auctioned or distributed however my executor see fit.

Item: I also have one *fanegada* of a planted wheat field, and that the proceeds be used for my soul and this is my will.

Item: I declare that I am in debt to the following people....

- Santiago Cayma, fifty-two (52) *patacones*
- Catalina Delgada, thirty (30) *patacones*
- Francisco Merlo, Spaniard, I am unsure, whatever the documents state, be paid
- Juan de Alba de Herao, farmer, two hundred and fifty (250) pesos, according to a written document I have made
- Juan Fernandes Vitarte, ten (10) *patacones*

Item: I also owe Juan de Parra two hundred (200) pesos, which also appears in writing

- Juan Fernandes, husband of Petrona, two (2) *fanegadas* of wheat
- Hernando Cayma, two (2) *patacones*
- The mother of don Esteban, a gold ring that she attached to the houses in Lima [Casapacsi's] in Lima

Item: I also declare that I have one plot of land and two houses in Lima, which the Spaniard, Miguel Pablo, has for six hundred pesos that I owed him according to our agreement, which stated that said six hundred pesos were to be deducted with said plot of land and in this way comply with our agreement and once this amount is paid in full my daughter, doña Magdalena Salla, shall inherit it.

Debts

Item: I owe María Bilbao's son-in-law fifty *patacones*, and he holds as collateral an altarpiece until the thirty *patacones* are paid and it returned to my heirs.

- Juan Tanta, sacristan, not sure what I owe, pay him what he says
- María Mostin, three (3) *patacones*
- Lorenzo Moscoso, ten (10) *patacones*
- Miguel Cayma, three (3) *patacones*
- the wife of Alonso Toribio, twelve (12) reales
- Don Esteban Vacay, one (1) *patacón* for renting his lands
- Don Francisco Chayque, a *fanega* of wheat
- the wife of Juan Vinco, two (2) *patacones*

[fol. 15v] Item: I also declare that I have one sown *fanega* of maize ready to harvest, the proceeds of which be given to my wife, doña María, and to my daughter, doña Magdalena....

Item: I also declare that I have some land called Vachicolli that is held by the widow Francisca de Salas in which she agreed upon six hundred and twenty pesos; Four hundred a *censo* [lien] [and] two hundred and twenty remaining that she had to pay me immediately, and of the *censo* of the four hundred pesos she has to pay me thirty pesos per year for the transaction and the agreement of the debt and litigation with aforementioned woman, as promised in the written document that was witnessed by Diego Nieto Maldonado, royal notary public. I order that my executors make an account with said Francisca de Salas, widow, in agreement with what was written, on the twenty-ninth day of the month of March of one thousand six hundred and seven, and once this account is made, that the debts be paid in agreement with the account. This is my will and testament that once these debts are paid my heirs inherit what remains....

Executors pay their debts

In order to comply with and pay this, my will, I leave and name as my executors and executrix, the Spaniard Miguel Galas, my godfather, who resides in this town of Magdalena, and don Esteban Vacay, and to each one I give them my complete power so that they may have access to and sell

or auction my property as they see fit. And of the proceeds of it fulfill and
pay my alms for the masses that will be said for the good of my soul, and
collect from the people who owe me and pay the people to whom I owe,
according to what is stated in different clauses. And I revoke and disregard
any will or codicil made before this one, that it have no value nor should
anyone have faith in it, save the will and testament that I presently make. I
want it to have value and be entrusted as my last will and testament, with
the form made in a place of law, with the witnesses being Diego Cayma,
alcalde, and don Francisco Chatan and Alonso Vallahunan and don Diego
Vaza and don Francisco Chazque and Juan Tacuri. And to verify, those
who knew how to sign their name, signed in the town of Magdalena, this
fourteenth day of the month of October of one thousand six hundred and
eight. And I also declare as my legitimate heirs my daughter, doña Magdalena Salla, and my

grandsons don Juan Casapacsi and Pedro Calpa.

[fol. 16r] I, the present public notary of said town give faith that this
will pass before me, and I know the one who grants it did not sign because
he said that he was unable, and implored that one of his witnesses sign on
his behalf.

In the presence of don Felipe Chantan
Town public notary

Notes

1. Although not exhaustive, the following is a select sample: Von Germeten
   2003; Wood 1991; Charney 1998; Salomon 1998; Lévano Medina 2002;
   Retamal Ávila 1986; Kellogg and Restall 1998; Pease 1981; Rostworowski de
   Diez Canseco 1989; Dunbar 1949–1950.
2. See also Espinoza Soriano 1987, which lists dozens of Quechua terms culled
   from colonial lexicographers that relate to commerce; his documented
   analysis convincingly shows that exchanges of goods took place outside of the
   socioethnic-based "archipelago model." Skepticism over markets and trade is
   expressed in the articles in part 2 of Larson and Harris 1995. In today's Cauca
   Valley, Colombia, peasants believe in *el bautizo del billete*, in which a bill is
   baptized instead of a child in the hope that it will return to the owner with
   interest, thus enriching the owners at the expense of others. See Taussig 1980,
   126–129.
3. In colonial Mexico, there was a similar pattern of loans executed among persons of different social and racial backgrounds (Couturier and Lavrin 1979,

302). Among fairly wealthy Chileans during the seventeenth century, women played an important role as creditors, while men were in constant need of capital (Muñoz Correa 2002, 111–132).

4. Today women carry the paternal name (Isbell 1978, 107, 111).

5. For Caxaquilla, see Castillejo 1597-1598, AGN, Protocolos Notariales (hereafter PN) 21, fols. 1473r–1475v; Castillejo 1599-1602, AGN, PN 22, fols. 159r, 161r, 163v; Francisco García 1598, AGNP, PN 164, fols. 478r–483v.

6. For Nacara, see Castillejo 1599–1602, AGNP, PN 22, fols. 673r–674v.

7. For Guacha, see Castillejo 1599–1602, AGNP, PN 22, fols. 899v-901v.

8. Ibid., fols. 899v–901v.

9. All six commoners's testaments discussed in this section are in AGN, Lima, "Testamentos de indios."

10. Arnold Bauer (2001, 42, 97) argues that women mainly produced *chicha*. Even today the first planting ritual is accompanied with *chicha* (Isbell 1978, 73).

11. In the highlands, *chumbi* (or *chunbe*) was a sash worn by noblewomen (Poma de Ayala [1615] 1992, 96, 115).

12. Cobo ([1609] 1990, 242) observed that fishing nets were made of cotton thread and required at least two individuals in separate balsa craft to drag the net. See also Rostworowski de Diez Canseco 1981.

References

Arriaga, Father Pablo José. [1621] 1920. *La extirpación de la idolatría en el Peru.* Vol. 1. Lima: Colección de Libros y Documentos Referentes a Historia del Perú.

Bauer, Arnold. 2001. *Goods, Power, History: Latin America's Material Culture.* New York: Cambridge University Press.

Bruins, Karen Olsen. 1994. *Ancient South America.* New York: Cambridge University Press.

Charney, Paul. 1991. "A Sense of Belonging: Colonial Indian Cofradías and Ethnicity in the Valley of Lima, Peru." *The Americas* 54: 379–407.

———. 1998. "A Sense of Belonging: Colonial Indian *Cofradías* and Ethnicity in the Valley of Lima, Peru." *The Americas* 54(3): 379–407.

———. 2001. *Indian Society in the Valley of Lima, Peru, 1532–1824.* Lanham, Md.: University Press of America.

Cieza de León, Pedro. [1553] 1984. *Primera parte de la Crónica del Perú.* Lima: Pontificia Universidad Católica del Perú.

Cline, S. L. 1986. *Colonial Culhuacan, 1580–1600: A Social History of an Aztec Town.* Albuquerque: University of New Mexico Press.

Cobo, Father Bernabé. [1609] 1990. *Inca Religion and Custom.* Translated by Roland Hamilton. Austin: University of Texas Press.

Couturier, Edith, and Asunción Lavrin. 1979. "Dowries and Wills: A View of Women's Socioeconomic Role in Colonial Guadalajara and Puebla, 1640–1790." *Hispanic American Historical Review* 59: 280–304.

Dunbar, Ella. 1949–1950. "Los testamentos inéditos de Paulla Inca, don Carlos y
don Melchor Carlos Inca." In *Documenta* 2: 630–651.

Espinoza Soriano, Waldemar. 1987. *Artesanos, transacciones, monedas y formas de
pago en el mundo andino, siglos XV y XVI.* Lima: Banco Central de Reserva
del Perú.

Garofalo, Leo J. 2005. "La sociobilidad plebeya en las pulperías y tabernas de
Lima y el Cuzco, 1600–1690." In *Más alla de la dominación y la resistencia:
Estudios de historia peruana, siglos xvi–xx,* edited by Paulo Drinot and Leo
Garofalo, 104–135. Lima: Instituto de Estudios Peruanos.

Graubart, Karen B. 2007. *With Our Labor and Sweat: Indigenous Women and the
Formation of Colonial Society, 1550–1700.* Stanford, Calif.: Stanford University
Press.

Gunther Doering, Juan, ed. 1983. *Planos de Lima, 1613–1983.* Lima: Industrial
Gráfica.

Guzzi-Heeb, Sandro. 2004. "Close Relatives and Useful Relatives: Welfare, Inheritance and the Use of Kinship in an Alpine Dynasty, 1650–1800." In *Family
Welfare: Gender, Property and Inheritance Since the Seventeenth Century,* edited
by David Green and Alastair Owens, 97–120. Westport, Conn.: Praeger.

Horn, Rebecca. 1998. "Testaments and Trade: Interethnic Ties among Petty
Traders in Central Mexico, Coyocan, 1550–1620." In *Dead Giveaways: In-
digenous Testaments of Colonial Mesoamerica and the Andes,* edited by Susan
Kellogg and Matthew Restall, 59–83. Salt Lake City: University of Utah Press.

Isbell, Billie Jean. 1978. *To Defend Ourselves: Ecology and Ritual in an Andean
Village.* Prospect Heights, Ill.: Waveland Press.

Keith, Robert G. 1971. *Conquest and Agrarian Change: The Emergence of the Hacienda System on the Peruvian Coast.* Cambridge, Mass.: Harvard University
Press.

Kellogg, Susan, and Matthew Restall, eds. 1998. *Dead Giveaways: Indigenous
Testaments of Colonial Mesoamerica and the Andes.* Salt Lake City: University
of Utah Press.

Larson, Brooke, and Olivia Harris, eds. 1995. *Ethnicity, Markets, and Migration in
the Andes: At the Crossroads of History and Anthropology.* Durham, N.C.: Duke
University Press.

Lévano Medina, Diego E. 2002. "De castas y libres: Testamentos de negras, mu-
latas y zambas en Lima Borbónica, 1740–1790." In *Etnicidad y discriminación
racial en la historia del Perú,* edited by Ana Cecília Carrillo, 127–145. Lima:
Pontificia Universidad Católica del Peru.

Mangan, Jane E. 2003. "Prendas y pesos en el Potosí colonial: Colocando las prác-
ticas urbanas en un contexto social." *Revista Andina* 36: 101–130.

———. 2005. *Trading Roles: Gender, Ethnicity, and the Urban Economy in Colonial
Potosí.* Durham, N.C.: Duke University Press.

Muñoz Correa, Juan Guillermo. 2002. "Acreedoras y deudoras en testamentos
Colchagua, siglo XVII." *Boletín de la Academia Chilena de la Historia* 3: 111–132.

Pease, Franklin. 1981. "Las relaciones entre las tierras altas y la costa del sur del Perú: Fuentes documentales." In *Estudios etnográficos del Perú Medridional*, edited by Shozo Masuda, 193–221. Hinode, Japan: Hinode University.

Poma de Ayala, Felipe Guaman. [1615] 1992. *El primero nueva corónica y buen gobierno.* 3rd ed. Mexico City: Siglo Veintiuno.

Ramírez, Susan E. 1996. *The World Upside Down: Cross-Cultural Contact and Conflict in Sixteenth Century Peru.* Stanford, Calif.: Stanford University Press.

Restall, Matthew. 1998. "Interculturation and the Indigenous Testament in Colonial Yucatan." In *Dead Giveaways: Indigenous Testaments of Colonial Mesoamerica and the Andes*, edited by Susan Kellogg and Matthew Restall, 115–162. Salt Lake City: University of Utah Press.

Retamal Ávila, Julio. 2000. *Testamentos de indios en Chile colonial, 1564–1801.* Santiago: Departamento de Derechos Intelectuales de Chile.

Rivera Serna, Raúl. 1975/1976. "El cultivo de la vid: La producción de vino y chicha en Lima en el siglo XVI." *Boletín del Instituto Riva-Aguero* 10: 175–187.

Rostworowski de Diez Canseco, María. 1974. "Coastal Fishermen, Merchants, and Artisans in Pre-Hispanic Peru." In *The Sea in the Pre-Columbian World*, edited by Elizabeth Benson, 167–186. Washington, D.C.: Dumbarton Oaks Research Library.

———. 1977. *Etnia y sociedad: Costa peruana prehispanica.* Lima: Instituto de Estudios Peruanos.

———. 1978. *Señoríos indígenas de Lima y Canta.* Lima: Instituto de Estudios Peruanos.

———. 1981. *Recursos naturales renovables y pesca, siglos xv y xviii.* Lima: Instituto Estudios Peruanos.

———. 1989. *Doña Francisca Pizarro: Una ilustre mestiza, 1532–1598.* Lima: Instituto de Estudios Peruanos.

Saignes, Thierry. 1999. "The Colonial Condition in the Quechua-Aymara Heartland (1570–1780)." In *The Cambridge History of the Native Peoples of the Americas*, vol. 3, *South America, Part 2*, edited by Frank Salomon and Stuart Schwartz, 59–137. New York: Cambridge University Press.

Salomon, Frank. 1988. "Indian Women of Early Colonial Quito as Seen through Their Testaments." *The Americas* 44: 325–341.

Taussig, Michael T. 1980. *The Devil and Commodity Fetishism in South America.* Chapel Hill: University of North Carolina Press.

von Germeten, Nicole. 2003. "Death in Black and White: Testaments and Confraternal Devotion in Seventeenth Century Mexico City." *Colonial Latin American Historical Review* 12: 282–330.

Wood, Stephanie. 1991. "Adopted Saints: Christian Images in Nahua Testaments of Late Colonial Toluca." *The Americas* 47: 259–293.

The Irreplaceable Window

Reflections on the Study of Indigenous Wills

SUSAN KELLOGG AND MATTHEW RESTALL

If you had asked us in 1998, when the first *Dead Giveaways* came out, whether a second iteration of the volume would see the light of day, we are quite certain that we would have answered no. We were pleased when Louise Burkhart (1999, 838–840) wrote in *Ethnohistory* that *Dead Giveaways* was "a particularly good resource for graduate students seeking current research models and ideas for further development." But we dared not imagine that almost two decades later the book would still be a model worth consulting, let alone emulating. However, *Native Wills from the Colonial Americas: Dead Giveaways in a New World* now exists, so it seems appropriate to ask why a sequel volume is justified and why the first book has endured as a scholarly contribution.

We suggest there are two answers. First, as Burkhart stated in the final line of her review of *Dead Giveaways*, "indigenous testaments still have much more to reveal." If *Dead Giveaways* suggested as much, *Native Wills from the Colonial Americas* confirms it in rich detail. Second, the chapters in this volume do not merely repeat the themes, methods, and findings of the earlier volume. They also reflect recent historiographical trends. All the essays mirror the linguistic or, what one of us would term, "the philological turn" in ethnohistory. Some essays continue the ethnohistoric trend, well illustrated in the first volume, to use women's wills as a way to explore their lives in great detail, especially their economic and political roles; others turn to the question of elite strategies for maintaining status and privileges; and another set confronts issues around death and dying. All reveal the rich complexities and paradoxes of individual colonial subjects navigating urban and rural colonial cultures. All of the chapters, one way or another, deeply probe the use of language and/or images to convey or contest cultural changes as the individual testators actually experienced them. Furthermore, the analysis in these essays of wills and those who wrote them provides insights into particular people beyond the Nahua and mestizo intellectuals—such as Chimalpahin, Alva Ixtlilxochitl, and Alvarado Tezozomoc—who have been a focus of recent scholarship.[1]

The book as a whole draws on the ever-expanding geographic and conceptual boundaries of Latin American history. Both Atlantic and transnational histories confront Latin Americanists today with the need to broaden our comparative geographic perspectives; *Native Wills from the Colonial Americas* takes on a more (if not wholly) continental perspective. Its essays show how individuals both embodied and enacted the changing times in which they lived, even when they used this legal instrument introduced by Europeans—the last will and testament—to conserve property and maintain, when possible, practices rooted in non-European cultural systems.[2] In providing an overview of the chapters preceding this one, we offer not only a summary of their main themes, but we also seek to suggest ways that future research into testaments might further probe questions of language and identity, as well as issues of cultural change and death and dying.

How, exactly, do these essays reflect an ever-evolving Latin Americanist historiography? Part 1, "Women of Native America," explores how women, as active agents, sought economic stability. We see how the languages used in these particular wills, whether Spanish or indigenous (Mixtec, or Ñudzahui to be precise), captured both hybridity and efforts to enact cultural persistence. Karen Graubart's essay explicitly takes up the idea of hybridity in Trujillo, Peru. Catalina de Agüero's 1570 will shows how she mediated newly linked indigenous and Atlantic cultures. Catalina's life spanned the turbulent middle decades of the sixteenth century in which new physical and transactional "go-betweens"—to borrow Alida Metcalf's useful typology—emerged to play crucial roles in the development of colonial Andean society. While her life in Trujillo began in servitude in a novel urban environment, that servitude allowed Catalina to maintain property in the rural community of her birth, wearing clothing of a style that perhaps reminded her of her rural origins, even as the new materials from which her clothing was made symbolized her mediation between American and Atlantic worlds, and urban and rural cultures (Metcalf 2005, 9–12).

The 1677 joint testament of Miguel da Silva, labeled a *chino*, and María de la Concepción, a free *mulata*, as evocatively described by Tatiana Seijas, is an unusual kind of will, to be sure. It reinforces the image of seventeenth-century Mexico City as a place of economic uncertainty and social variability, in which political and gender hierarchies had to be carefully navigated. Navigable they were, though, as Miguel and María fostered two children, one of whom was Spanish. More remarkable still was María's marital history: she married twice, first to a wealthy man of unknown ethnicity who left her the considerable sum of 5,000 pesos; she then used some of that money to free her second husband, a man of likely Filipino origin, from his enslavement. Did the limited "liberation" this sometimes anomic urban atmosphere granted María come at the cost of deeper religious or communal ties, leaving her estranged from any of the political or religious structures to which communal identities were connected? María was able to purchase her new husband's freedom, but the interpersonal tension that came to characterize their family reflected the mix of racial and class differences embedded in that single family unit.

Jonathan Truitt explores the theme of popular religious belief and practice through the 1640 will of one female testator. Neither a "particularly wealthy nor destitute" woman, she owned a variety of saints' images, several of which she disposed of through burning, a potent prehispanic Mesoamerican symbol of both death and rebirth. Yet Nicolasa Juana does not appear to have had rebellious tendencies. Her will suggests her piety, and she refers respectfully to a woman named Ana, the *tenantzin* or "beloved mother" of the barrio of Teocaltitlan, who held the wills of her parents; this Ana enjoyed a position of some authority—whether formal or informal—to guard the written records of family and kin, a position recognized by residents such as Nicolasa Juana. No doubt her unclear indigenous, yet ethnic, identity exemplified the cultural hybridity that frequently characterized indigenous life in seventeenth-century Mexico City, especially in the particular parish in which she lived.

Hybridity also characterizes the seventeenth-century will of Lucía Hernández Ñuquihui. Far from powerless (as can be said of all three women whose wills are in this part of the book), her good fortune was based on continuities of life in the towns and villages of the Mixteca Alta. Her ability to amass some wealth and navigate the more transcultural seventeenth-century economy of that region of New Spain was rooted in marital connections and in her success at adapting a traditional craft—weaving—to new forms of transport and exchange. As Kevin Terraciano explains, Lucía, her family, and her social network thrived within a political culture that retained significant structural similarities to that of the late prehispanic period. Mexico City and Trujillo, Peru, on the other hand, were places where indigenous people—native or migrant—faced an array of challenges in adapting to a transformed political world.

The chapters in part 2, "Strategies of the Elite," examine the testaments of people of noble status—that is, descendants of the ruling dynasties of the late prehispanic era, families whose members often still held positions of authority or status—or look at the political culture elites sought to model and shape. Through such wills, we see how old, noble families acted strategically to use new vehicles like will making to reinforce traditional hierarchies and privileges—such as the Pech elite family in the small Yucatec town of Ixil, still maintaining economic and political status two centuries and more after the Spanish arrival, as uncovered by Mark Christensen. We also see this process at work in the use of the pictorial representations that sometimes accompanied wills, designed to reinforce legal claims to property, as described by Richard Conway for Xochimilco in the Valley of Mexico. Visual images had long been used to support oral performances in Mesoamerican cultures. Colonial pictorial documents also illustrate how new types of conflict and legal practice influenced the nature of such texts as they became legal instruments; as such, they were no longer just records of ownership, but also rhetorical devices intended to persuade Nahua and Spanish colonial officials. Conway's emphasis on visual images reflects the way scholars of ethnohistory have deepened their analysis of pictorial representations in the late preconquest and postconquest Mesoamerican world, in conjunction with our now much greater knowledge of colonial indigenous language.

The bounty of Ixil testaments analyzed by Christensen illustrates how Maya nobles used new legal and social strategies to enhance their status in a system of prestige that conquest events and colonial power structures often undermined. The result was the emergence of novel practices, such as *chibal* (patronym group) endogamy, developed to allow the Pech family to maintain wealth and position in an increasingly competitive eighteenth-century political context. Because the Maya continued to govern their own towns and villages through the *cabildo* system, and because *cabildo* officers signed their names and titles to every will, documents such as the Ixil testaments offer a unique insight into the inner workings of Maya community politics.[3]

The exquisite sensitivity to sociopolitical terminology shown in some of these chapters, such as those by Terraciano and Christensen, can also be found in the chapter by Owen Jones. His focus is on indigenous language terminology, using his extraordinary knowledge of the K'iche Mayan tongue to compare wills from three Guatemalan communities. He shows that the language in which these testaments were written does not merely capture the individual testator's voice, but also the voices of community leaders, including those of local scribes trained in practices specific to the locales that Jones discusses. But, beyond all that, even a highly individuated textual production like a will could represent, Jones shows, a communal act with strong social and political implications for Maya property relations and authority structures, judicial practices, and spiritual beliefs. The new thus became a vehicle to reenact the old.

The third part of the book, "The Individual and Collective Nature of Death," treats death and dying as an experience on two distinct levels, that of the individual testator and that of the group. In their introduction to the book *Death and Dying in Colonial Spanish America*, Martina Will de Chaparro and Miruna Achim (2011, 5) argue that in the early modern Atlantic world "death permeated the meaning of life," with many seeing themselves as "living in a community that they shared with the dead." Kathleen Bragdon uses ethnohistory, archaeology, and ethnography to suggest how, in a Christianizing eighteenth-century southern New England, death and dying became more individual experiences. As communities experienced Christian influence variously and at different times, the beliefs, goods, and legal practices that were introduced began to reshape the conception of personhood. Bragdon's article illustrates how the mortuary practices she describes began to vary within and between communities as new forms of property and legal conventions influenced socially defined concepts of personhood and community.

In her chapter, Lisa Sousa takes us back to Oaxaca, bringing to light the intriguing use of Nahuatl by Mixe testators in the Villa Alta region.

Nahuatl as a lingua franca is now coming into focus as a process of colonial language change that is being studied in greater depth by historians and linguists.[4] What Sousa conclusively shows is that Mixe and Nahua land-holding practices were quite different well into the colonial era, with the rotational patterns of office holding and political organization that characterized the Nahua extending deeply into customary practices of land use and ownership among the Mixe. Sousa's remarkable body of documents includes a number of wills that show the Mixe faced the issue of how to use Nahuatl to express their own concepts of social organization. Nahuas had themselves faced this issue as they began to use their language in texts whose forms emanated from a legal system with different categories of land tenure and forms of transmission of property rights, to give just two examples. Although in the Mixe case a *novel* language was adopted, the practice of will making became a powerful means to conserve Mixe ways of owning, sharing, and working land, even as new classifications and forms of property entered into the lexicon and everyday practices in this remote part of New Spain.

Like Bragdon, Erika Hosselkus explores indigenous burial practices, focusing on the Nahua community of Huexotzinco. She also finds compelling evidence that local, community-based norms and social networks shaped the practices of burial location and devotion to the saints. While testaments, as she notes, to a large extent "organized and standardized the spiritual directives of the dying" in this and other Nahua communities, she is able to tease out "the personal, regional, and ethnic concerns" that influenced the decisions—especially about burials and the connections to the emerging cult of saints[5]—made by testators in the increasingly ethnically and racially diverse community of early seventeenth-century Huexotzinco.

Paul Charney likewise explores the relationships among the individual, local or regional, and cultural in his exploration of a small number of wills from rural communities around Lima, covering the years 1596 to 1607. One of the fascinating features of his corpus is that both nobles and commoners are almost equally represented. Focusing especially on debt and credit, Charney shows how "networks of trust" undergirded local and regional economies, allowing traditional commodities and forms of exchange and reciprocity to be integrated into a colonial economy. In such an economy, some labor and wealth were siphoned off into a market system in which Spaniards, Africans, and individuals of mixed ethnicity participated.

Indigenous nobles interacted with Spaniards through credit more than
commoners, in part because of their responsibility for tribute payment.
Whereas kin- and community-based forms of sharing and reciprocity did
not disappear, ties among debtors and creditors played a role in the shift
to a more monetized economy that linked villages in the Valley of Lima to
the city of Lima and beyond.

As much as these essays illustrate recent historiographical trends
in ethnohistory, they also reflect the enduring appeal of testaments as a
source for colonial history, pointing toward the potential for wills to contribute further to numerous current trends in the field. One example is that
of language and literacy. The approach known as the New Philology has
arguably exploded into a nexus of investigative subfields and foci; many
of the resulting studies emphasize the philological analysis of terms used
by native protagonists, whether in Spanish or in an indigenous language,
in vernacular speech or legalese, in a local tongue or lingua franca.[6] In parallel, but closely related, are studies of writing and literacy. The similarities
and differences in literacy traditions and trends in Mesoamerica and the
Andes have long challenged and stimulated scholars of the two regions to
think more deeply about each other's fields—and thereby their own too—
and wills offer opportunities for such contemplation.[7]

Another example is that of the above-mentioned theme of cultural hybridity, which bears further study. In recent years, there have been some
sophisticated musings on its relevance by nonhistorians and historians
alike; to borrow Martin Nesvig's (2012, 190) conclusion to the study of a
topic not related to wills, if something is "very Mexican, neither Spanish
nor indigenous, a hybrid religious and cultural practice," then can we say
that religious and cultural hybridity is something very Spanish American,
both Spanish and indigenous?[8]

With wills as a source base—or as part of a set of source bases—culture
change can be profitably examined using various concepts of hybridity,
nonlinear change, collective memory, and so on. For example, while to
some extent embracing James Lockhart's (1991, 22) observation that "continuity and change are often to a large extent the same thing," Caterina Pizzigoni's (2012, 10) recent monograph, based on a large corpus of wills from
the Toluca area, suggests that while important continuities can be seen in
indigenous culture, the idea that "a new whole created from indigenous
and Spanish components, a different world even though it embodies im-

portant elements of continuity from both antecedents," should be further explored.

While examples abound in this volume, here two will suffice. Richard Conway (first) shows how the prehispanic practice of pictorial record keeping became *repurposed*, with such records turned into documents that carried not just legally relevant information but legal power. But (second) just as the old became new, the new could become old—*repackaged*, we might say—as Kathleen Bragdon illustrates with metal goods bearing a potential for animacy. This "old" characteristic of new metal objects relates to the theme of social regeneration, which she ties to the chiefdoms of Late Woodland and early colonial New England native peoples. Social regeneration implies an effort, whether conscious or not, to maintain the past in the future.

Memory studies, especially those focusing on cultural memory, suggest communally rooted efforts to achieve the same thing. Do we find evidence for the idea that testators often, though not necessarily always, participated in propagating "shared memories of the past [that] are not accidentally produced by social groups but [as] a consequence of cultural mediation, primarily of textualization and visualization" (Tamm 2013, 461)?[9] Wills propagated not just individual but family memories, and they could draw on community-based memories of, for example, property, land, and who used or owned it.

Jones's virtually community-produced K'iche testaments suggest efforts to reinforce communal understandings—rooted in the past—of family, sociopolitical units, and the role of community officials. These memories were socially activated through making wills and carrying out their instructions, not simply for practical reasons but also with the goal of forestalling familial and community strife. Sousa's Mixe testators showed an interest in maintaining the practice of *shared* use rights to land. She also suggests that testators tried to create a sense of "long-term obligation," so that heirs would continue to care for the souls of those who had passed on and, in the process, propagate the memory of those from whom rights to use land came. This new practice—making a will and having it recorded neither in Mixe nor in Spanish, but in Nahuatl—not only reminds us of the complexities of change but points to what Restall (1998, 144) calls "interculturation," a term that "does not restrict culture change to a single direction or a single end result, nor does it overemphasize culture loss or acquisition, expressing instead the colonial-era process of cultural intercourse."

The idea of interculturation not only encompasses the notion that responses to colonialism were highly variable and often included cultural creativity and innovation—points made especially well in this volume by Graubart, Charney, and Seijas—but also that change could be nonlinear, with no fixed endpoint. Indigenous residents of cities such as Trujillo made efforts to create or maintain strong ties to rural communities of origin; migrants such as Catalina de Agüero wore clothing that spoke to their birth identity, kept property, and maintained other ties to their natal communities. While such examples might be seen as an incomplete acculturative process, they can just as easily be understood as a way for a woman like Agüero to reinforce her sense of Andean-ness, her indigeneity, in the new multiethnic environment in which she lived and seemingly thrived. Cities could be places where indigenous identities flourished, however "reformulated" those identities became.[10]

Truitt's chapter speaks to this point particularly well. His Spanish-language but indigenous-made testament shows clearly how indigenous women continued to play community-based leadership roles, perhaps repurposed to deal with new realities of disease, death, geographic mobility, and displacement. Caring for children, documents, and saints, the woman Ana, *tenantzin* of Teocaltitlan, points to ways that the urban indigenous of the largest Mesoamerican city adapted, adjusted, yet conserved communally based ways of doing things—despite urban, acculturative pressures that we think of as individuating, if not anomic, and often overwhelming. What if it was the case that a Mixtec-descended woman—*india ladina* though Nicolasa Juana appears to have been—found security and comfort in the Nahua-based cultural environment that at least partly shaped her life? Does this not, to some extent, undermine assumptions about acculturative processes' centers and peripheries?

If the overall trend of change was toward the hybrid and acculturated, wills such as Nicolasa Juana's and the Nahuatl testaments of Mixe testators show how complex intercultural processes could lead to nonlinear patterns of change. The contrasts among K'iche testaments from Rab'inal, Xelajú, and San Miguel Totonicapán suggest that—regardless of the impact of acculturative influence (less in Rab'inal, more in the other two communities)—individuals, communities, and their leaders were preoccupied by the idea of avoiding future conflict. Community leaders appear to have seen wills as a highly utilitarian means to reinforce this value. The K'iche desire to influence the future went beyond passing along property and settling debts; it extended to avoiding conflict and to maintaining relationships to kin who then became ancestors (but whose being remained very present and real).

Jones's chapter, as well as Terraciano's, also suggests how important local traditions and practices could be, despite the fact that no communities writing wills in colonial Spanish America were immune to the influence of global processes and changes. For the K'iche towns that Jones examines, scribal schools were a notable local tradition. For other communities, localized culture might include attitudes toward death, the soul, bodies, and corpses.

Hosselkus, for example, takes up the issue of bodies in particular and what happened to them after death. Knowing that the sixteenth-century residents of Madrid were usually buried in churches (Eire 1995, 94–103), perhaps it is not surprising that the practice of church burial for Nahuas became well established by the last quarter of the sixteenth century.[11] As Hosselkus suggests, local practices shaped the burial instructions of Huexotzinco's Nahua residents, who often specified burial near particular saints; this concern over placement near saints suggests an early manifestation of what later became a more general practice (Pizzigoni 2007, 16–17; 2012, 188–190). But if it took some time to sort out what might become of Christian Nahua bodies, the need for masses for souls did not. The earliest Mexico City testaments offer evidence of testators providing funds for masses, as do those of Culhuacan (Kellogg 1995, 141; Cline 1986, 28–29). Thus concern for the care of the soul existed—and perhaps built upon Nahua beliefs—about the journeys that souls or spirits took upon death (Berdan 1982, 94–96; Kellogg 1995, 122–123).

Death, it seems to us, was a particularly pivotal moment of potential change, a window that could be opened to let in new beliefs and new rituals surrounding death. Such shifts in death-related perspectives and practices played a key role in the emergence of indigenous Christianities. Indeed, the Christianizing of death proved to be a crucial feature of conversion, not just in the Andes—as eloquently argued by Gabriela Ramos in her recent book, *Death and Conversion in the Andes*—but throughout the Americas, in both Catholic and Protestant communities.[12] As crucial as baptism and marriage were to the formation of new Christians and Christi-anities, death provided perhaps the most significant means of teaching and reinforcing new ideas and arranging or rearranging family and community (as both lived space and/or a network of social relations), along with so-cial and property organization. These changes were nonlinear in the sense that once interculturative practices began, they occurred in variable ways across the times and places dealt with in this book, never reaching a fixed endpoint.

Wills still have great potential for further exploration of the experi-ences and the cultural meanings of death and dying. But—in the wake of Carlos Eire's inspiring use of the wills of sixteenth-century Madrileños—wills by native peoples of the colonial Americas need to be put in further dialogue with many other types of texts, annals, chronicles, pictorial his-tories, funerary descriptions, burial records, legal cases covering not just property distribution but burial or other death-related conflicts, as well as the rich death-related sodality records from across the Iberian Americas.[13]

We have seen in this volume that because will making and dying could never be wholly individual affairs, for many indigenous testators, produc-ing a will could offer means, material and social, to strengthen familial and communal values and practices. Testament production always connected an individual, of whatever time and place, to other family and community members, including officials who represented the community. Many colo-nial testators—of all races, ethnicities, and backgrounds—left bequests to honor and aid families and a variety of institutions. Such bequests became basic to the socially regenerative, even reproductive, nature of death that Bragdon mentions in her essay. Part of the future of testamentary analysis, then, is to explore questions of changing mortality and mortuary patterns, death as experience and symbol, and regenerator of material and social value in ways that reflect the complex local, temporal, ethnic, class, and status patterns that existed across the colonial Americas.

This sequel to *Dead Giveaways* offers the historiographical version of such a regenerative future. The testaments and essays in both volumes cap-ture individuals, families, and communities at moments of crisis, grief, and sometimes conflict. Explorable through both their forms of expression and for the social relationships, economic practices, and patterns of political authority that they reveal, these documents are also highly idiosyncratic. Even as the role of the scribe in mediating colonial textual production must

Finaline re.

be acknowledged—as shown so persuasively in Kathryn Burns's (2010) book—testaments capture people's voices and offer a kind of chronicle of individual lives through a dramatic period of change in world history.

As Truitt and Christensen observe in the introduction, many more indigenous-language wills have come to light since *Dead Giveaways* was published, and the exploration of testaments from a greater number of areas and among other subaltern groups has progressed. This new volume captures that shift. But as we pointed out in the introduction to *Dead Giveaways*, testaments represent the conjunction of so many elements: moments just prior to death and an individual's life course, the person and the community, the material and the spiritual, the customary and the legal, the old and the new (Restall and Kellogg 1998, 2–5). If testators "conceived of death and the hereafter as intricately bound to earthly life" (to borrow a phrase of Eire's [1995, 249]), then ethnohistorical wills were intricately bound to life in their creators' communities.

The great collective corpus of indigenous wills is an irreplaceable and invaluable window onto an early modern American world, revealing how its inhabitants experienced that changing world in particular corners of tiny towns and huge cities. The men and women whose names we know and whose stories we glimpse—because they left a record of their piety, property, families, and friends—hoped to record a past that would influence the future. That hope endures even as our tools of analysis develop and change.

Notes

1. The rich scholarship on Chimalpahin and Alva Ixtlilxochitl, in particular, can be sampled in the Schroeder and Brian essays in Schroeder 2010.
2. For discussions of recent historiographical trends in Latin American ethnohistory and colonial history, see Kellogg 2003 and Restall 2003, 2012. On the variety of comparative frameworks available to historians, including Atlantic world and transnational, see Hinderaker and Horn 2010.
3. Christensen here uses wills newly discovered by him to build on a testament-based analysis of Maya politics by Restall (1997) and by its pioneer (despite the later date of the eventual publication of the study), Thompson (1999).
4. A special issue of *Ethnohistory* ([Fall 2012] 59: 4) titled *A Language of Empire, a Quotidian Tongue: The Uses of Nahuatl in Colonial Mexico*, edited by Robert Schwaller, and also marketed as an edited volume (Durham, N.C.: Duke University Press, 2012), focuses on the topic of Nahuatl as a lingua franca in New Spain.

5. There is a vast literature on saints in the Americas. Some especially relevant works include Morgan 2002; Greer and Bilinkoff 2003; Rubial García 2006a, 2006b; Taylor 2010; and Pizzigoni 2012, esp. 36–45, 180–181, 188–189, 222–224, 234–235.

6. On Nahuatl as a lingua franca, see Schwaller 2012.

7. See, for example, Rappaport and Cummins 2011 and Salomon and Niño-Murcia 2011.

8. A compelling essay by nonhistorians (albeit ethnohistorians who have written eloquently on historical topics) on the relevance of hybridity to the study of colonial Latin America is Dean and Leibsohn 2003.

9. Also see Megged 2010 and Megged and Wood 2012.

10. This idea owes something to Alan R. Sandstrom's (2008, 160) observation, based on his own ethnographic research and that of others, that "Native American [Mesoamerican] villages closest to urban centers can be more conservative of ancient cultures that villages farther removed."

11. See Cline 1986, 21–24 on the beginnings of church burials in Culhuacan in central Mexico. For the Andes (Lima and Trujillo in particular), Ramos (2010) discusses the issue of church burials in detail.

12. Burkhart (2004) has commented that "Perhaps as much as or even more than formal preaching, will-making familiarized Nahuas with Catholic practices and discourse related to death." The plays collected in this volume include one that expressly deals with will making: "Souls and Testamentary Executors," 164–189. Also see Cline 1998. For very recent work on the creation of new indigenous Christianities in Mexico and Yucatan, see Christensen 2013.

13. The amount of work on death using such records is growing; the recent collection edited by Martina Will de Chaparro and Miruna Achim (2011) contains a number of examples. Other important works on death in New Spain (where the literature has grown exponentially) include Malvido, Pereira, and Tiesler 1997; Zárate Toscano 2000; Voekel 2002; Roselló Soberón 2006; Von Wobeser and Vila Vilar 2009; and, of course, Lomnitz 2005, which discusses death throughout Mexican history.

References

Berdan, Frances. 1982. *The Aztecs of Central Mexico: An Imperial Society.* New York: Holt, Rinehart, and Winston.

Burkhart, Louise. 1999. "Review of Susan Kellogg and Matthew Restall, eds., *Dead Giveaways: Indigenous Testaments of Colonial Mesoamerica and the Andes* (Salt Lake City: University of Utah Press, 1998)." *Ethnohistory* 46(4): 838–840.

———. 2004. "Death and the Colonial Nahua." In *Nahuatl Theater,* vol. 1, *Death and Life in Colonial Nahua Mexico,* edited by Barry D. Sell and Louise M. Burkhart, 29–54. Norman: University of Oklahoma Press.

Burns, Kathryn. 2010. *Into the Archive: Writing and Power in Colonial Peru.* Durham, N.C.: Duke University Press.

Christensen, Mark Z. 2013. *Nahua and Maya Catholicisms: Texts and Religion in Colonial Central Mexico and Yucatan.* Stanford, Calif.: Stanford University Press.

Cline, S. L. 1986. *Colonial Culhuacan, 1580–1600: A Social History of an Aztec Town.* Albuquerque: University of New Mexico Press.

———. 1998. "Fray Alonso de Molina's Model Testament and Antecedents to Indigenous Wills in Spanish America." In *Dead Giveaways,* edited by Kellogg and Restall, 13–33.

Dean, Carolyn, and Dana Leibsohn. 2003. "Hybridity and Its Discontents: Considering Visual Culture in Colonial Spanish America." *Colonial Latin American Review* 12(1): 5–35.

Eire, Carlos M. N. 1995. *From Madrid to Purgatory: The Art and Craft of Dying in Sixteenth-Century Spain.* Cambridge, U.K.: Cambridge University Press.

Greer, Allan, and Jodi Bilinkoff, eds. 2003. *Colonial Saints: Discovering the Holy in the Americas, 1500–1800.* New York: Routledge.

Hinderaker, Eric, and Rebecca Horn. 2010. "Territorial Crossings: Histories and Historiographies of the Early Americas." *William and Mary Quarterly* (3rd series) 66: 395–432.

Kellogg, Susan. 1995. *Law and the Transformation of Aztec Culture, 1500–1700.* Norman: University of Oklahoma Press.

———. 2003. "Encountering People, Creating Texts: Cultural Studies of the Encounter and Beyond." *Latin American Research Review* 38: 261–274.

Lockhart, James. 1991. "Postconquest Nahua Society and Culture Seen through Nahuatl Sources." In *Nahuas and Spaniards: Postconquest Central Mexican History and Philology,* 2–22. Stanford, Calif.: Stanford University Press.

Lomnitz, Claudio. 2005. *Death and the Idea of Mexico.* New York: Zone Books.

Malvido, Elsa, Gregory Pereira, and Vera Tiesler, eds. 1997. *El cuerpo humano y su tratamiento mortuorio.* Mexico City: INAH.

Megged, Amos. 2010. *Social Memory in Ancient and Colonial Mesoamerica.* Cambridge: Cambridge University Press.

Megged, Amos, and Stephanie Wood, eds. 2012. *Mesoamerican Memory: Enduring Systems of Remembrance.* Norman: University of Oklahoma Press.

Metcalf, Alida. 2005. *Go-Betweens and the Colonization of Brazil, 1500–1600.* Austin: University of Texas Press.

Morgan, Ronald J. 2002. *Spanish American Saints and the Rhetoric of Identity, 1600–1810.* Tucson: University of Arizona Press.

Nesvig, Martin. 2012. "Peyote, Ever Virgin: A Case of Religious Hybridism in Mexico." In *A Linking of Heaven and Earth: Studies in Religious and Cultural History in Honor of Carlos M. N. Eire,* edited by Emily Michelson, Scott K. Taylor, and Mary Noll Venables, 175–190. Farnham, U.K.: Ashgate.

Pizzigoni, Caterina. 2007. *The Testaments of Toluca.* Stanford, Calif.: Stanford University Press.

———. 2012. *The Life Within: Local Indigenous Society in Mexico's Toluca Valley, 1650–1800.* Stanford, Calif.: Stanford University Press.

Ramos, Gabriela. 2010. *Death and Conversion in the Andes: Lima and Cuzco, 1532–1670.* Notre Dame, Ind.: University of Notre Dame Press.

Rappaport, Joanne, and Tom Cummins. 2011. *Beyond the Lettered City: Indigenous Literacies in the Andes.* Durham, N.C.: Duke University Press.

Restall, Matthew. 1997. *The Maya World: Yucatec Culture and Society, 1550–1850.* Stanford, Calif.: Stanford University Press.

———. 1998. "Interculturation and the Indigenous Testament in Colonial Yucatan." In *Dead Giveaways*, edited by Kellogg and Restall, 141–162. Salt Lake City: University of Utah Press.

———. 2003. "A History of the New Philology and the New Philology in History." *Latin American Research Review* 38: 113–134.

———. 2012. "The New Conquest History." *History Compass* 10. history-compass .com/caribbean-latin-america.

Restall, Matthew, and Susan Kellogg. 1998. Introduction to *Dead Giveaways*, edited by Kellogg and Restall, 1–11. Salt Lake City: University of Utah Press.

Roselló Soberón, Estela. 2006. *Así en la tierra como en el cielo: Manifestaciones religiosas de la culpa y el perdón en los siglos XVI y XVII en la Nueva España.* Mexico City: El Colegio de México.

Rubial García, Antonio. 2006a. "Icons of Devotion: The Appropriation and Use of Saints in New Spain." In *Local Religion in Colonial Mexico*, edited by Martin A. Nesvig, 37–62. Albuquerque: University of New Mexico Press.

———. 2006b. *Profetisas y solitarios: Espacios y mensajes de una religión dirigida por ermitaños y beatas laicos en las ciudades de Nueva España.* Mexico City: UNAM and FCE.

Salomon, Frank, and Mercedes Niño-Murcia. 2011. *The Lettered Mountain: A Peruvian Village's Way With Writing.* Durham, N.C.: Duke University Press.

Sandstrom, Alan R. 2008. "Blood Sacrifice, Curing, and Ethnic Identity among Contemporary Nahua of Northern Veracruz, Mexico." In *Ethnic Identity in Nahua Mesoamerica: The View from Archaeology, Art History, Ethnohistory, and Contemporary Ethnography*, edited by Frances F. Berdan et al., 150–182. Salt Lake City: University of Utah Press.

Schroeder, Susan, ed. 2010. *The Conquest All Over Again: Nahuas and Zapotecs Thinking, Writing, and Painting Spanish Colonialism.* Brighton, U.K.: Sussex Academic Press.

Schwaller, Robert, ed. 2012. *A Language of Empire, a Quotidian Tongue: The Uses of Nahuatl in Colonial Mexico.* Durham, N.C.: Duke University Press.

Tamm, Marek. 2013. "Beyond History and Memory: New Perspectives in Memory Studies." *History Compass* 11: 461. DOI:10.1002/HIC3.12050.

Taylor, William B. 2010. *Shrines and Miraculous Images: Religious Life in Mexico before the Reforma.* Albuquerque: University of New Mexico Press.

Thompson, Philip C. 1999. *Tekanto, a Maya Town in Colonial Yucatan.* New Orleans: Tulane University Middle American Research Institute.

Voekel, Pamela. 2002. *Alone before God: Death and the Origins of Mexican Modernity.* Durham, N.C.: Duke University Press.

Von Wobesar, Gisela, and Enriqueta Vila Vilar. 2009. *Muerte y vida en el más allá: España y América, siglos XVI–XVIII.* Mexico City: UNAM, 2009.

Will de Chaparro, Martina, and Miruna Achim, eds. 2011. *Death and Dying in Colonial Spanish America.* Tucson: University of Arizona Press.

Zárate Toscano, Veronica. 2000. *Los nobles ante la muerte: Actitudes, ceremonias y memoria, 1750–1850.* Mexico City: El Colegio de México, Instituto de Investigaciones Dr. José María Mora.

Glossary

alcalde. Mayor
alguacil mayor. Constable
altepetl. A central Mexican ethnic-state
amatl. Indigenous-style paper
ayllu. A sociopolitical unit headed by a leader whose members are linked to a
    common lineage or ancestor-deity
barrio. Neighborhood
cabildo. City council
cacica. Female indigenous leader
cacique. Indigenous leader
cah. Maya sociopolitical unit or town
casta. People of mixed ancestry
chibal. Patronym group
chinamit. Ward of a Mayan indigenous township
chinampas. Fertile aquatic gardens
cofrade. Member of a confraternity
cofradía. Confraternity
corregidor. Crown liaison to Native Americans
doctrina. A parish for people new to the Catholic faith
don. Elite title for a man
doña. Elite title for a woman
encomendero. Individual, usually a Spaniard, who collects tribute from his
    assigned *encomiendas* (or indigenous communities).
escribano. Notary
gobernador. Governor
gremio. Guild
ladino/a. A Spanish-speaking native
mayordomo. Majordomo
mestizo. Individual of mixed indigenous and Spanish ancestry
mita. Forced labor rotation
mulato/a. Person of mixed African and Spanish ancestry
ñuu. Sociopolitical unit, or town, of the Mixteca Alta.
pedazo. Piece or parcel
pinturas. Pictorial documents

reales. "Pieces of eight." Eight reales was the equivalent of a peso.
regidor. Councilman
santos. Saints
solares. Urban plots of land
teniente. Lieutenant
tlacuiloque. Painters of books from precontact central Mexico
tomines. Coins worth one-eighth of a peso
traza. Plan or grid; layout.
vecino. Citizen

Contributors

Kathleen J. Bragdon
The College of William and Mary
Department of Anthropology
Williamsburg, Virginia

Paul J. Charney
Frostburg State University
Department of History
Frostburg, Maryland

Mark Christensen
Assumption College
History Department
Worcester, Massachusetts

Richard Conway
Montclair State University
Department of History
Montclair, New Jersey

Karen B. Graubart
Johns Hopkins University
Baltimore, Maryland

Erika R. Hosselkus
Southeast Missouri State University
Department of History
Cape Girardeau, Missouri

Owen H. Jones
Valdosta State University
Department of History
Valdosta, Georgia

Susan Kellogg
University of Houston
Department of History
Houston, Texas

Matthew Restall
Pennsylvania State University
History Department
University Park, Pennsylvania

Tatiana Seijas
Pennsylvania State University
History Department
Oxford, Ohio

Lisa Sousa
Occidental College
Department of History
Los Angeles, California

Kevin Terraciano
UCLA
Department of History
Los Angeles, California

Jonathan Truitt
Central Michigan University
Department of History
Mt. Pleasant, Michigan

Index

Page numbers in *italics* indicate figures and tables.